Are You Watching Closely?

THE SUNY SERIES

HORIZONS OF CINEMA

MURRAY POMERANCE | EDITOR

Also in the series

William Rothman, editor, *Cavell on Film*
J. David Slocum, editor, *Rebel Without a Cause*
Joe McElhaney, *The Death of Classical Cinema*
Kirsten Moana Thompson, *Apocalyptic Dread*
Frances Gateward, editor, *Seoul Searching*
Michael Atkinson, editor, *Exile Cinema*
Paul S. Moore, *Now Playing*
Robin L. Murray and Joseph K. Heumann, *Ecology and Popular Film*
William Rothman, editor, *Three Documentary Filmmakers*
Sean Griffin, editor, *Hetero*
Jean-Michel Frodon, editor, *Cinema and the Shoah*
Carolyn Jess-Cooke and Constantine Verevis, editors, *Second Takes*
Matthew Solomon, editor, *Fantastic Voyages of the Cinematic Imagination*
R. Barton Palmer and David Boyd, editors, *Hitchcock at the Source*
William Rothman, *Hitchcock: The Murderous Gaze, Second Edition*
Joanna Hearne, *Native Recognition*
Marc Raymond, *Hollywood's New Yorker*
Steven Rybin and Will Scheibel, editors, *Lonely Places, Dangerous Ground*
Claire Perkins and Constantine Verevis, editors, *B Is for Bad Cinema*
Dominic Lennard, *Bad Seeds and Holy Terrors*
Rosie Thomas, *Bombay before Bollywood*
Scott M. MacDonald, *Binghamton Babylon*
Sudhir Mahadevan, *A Very Old Machine*
David Greven, *Ghost Faces*
James S. Williams, *Encounters with Godard*
William H. Epstein and R. Barton Palmer, editors, *Invented Lives, Imagined Communities*
Lee Carruthers, *Doing Time*
Rebecca Meyers, William Rothman, and Charles Warren, editors, *Looking with Robert Gardner*
Belinda Smaill, *Regarding Life*
Douglas McFarland and Wesley King, editors, *John Huston as Adaptor*
R. Barton Palmer, Homer B. Pettey, and Steven M. Sanders, editors, *Hitchcock's Moral Gaze*
Will Scheibel, *American Stranger*
Nenad Jovanovic, *Brechtian Cinemas*
Steven Rybin, *Gestures of Love*
Amy Rust, *Passionate Detachments*

Are You Watching Closely?

Cultural Paranoia, New Technologies, and the Contemporary Hollywood Misdirection Film

Seth Friedman

SUNY PRESS

Cover image: From *The Prestige*. Credit: Newmarket/Photofest

Published by State University of New York Press, Albany

© 2017 State University of New York

All rights reserved

Printed in the United States of America

No part of this book may be used or reproduced in any manner whatsoever without written permission. No part of this book may be stored in a retrieval system or transmitted in any form or by any means including electronic, electrostatic, magnetic tape, mechanical, photocopying, recording, or otherwise without the prior permission in writing of the publisher.

For information, contact State University of New York Press, Albany, NY
www.sunypress.edu

Production, Eileen Nizer
Marketing, Anne M. Valentine

Library of Congress Cataloging-in-Publication Data

Names: Friedman, Seth, 1976– author.
Title: Are you watching closely? : cultural paranoia, new technologies, and the contemporary Hollywood misdirection film / by Seth Friedman.
Description: Albany : State University of New York Press, [2017] | Series: SUNY series, horizons of cinema | Includes bibliographical references and index.
Identifiers: LCCN 2016039673 (print) | LCCN 2016056195 (ebook) | ISBN 9781438465913 (hardcover : alk. paper) | ISBN 9781438465906 (pbk. : alk. paper) | ISBN 9781438465920 (ebook)
Subjects: LCSH: Motion pictures—Philosophy. | Space and time in motion pictures. | Narration (Rhetoric)
Classification: LCC PN1995 .F7445 2017 (print) | LCC PN1995 (ebook) | DDC 791.4301—dc23
LC record available at https://lccn.loc.gov/2016039673

10 9 8 7 6 5 4 3 2 1

For Leo and Clark Friedman

Contents

Illustrations

Acknowledgments

As with Hollywood film production, virtually any academic book is a highly collaborative effort in which key contributors often do not receive the full credit that they deserve. Although devoting this section to thanking those who supported me might not jibe entirely with a book devoted partly to how innovation occurs amid standard genre, narrative, and formal conventions, I chose to leverage it traditionally because it is the least I can do to provide those backers with the recognition that they earned. This book would not have been possible without the valuable assistance of the following people.

This project began with the guidance of my MA thesis director, Matthew Solomon, who generously dedicated hours of his time to helping both to generate and shape the idea into a viable scholarly project. In fact, early work I wrote under his tutelage became an article in *Journal of Film and Video* 58.4 (Winter 2006): 16–28, portions of which appear in chapter 1. Matthew taught me how to be a professional academic and has graciously continued to mentor me. David Gerstner also developed that thesis into a rigorous piece of scholarship and remains a staunch supporter. Under the assured direction of Barbara Klinger, I transformed that thesis into a dissertation, some of which was derived from essays produced in her seminars, including one that was the source for an article in *Genders* 59 (Spring 2014) that is the basis of chapter 3. Barb's thorough and perceptive editorial suggestions consistently made my arguments more clear, concise, and persuasive. I am grateful that she lent so much of her seemingly endless energy and prodigious expertise to helping make the dissertation into a readily marketable book. I also want to thank the other prominent members of my dissertation committee—Joan Hawkins and Gregory Waller—for their insightful and influential feedback throughout the process.

Many of my peers, colleagues, and other professionals provided crucial comments on various iterations of the project that greatly improved it. Travis Vogan and Andrea Kelley both read numerous chapters of the manuscript and gave me sharp suggestions that strengthened a variety of key arguments. Additional peers from my graduate school community deserve special recognition for their generosity when this project was a dissertation and beyond, including Shelley Bradfield, Antonio Golán, Michael Lahey, James Paasche, and Justin Rawlins. During the dissertation phase, Shira Segal was a champion of my work as well as a loyal confidant and comrade in Joan's dissertation reading group. I also want to acknowledge the other members of that group throughout my tenure in it for their contributions. Joan again deserves special recognition for sacrificing many of her Saturdays to enhance the work of graduate students. At DePauw University, my colleagues in the Department of Communication and Theatre have graciously welcomed me into a group that is uncommonly supportive and compassionate. Finishing this book was a lot easier than it likely would have been elsewhere because I am fortunate to have found a home in which it is a genuine pleasure to work with each of my colleagues. Of those spectacular peers, Andrew Hayes, Kevin Howley, and Jonathan Nichols-Pethick were particularly instrumental to ensuring that DePauw became the place where I could complete this project with adequate support. Finally, thanks to Murray Pomerance for including me in the Horizons of Cinema series and for handing me over to Eileen Nizer, James Peltz, and Rafael Chaiken, who have been fantastic editors at SUNY Press. I also want to thank them for recruiting the anonymous readers of the manuscript, who offered astute feedback that bolstered the quality of the final product.

Finally, I want to thank my family and non-academic friends for their backing. Yona Belfort, Rich Caponetti, Steve Dorman, and Matt Morgan read papers on this subject in its earliest phases and have consistently believed in my abilities as a scholar. Jeremy Harmon gave me access to numerous films that I needed to use to complete the project. My parents, Jerry and Cheryl Friedman, and my brother, Justin Friedman, have been there for me every step of the way. My sons, Leo and Clark Friedman, provided the inspiration I needed to complete the project. Those two scoundrels immeasurably amplify the quality of everything I do each day.

Introduction

Since the early 1990s, there has been a spate of Hollywood films that uncharacteristically inspire viewers to reinterpret them retrospectively. Films employing this narrative mode are hardly new in Hollywood and other cinema contexts. Numerous Hollywood and world cinema classics, such as *The Cabinet of Dr. Caligari* (1920), *The Wizard of Oz* (1939), and *Citizen Kane* (1941), contain a late revelation that encourages spectators to reassess the meaning of a majority of what has come before. As part of the recent upcropping of films, Hollywood also remade three of the most celebrated twist-ending films released before the 1990s: *Diabolique* (1955; 1996), *Psycho* (1960; 1998), and *Planet of the Apes* (1968; 2001). In addition to *Diabolique* (a remake of the French film, *Les diaboliques*), contemporary titles, like *The Crying Game* (1992, an Irish film) and *Vanilla Sky* (2001, a remake of *Abre los Ojos*, a 1997 Spanish film), indicate that these films have never been linked exclusively to the U.S. commercial film industry. Yet, between 1990 and 2010, Hollywood backed over 40 films that encourage viewers to reinterpret them retrospectively, making it the most fertile period for such films in history. Many of these films were commercial and critical successes, including *The Sixth Sense* (1999), *A Beautiful Mind* (2001), and *Inception* (2010), which each garnered significant box-office returns and considerable Academy Award attention. This book explores the reasons for this production trend. I examine these films in their cultural, industrial, and technological contexts to explain why they became unprecedentedly attractive to Hollywood producers and some audiences at the time.

Regardless of how they are packaged by the industry, these films constitute a genre defined partly by narrative structure. I use the term "misdirection" to describe them because it effectively captures how they provoke spectators to understand narrative information initially in one manner and subsequently comprehend it in drastically new ways. Despite this common element, they are not a clear-cut industrial genre. As with other genres, most notably film noir, no one set out to make a misdirection film per se because there is yet to be an agreed-upon label for them. The discursive evidence I chart throughout this book, however, shows that audiences, critics, and producers engage with misdirection films in a manner that differentiates them from other Hollywood fare. The ways in which these films are designed and packaged to prompt various groups to interact with them distinctly make them a viable cultural category set apart from other generic classifications.

What is in a Name?: The Misdirection Film Genre in its Contexts

Existing scholarly literature begins to provide discursive evidence that demonstrates these films constitute a genre. A number of works have been recently published on increasing narrative complexity in commercial U.S. film and television, a few of which even grapple with some of the sociocultural, industrial, and technological circumstances contributing to its growing popularity. No book-length study and only a handful of articles, though, focus exclusively on misdirection films in relation to their contexts. Instead, scholars generally lump misdirection films into larger categories that encompass an array of contemporary, narratively complex media texts. In a rare essay that wrestles with these particular films directly, Cornelia Klecker deploys the term "mind-tricking narratives" to describe how misdirection films are constructed and interpreted. Like Klecker, I contend that the classification "complex storytelling," which Aristotle originally devised in *Poetics*, is too "vague" because it merely signifies that a film somehow "does *not* adhere to a classical narrative structure" (emphasis in original, 121). Other scholars have also created categories to distinguish specific storytelling developments in contemporary Hollywood cinema from the broader trend of increasing narrative complexity. Perhaps most influentially, in *Convergence Culture*, Henry Jenkins coined the concept of "transmedia storytelling" to identify the proliferation of contemporary U.S. films and television shows that migrate viewers across media by encouraging virtual communities to master their complexities. Similarly, David Bordwell and Barbara Klinger employ the term "puzzle film" in individual chapters of *The Way Hollywood Tells It* and *Beyond the Multiplex*, respectively, to describe contemporary Hollywood films that inspire spectators to gain deeper appreciations by engaging in repeated viewings. My definition of the misdirection film, however, does not include many of the devices that also prompt this activity, such as the creation of eminently quotable dialogue and elaborate fictional worlds, encompassed by these more amorphous categorizations.

As one sign of how influential the puzzle film moniker has become in Film Studies, Warren Buckland edited an anthology, entitled *Puzzle Films*, just three years after Bordwell and Klinger mobilized the term. A majority of essays in that collection are, like the preponderance of extant scholarship, almost exclusively preoccupied with issues of narrative construction and comprehension; however, Thomas Elsaesser's chapter on the "mind-game film" constitutes the most significant prior publication to connect these films to some of the cultural and technological conditions, including anxieties about the persistence of traditional ways of thinking and the ramifications of the advent of the World Wide Web, that I explore throughout the majority of this book. However, his categorization includes films that play games with *either* unwitting characters or both those characters and audiences by withholding important narrative information. In addition to conflating films that deceive actual audiences with ones in which only characters are tricked, his culturally attuned analysis underplays the importance of the industrial shifts contributing to their relative appeal to producers. My focus solely on films that inspire retrospective reinterpretations only by spectators, in contrast, isolates one of Hollywood's most successful responses to the ways that some viewers now commonly interact with its products. Misdirection, therefore, also provides an important historical dimension that links the genre's contemporary constituents to notable antecedents, setting up key comparisons and distinctions between the period under study and earlier moments in Hollywood.

There are a number of reasons why "misdirection" is more appropriate than the "puzzle film," the "mind-game film," "mind-tricking narratives," and other labels used to classify these films. Whereas such alternatives reduce these films to gimmicks and ostensibly trivial leisure time diversions, misdirection instead alludes expressly to "direction." It thus intimates how filmmakers working in the genre encourage initial misapprehensions of narrative information. Misdirection captures how these films are often created and promoted as contests of wits between filmmakers and audiences. In fact, the directors most closely associated with the misdirection film—M. Night Shyamalan and Christopher Nolan—have tried to bolster their reputations as self-styled masters of the genre through marketing and by incorporating references into the films themselves that alert audiences to the intellectual competition. Shyamalan, for instance, followed up Cole Sear's (Haley Joel Osment) humorous observation in *The Sixth Sense* that great storytelling needs "lots of twists" by having Elijah Price's mother (Charlayne Woodard) in *Unbreakable* (2000) tell her son that a comic book gift "has a surprise ending." Similarly, after the opening credits in Nolan's *The Prestige* (2006), a film about rival magicians, Alfred Borden (Christian Bale) asks in voiceover "Are you watching closely?," which is followed by many self-referential insinuations to its narrative structure, including John Cutter's (Michael Caine) exclamation that "a pretty assistant's the most effective form of misdirection." These meta-generic references are especially apt in a magic-themed film and serve as a telling evocation of the category as a whole because misdirection also invokes illusionism. Filmmakers both flaunt the trickery and conceal it. As Matthew Solomon documents in *Disappearing Tricks*, the historical links between magic and early cinema are underappreciated. Misdirection is also the appropriate moniker, then, because it indicates the persistent ways that magic and cinema relate, connoting the enduring connections between conjuring and film form and narrative.

A strong reliance on Hollywood principles is central to the particular brand of magic that most misdirection films employ, revealing a primary reason why they have already been of considerable interest to some film and media scholars. The release of an uncharacteristically high number of Hollywood films with similar unconventional narrative structures raises questions about the endurance of Hollywood's foundational storytelling and associated representational standards. Such issues make it valuable to grapple with questions associated with narrative and genre in relation to these films to link them to their contexts. Although connecting these films to their historical conditions of production and reception is my primary objective, identifying the properties that make them a distinct set that

Figure. I.1. Young Elijah Price's mother explains that her comic book gift contains a surprise ending in *Unbreakable*.

Figure. I.2. *The Prestige*'s Robert Angier uses his assistant, Olivia Wenscome, to distract the audience from detecting the trick's secret.

can be separated from other Hollywood fare first begins to provide the evidence as to why various groups might conceive of them as a genre.

Many assessments that already engage with these issues support the argument that, regardless of their ostensibly atypical properties, misdirection films buttress the storytelling and representational conventions that theorists, like Bordwell, claim have been dominant in Hollywood since the classical mode of narration calcified in the 1910s. As Bordwell explains in *Narration in the Fiction Film*, the "classical" Hollywood film's focus on "psychologically defined individuals who struggle to solve a clear-cut problem or attain specific goals" distinguishes it from alternatives (157). Formal devices in virtually all Hollywood films since the late 1910s have been compositionally motivated because they are subservient to narrative and used invisibly to forward a canonic story in which a typically white, heterosexual, male protagonist with consistent traits strives to overcome obstacles until all causal lines of action are tied up predictably and unambiguously. In spite of the misdirection film's unexpected or ambiguous conclusions, narrative causality is not typically revealed as being ultimately attributable to the random forces of chance. Rather, once the epiphany is exposed or its meaning is discovered, it usually shows, in conspiratorial fashion, that narrative causality can be reinterpreted as being driven by the actions of clearly identifiable agents, who appeared incapable of having such authority. This alternative explanation can provide consolation to viewers accustomed to Hollywood's standard storytelling and representational practices that generally support the status quo, indicating a major reason why they often resonate with mass audiences. Of course, the retrospective reinterpretations that misdirection films inspire are not always this clear-cut in relation to what "really" happened and the plurality of potential readings that they can prompt render proclamations about their cultural politics being monolithic as suspect. Yet, the atypical ways in which they generally encourage viewers to discover the actual "truth" distinguishes them from other Hollywood films and ultimately appeals to audiences seeking to make order out of chaos.

Regardless of this and other connections between these films and their contexts, almost all existing studies of them focus primarily, if not exclusively, on issues associated with narrative construction and comprehension to assess their relationship to the classical paradigm. Bordwell, for instance, uses these films to refute those who declare that the fall of the studio system has ushered in a postclassical era in Hollywood. Such arguments, he charges, typically focus too much on anomalies and ignore the continued dominance of the classical Hollywood film. Moreover, he claims that virtually all Hollywood films that seem to break with the classical mode of narration, including misdirection films, actually do nothing of the sort. In support of this assertion, Bordwell analyzes how the contemporary "puzzle film," keeps "one foot in the classical tradition" by providing "legible variants on well-entrenched strategies for presenting time, space, goal achievement, causal connection, and the like" (*The Way* 73, 75). As his examination of *Memento* (2000) reveals, Hollywood films that seemingly contain the most confounding narrative and formal innovations, paradoxically, typically rely most on classical devices to stay intelligible. *Memento*, therefore, hits spectators over the head with redundancy to orient them in time and space as well as remind them that the narrative unfolds backwards because it is compositionally motivated by the protagonist's short-term memory loss.

Although there is considerable research on how misdirection films operate narratively and are interpreted, there is surprisingly little interest in the reasons for their increasing appeal. Bordwell, for example, contends that to determine why Hollywood experienced a "narrative experimentation surge in the 1990s," the impulse "to look for some broad cultural change as the trigger" should be avoided (*The Way* 73). Moreover, even though he subsequently admits that Hollywood storytelling has recently been "enhanced by DVD," Bordwell only discusses the links between the development of new technologies and Hollywood's shifting narrative strategies fleetingly so that he can attempt to prove that the classical film still reigns supreme (*The Way* 103). Likewise, in his study of narrative in *The Sixth Sense*, Erlend Lavik initially remarks that "it is tempting to speculate that this boom in twist movies is related to the rise of the DVD"; however, he cuts off that line of inquiry to conduct a formalist analysis of its narrative structure (60). Yet, I contend that by examining these very sorts of issues, it is possible to determine how the contemporary misdirection film exemplifies the ways in which Hollywood production remains consistent in some regards and, importantly, shifts with the times in other fashions.

Rather than primarily investigate misdirection films in relation to the classical paradigm, after mapping their narrative properties and generic links at the outset of this book, I devote subsequent chapters to an assessment of how and why they epitomize a kind of narrative experimentation that has become a crucial facet of twenty-first-century audiovisual storytelling. This focus fills the gap in the scholarly literature on these films by highlighting their historical and cultural significance. Undoubtedly, as Jenkins, Klinger, and others argue, this spate of films is connected to the advent of new media technologies that make complex narratives designed to be watched repeatedly and dissected online attractive to an industry that depends exceedingly on post-theatrical markets. The development of new communication and film exhibition technologies has created profitable revenue streams that give industry executives financial incentive to back misdirection films. Neither changing industrial motives nor technological determinism, however, fully explains why these films have become more attractive.

There are also key cultural conditions contributing to the appeal of the contemporary Hollywood misdirection film. Most of these films, even those few that initially appear to be narratively incoherent, such as *Magnolia* (1999), *Memento*, and *Mulholland Dr.* (2001), can be reinterpreted along the lines of classical Hollywood storytelling, usually by making recourse to authorship. This is culturally relevant because although these films initially appear to interrogate traditional ways of thinking by seeming to support the discourses of relativity, subjectivity, and multiculturalism, the retrospective reinterpretations that they often inspire articulate a stronger reluctance to abandon familiar epistemologies, including a belief in absolute fact, faith in teleological narratives, as well as the notion that identity is static and biologically determined. In particular, although many misdirection films ostensibly present challenges to the social order, on further review they usually end up encouraging reinterpretations that reassure viewers that foundational American ideologies, such as white patriarchal capitalism, are still dominant. In addition to referencing the connections between these films and magic as well as the ways they prompt filmmakers and viewers to engage in cerebral competitions, the misdirection moniker expresses nostalgia for a bygone era that many people still want to exist. The term is thus also most appropriate because it references how these films can assuage growing cultural anxieties about the unknowability of the "truth" by diverting viewers away from the cognitive crises of relativity and subjectivity with the fantasy that it is possible to determine what "actually" occurred and who was "really" responsible for events.

That is not to say that all misdirection films uphold dominant ways of thinking indisputably or inspire retroactive readings that render their meanings absolute. As in virtually all Hollywood films, ideological contradictions abound in the genre's constituents, and they can prompt clashing interpretations that are often persuasively supported by textual and/or extratextual evidence to vastly different ends. Neither my own readings nor the ones produced by fans that I present throughout this book, then, are definitive. In fact, one of the reasons I devote so much space to both is to demonstrate the myriad and often compelling responses that these films can inspire, even when they contradict each other. Yet, like all readings, those that follow are contingent on the contexts that shape creative decisions and viewer comprehensions because they represent tendencies in artistic creation and audience interpretation that are framed by historically specific circumstances of production and reception.

My exploration of the genre's historical significance is thus driven by the "context-activated" theory of reception that Janet Staiger outlines in *Interpreting Films*, which rejects more traditionally employed "text-activated" or "reader-activated" alternatives. Rather than deem meaning as being determined by the author, the text, or the viewer, Staiger contends that "the interpretive event occurs at the intersection of multiple determinations," which means that "*interpretation is contradictory* and not coherent" (emphasis in original, 48). The film analyses that ensue highlight how all interpretations, including my own, are always contestable.

This does not imply, however, that reception studies disregards the importance of textual properties, is governed by relativism, or proves the futility of historical research because it is inexhaustible and subject to the whims of the critic. As Klinger acknowledges, "Without question, historical reception studies has a strong interpretive dimension" ("Film" 112). Although privileging context rather than texts, authors, or readers does not isolate a film's conclusive significance because it is still beholden to the researcher's interpretations, it productively means, as Klinger posits, "the aesthetic or political value of a film is no longer a matter of its intrinsic characteristics, but of the way those characteristics are deployed by various intertextual and historical forces" ("Film" 112). Examinations of how the films themselves mobilize or repress discourses in circulation when they are created and the various moments that they are consumed renders intertextuality compatible with reception studies. Textual analysis and reception studies are not irreconcilable and can coexist, then, provided that textual properties are considered just one discursive element in the complex meaning-making matrix. My own readings and the ones forwarded by fans negotiate this tension by situating these interpretations in the particular contexts that shape them. As with all comprehensions, my own exhuming of textual significance and my summaries of fan readings of these films are underscored by how conditions of production and reception influence meaning-making activities at given historical moments. To begin this contextual analysis, I thus turn to a discussion of how misdirection films are constructed and understood in relation to the dominant production logic of the time.

Subsets of Misdirection: Defining the Changeover and the Master Key Films

In misdirection films the manner in which the viewer is encouraged to reinterpret narrative information retrospectively materializes in two primary ways. I use the terms "changeover" and "master key" to differentiate these two discernable, though not always mutually exclusive, narrative forms. Inspired by *Fight Club*'s (1999) revelation in which the protagonist, in voiceover, uses the term to explain what is transpiring, the changeover is an incident that occurs within the narrative flow that *forces* a primary character and the spectator to question the validity of almost all that precedes its emergence. It has a recognizable lineage in Hollywood, from films like *The Wizard of Oz*, in which the changeover reveals that the Technicolor Oz sequences were a dream, to recent films, such as *The Usual Suspects* (1995), in which it exposes the fact that Verbal Kint (Kevin Spacey) evades the authorities and augments his criminal legend by constructing a cover story from the contents of a bulletin board. Changeover films *explicitly* signal that there is another way to reassess the meaning of a majority of narrative information by incorporating an explanatory sequence into the narrative itself.

In the master key film there is no single moment within the narrative that blatantly reveals that an alternative explanation exists. The master key film instead contains a subtext that, when its meaning is discovered, provides spectators with a different way to comprehend the meaning of a majority of narrative information. Mysterious objects or bizarre narrative occurrences remain unexplained by the master key film's conclusion. The existence of these enigmatic properties only *alludes* to the possibility that there is an alternative way to interpret the narrative significance of what has come before. However, once the meanings of clues related to these lingering ambiguities are discovered and understood, it becomes possible to reinterpret the significance of most narrative information. As with the changeover, this narrative form has appeared in Hollywood for decades, from studio-era films, like *Citizen Kane*, in which the belated identification of Rosebud *may* provide a totalizing explanation for the reasons for Charles Foster Kane's (Orson Welles) befuddling character traits, to contemporary titles, such as *Magnolia* (1999), in which the master key of Exodus 8:2 strongly suggests the significance of the film's seemingly inexplicable rain of frogs and its other puzzling elements. The master key, though, has a less discernable genealogy than the changeover because although the existence of an alternative narrative explanation can be obvious (*Citizen Kane*), there are instances in which it is never clearly present (*Magnolia*). In the latter case, it is only discovered if groups, like critics and audiences, unearth the secrets and communicate their findings to others persuasively enough to convince them that there is, in fact, a more compelling way to reassess narrative meaning.

Obviously, narrative devices like the changeover and the master key did not originate in cinema. The consistent use of similar narrative structures in print media makes it possible to use established terms from literary theory, such as a concealed "frame narrative" or an "allegory," to describe the ways that these films tell stories. As Shouhou Qi's PhD dissertation *The Shift of Emphasis and the Reception of Surprise Ending Stories* (1900–1941) reveals, the misdirection narrative appeared with its most prominence in print in the United States during the late nineteenth and early twentieth centuries. During that time, a handful of leading American authors, including Thomas Bailey Aldrich, Bret Harte, Frank Stockton, Ambrose Bierce, Richard Harding Davis, and, most famously, O. Henry, whose name is now synonymous with the ironic, twist ending, each published short stories, containing late revelations that encourage drastic retrospective reinterpretations of narrative information. In addition to illustrating the differences in the ways that the changeover and the master key film are constructed and interpreted, literary theory provides a framework for conceiving of the two devices as fundamentally similar. As Emma Kafalenos writes, renowned authors, like Edgar Allan Poe and Henry James, have long been considered masters of making meaning "functionally polyvalent" because the relevance of narrative information changes drastically in many of their works as readers "read, page by page, and acquire further information" (475). Both the changeover and the master key are functionally polyvalent narrative structures because they encourage reassessments of the significance of a majority of narrative information after the revelatory evidence is exposed or unearthed.

Literary theory is only a starting point for describing how misdirection films actually operate because it does not account for how they depend on particular cinematic techniques to render their narratives functionally polyvalent. *The Sixth Sense* exemplifies just how strongly many misdirection films rely on classical narrative and formal conventions to trick spectators into jumping to erroneous conclusions. To put it another way, *The Sixth Sense* typifies how these films often use classical principles as the magician's pretty assistant to distract viewers from discovering the secret. Up until the film's revelatory sequence, there is little reason for spectators accustomed to Hollywood standards to suspect that Malcolm Crowe (Bruce Willis) is dead. Instead, the quest narrative appears to center on the assistance that Malcolm provides to the tortured Cole Sear, who is cursed with the ability to see—hence the surname—dead people. Accordingly, spectators are led to believe that the narrative will be satisfactorily settled only when it builds to a climactic moment in which Malcolm helps the scared child finally cope with the spirits that haunt him and resolves the classical film's heterosexual coupling subplot that focuses on his attempts to reconcile with his wife, Hannah (Olivia Williams). This is exactly what seems to occur. Malcolm becomes Cole's pseudo-father as well as his mentor and appears to help the child overcome fears of his paranormal visions while trying to rekindle his marriage.

The exposure of the revelation, however, shows that narrative events are actually related to a much different causality. The changeover unexpectedly reveals that Malcolm did not survive the shooting that occurred at the film's outset. It exposes the fact that the narrative has not only focused on Malcolm's efforts to help Cole deal with his issues, but that Cole has also been helping Malcolm cope with a problem of his own. This causal line of action is not made explicit, though, because for most of the film the narrative appears to center primarily on Malcolm's efforts to convince Cole that the ghosts that haunt him are simply searching for closure, which, of course, remains significant upon reinterpretation because Malcolm is such a spirit himself. Consequently, at approximately the film's midpoint, when Cole famously mutters to Malcolm that he "see[s] dead people" everywhere and they do not realize that they are dead, it only becomes evident, in retrospect, that he is also referencing the film's hidden causal line of action. Ostensibly, his statement merely suggests he is finally opening up to Malcolm by providing him with the information that will help him conquer the demons. Yet, the changeover reveals that the confession has another meaning: Malcolm is unable to rest in peace until he comes to terms with his own death. Importantly, this duplicity operates at a formal level as well because the critical exchange between the two characters is filmed in standard shot/reverse shot manner that relies on quintessential techniques, like standard eye-line matches, making it seem as though it is simply a prototypical classical Hollywood conversation. In retrospect, though, the reasons for

Figure I.3. Cole Sear's perspective during a shot/reverse shot conversation with Dr. Malcolm Crowe in which the child divulges that he sees dead people in *The Sixth Sense*.

the camera focusing on Malcolm so exclusively when Cole divulges his ability to see ghosts is not only designed to display the doctor's reactions to the child's confessions. It also subtly reveals the doctor is dead because when Cole speaks about the ghosts that haunt him, the camera centers on Malcolm. In short, the changeover shows how classical storytelling and formal principles are deployed to trick viewers into drawing incorrect suppositions initially about narrative meaning.

As with the changeover film, the revelatory evidence in the master key film dramatically alters the significance of narrative information. *Pulp Fiction*, for instance, can be classified as a master key film because of a particular alternative reading that has been popularized by fans, which postulates that Jules Winnfield (Samuel L. Jackson) and Vincent Vega (John Travolta) have been sent from God to retrieve a briefcase that contains Marcellus Wallace's (Ving Rhames) soul from the devil's henchmen. Of course, like some master key films, the film's narrative is largely comprehensible to most audiences without this insider knowledge. Many observers claim that such an alternative reading is absurd and unverifiable because of this fact. Such debates proliferate in virtual communities, such as on the fan website PulpFiction.com, in which there is a discussion board devoted exclusively to this issue entitled "The Briefcase & The Band Aid." On one hand, some contributors argue that the master key interpretation is partly verified by the enigmatic Band-Aid on the back of

Wallace's neck because they claim the soul is removed from there by the devil. Furthermore, the briefcase is opened with the combination "666" and Vincent and Jules, the latter of who routinely quotes the Bible, are seemingly saved from a barrage of bullets by divine intervention when they attempt to recover it. Yet, on the other hand, some fans counter that the briefcase's exact contents are purposely never revealed because it is simply a quintessential MacGuffin. To support their position further, they cite numerous interviews in which Tarantino himself consistently maintains that what is in the briefcase is and should remain a mystery. This kind of disagreement about the correct way to understand *Pulp Fiction*'s meaning is one of the primary reasons why it can be difficult to identify master key films definitively. Any film can be read figuratively since it always can be interpreted in a multiplicity of ways. A film's status as a master key film, then, can be challenging to validate because the presence of an alternative narrative explanation is often vehemently denied by those who believe that overzealous fans have discovered connections never intended by its makers.

The existence of such alternative narrative explanations that render a film's ostensible ambiguities narratively significant undoubtedly raises questions about the misdirection film's relationship to the classical paradigm. Although these films can be distinguished from standard Hollywood fare, most are more closely aligned with the classical film than they are with other cinematic traditions, such as experimental film or art cinema, in which Bordwell argues that "the tight causality of classical Hollywood construction is replaced by a more tenuous linking of events" (*Narration* 206). As with art cinema, I grant that viewers often rely on suppositions about authorial intent to explain the causal relationship of events in the misdirection film. In contrast to art cinema, however, misdirection films typically do not feature psychologically ambiguous characters who remain uncertain about even their own motives. Instead, misdirection films generally can be retrospectively reinterpreted hyper-classically in spite of their seemingly non-classical tendencies precisely because the revelation often exposes how an indisputable cause—someone or something concrete—has been secretly orchestrating events behind the scenes. The misdirection film represents Hollywood's concerted attempt to appeal to a niche market seeking innovation within relatively secure confines. The narrative and formal experiments contained in misdirection films, like innovations associated with genre, are ultimately attractive to some audiences because they promise to be at once something that is comfortably familiar as well as something that is new and different. These films exemplify how Hollywood has historically striven to capture audiences by making a subset of films that are at once classical and something more.

Although the revised interpretations that misdirection films inspire do not necessarily abandon Hollywood's storytelling and representational principles, their growing popularity suggests that some contemporary viewers are drawn to films that explicitly expose the constructedness of the classical film. Bordwell, then, may go too far by claiming that the misdirection film's innovations are almost always completely contained by the classical paradigm. He is right that the classical mode is still dominant and that virtually all contemporary Hollywood releases, including misdirection films, are rooted in the classical tradition; however, misdirection films also have a crucial non-classical element. Whereas the classical film is supposed to conceal its storytelling and representational mechanics to suture viewers into the narrative, the misdirection film typically shows that those very principles have been employed to distract viewers from discovering the truth, shattering the façade of Hollywood's invisible style and drawing attention directly to it as a construction, in retrospect. The critical awareness that this epiphany fosters renders the narrative itself spectacular. The historical prominence of such excess is one of the primary reasons that it is difficult to maintain that the classical narrative is, or has ever been, what most characterizes the Hollywood film. Even during the height of the studio-era, Elizabeth Cowie writes, producers aimed to obtain "multiple guarantees," secured "through other elements of the package, notably stars and high production values, but also sensational and spectacular elements" (182). Narrative is just one variable that Hollywood has considered in its production formula and the historical role that spectacular attributes, like excessive narrative itself, have played in attracting audiences, especially over the past few decades, needs to be accounted for more thoroughly.

That does not mean that misdirection films jettison the classical paradigm entirely. As with most Hollywood films concocted with an indie sensibility to cater to niche audiences, misdirection films often seem to be more unconventional than they actually are. This can allow misdirection films to uphold dominant ideologies covertly, as their meanings often do not become fully evident until after repeated viewings. The cultural politics of indie films can be similarly difficult to ascertain because their supposed alternative status may function to obscure their core messages. The connections between mainstream and indie films make it notoriously slippery to define the genre, a phenomenon that is only compounded by Hollywood's growing interest in the sector. Consequently, Michael Newman's contention that the indie film is best conceived of as "a cultural category," determined by "a cluster of interpretive strategies and expectations shared among" various groups rather than by "industrial criteria or formal and stylistic conventions" is a useful analog for my study of the misdirection film (*Indie* 11). Like Newman, I justify my generic grouping by charting the ways in which misdirection films provoke various groups to engage with them differently than mainstream fare, which is itself also always a constructed category subject to change based on historical circumstances. Using the broad indie label to classify these films, then, would present the same problem as the "narrative complexity" classification because it does not specifically identify how misdirection films can be distinguished from other contemporary cinematic forms that are also known for both challenging and upholding Hollywood conventions.

The way in which indies encourage interpretive activities that depart from the classical film, however, is a good starting point for comparing it to the misdirection film. In *American Independent Cinema*, Geoff King documents how developments in the late 1970s and 1980s, such as the explosion of film festivals, the success of the VCR, and Hollywood's growing blockbuster conservatism, created a larger audience for offbeat films, providing independent producers with more distribution opportunities, albeit on a limited basis. These conditions paved the way for a string of successful independently produced films that got the industry's attention, including *Stranger Than Paradise* (1984), *She's Gotta Have It* (1986), and *sex, lies, and videotape* (1989). Hollywood's subsequent, direct involvement in many films typically classified as indies suggests why King theorizes that indies are often conceptually distinguished by their tendency "to employ devices designed to deny, block, delay, or complicate the anticipated development of narrative, to reduce clarity or resolution and in some cases to increase narrative self-consciousness" (*American* 63). In spite of these attributes, King notes that a majority of indies are readily comprehensible to most audiences, situating them "somewhere between" Bordwell's "classical" and "art cinema" modes of narration, but ultimately rendering them closest in spirit to the standard Hollywood film (*American* 101). Like most films labeled as indies, misdirection films, many of which are also categorized as indies, largely adhere to Hollywood principles. The indie and the misdirection film, though, can also be differentiated from classical films by how they play with those very conventions. King's notion of the indie, therefore, relates to the misdirection film for two reasons. First, it demonstrates that Hollywood genres are determined by how films are *perceived* as linked to one another by various groups, including film scholars. Second, it suggests that misdirection films are part of a larger production trend, characterized by Hollywood's increasing willingness to back films that challenge some classical conventions at the same time that they uphold others.

Although Hollywood has growing faith in supporting narrative complexity, the conditions that have made the misdirection film more appealing to producers and audiences are not exactly the same as those that contributed to the concurrent rise in indies. Of course, the indie and misdirection film genres only represent a small fraction of Hollywood's output since the early 1990s. Misdirection films have coexisted with many other types of Hollywood films since then, a majority of which are more closely aligned with industry standards because they play far less with classical conventions. Like the indie-era identified by Newman, the periodization in this book is somewhat unsystematic; however, there was a quantifiable increase in the number of misdirection films distributed by Hollywood since roughly the same moment that he identifies as the beginning of the "Sundance-Miramax era" at the very end of the 1980s. This starting point also marks the time in which the most recognizable prototypes of the genre, films like *The Usual Suspects*, *The Sixth Sense*, and *Inception*, were released. As Newman theorizes, all periodization is arbitrary, but he also shows how such conditions make it as logical of a starting point for the study of these films as any alternative. In an industry that prioritizes profit over everything else, it is also important to link the selected period to trends in Hollywood that made it more appealing to produce these films. As with the indie, the misdirection film's growth is partly connected to the changing revenue streams resulting from technological developments that altered the ways that Hollywood films are distributed, exhibited, and experienced. As a result, the chosen timeframe also dovetails with the rise and fall of media and communication technologies that impacted film production strategies and reception practices, most notably the DVD player, which was at the height of its popularity during the misdirection film's peak and was in steady decline by the end of the period under study. The circumstances that made this epoch well-suited for films that encourage retrospective reinterpretations of narrative information are what warrant further examination.

At the same time, it is important to note that neither indies nor misdirection films are solely products of the contemporary moment. Narratively complex and prominent independent films were backed by Hollywood during the studio-era. Additionally, the industry has largely outsourced production to independents since it transformed into its current role as primarily a distributor and financer after the end of vertical integration. As Bordwell admits, "Hollywood has long been a stylized filmmaking tradition" because even at the height of the studio system, "Fritz Lang and Orson Welles" consistently "put formal problems at the center of their work" and that "[Alfred] Hitchcock is virtually the patron saint of young filmmakers who want to tinker with storytelling" (*The Way* 74). Welles, Lang, and Hitchcock indeed each made films in the studio-era, such as *Citizen Kane*, *The Woman in the Window* (1944),

Beyond a Reasonable Doubt (1956), *Stage Fright* (1950), and *Psycho*, which encourage viewers to reinterpret a majority of narrative information retrospectively. The presence of these films reveals that misdirection films are not just a product of changing cultural, industrial, and technological contexts, as some audiences have long derived pleasure from films that challenge classical standards and producers found ways to make them successfully in previous periods.

Despite the historical persistence of the misdirection film, it has unquestionably become much more common of late. For Bruce Isaacs, such a production trend reveals that "narrative experimentation is no longer the privileged domain of the European art film but commonplace in American studio productions" (130). Yet, as Hitchcock's long struggle to make a commercially successful misdirection film suggests, there are key reasons why they were produced far less frequently prior to the 1990s. As I argued in "Misdirection in Fits and Starts," an array of evidence reveals that the director always aspired to make a successful misdirection film; however, after his belated entry into the genre with *Stage Fright*, Hitchcock was so reticent to direct another one because of that film's critical and commercial disappointment that he revealed *Vertigo*'s (1958) big secret only to the audience approximately two-thirds of the way through the film instead of at the conclusion, the time that it is exposed in the source novel. Instead of its remarkable success being most attributable to narrative construction, then, the famously effective reception of *Psycho*, which similarly contains a changeover, stems from other primary factors. In particular, the marketing campaign leveraged how *Alfred Hitchcock Presents* (1955–1965) made the director into a star and colloquially reshaped his reputation as the "Master of Surprise," largely explaining why he shot the film to look like an extended episode of the show to capitalize on his fame. Finally, *Psycho* was exhibited and marketed in ways that optimized its surprises. Such radical tactics were necessary when the movie theater was virtually the only venue for viewing Hollywood films, showcasing the obstacles inhibiting the misdirection film's effectiveness at the time as well as the roles that promotion and exhibition can play in its successful reception.

Clearly, much has changed in Hollywood since the release of *Psycho* that has made misdirection films more attractive to the industry. New film exhibition and media communication technologies have been a boon for the industry in a number of ways. For starters, they have helped to bolster the reputations of films that otherwise likely would not have received much attention after they disappeared from theaters. As of August 2015, for instance, *Fight Club* is listed as the 10th most popular film of all time on the *Internet Movie Database*'s (imdb.com) Top 250 list.

Fight Club's canonical status is significant, considering that it generated an underwhelming $37 million at the domestic box office on its $63 million budget (imdb.com). Such box-office disappointment is not uncommon for misdirection films, as many struggle to recover negative costs during their theatrical runs. Yet, *Fight Club*'s post-theatrical performance also indicates the potential rapid reversal of fortune associated with these films. *Fight Club* has since become renowned for being both one of the best DVDs available and among the best Hollywood films ever made. *Entertainment Weekly*, for example, put the film's two-disc special edition atop its 2001 list of "50 Essential DVDs" (ew.com). *Total Film Magazine* readers similarly ranked *Fight Club* as the second best film of all time on its 2006 Top 100 list (totalfilm.com). This swift appreciation has not only elevated *Fight Club*'s reputation; it also transformed the film into a moneymaker. In April 2001, *Variety* reported that *Fight Club* grossed $55 million in home video revenues ten months after the two-disc special edition DVD became available (Bing). This small fragment of the film's post-theatrical revenues, which does not include subsequent earnings from home-video sales and rentals, epitomizes Hollywood's economic logic at a time when the theatrical take can have little impact on overall profitability.

A film's box-office performance is not now insignificant, however, as Hollywood films have a much greater chance of becoming hits in the aftermarket if they do well in U.S. theaters. Additionally, not all misdirection films only become canonized or profitable after their theatrical runs. To wit, *Inception* grossed nearly $300 million at the domestic box office and over $800 million theatrically worldwide, helping it immediately secure a spot near the top of the imdb.com 250 list, where it still resided in the lofty 14th position in August 2015 (imdb.com). *Inception* is the exception rather than the rule, though, as some of its success is attributable to its atypical blockbuster status. No other contemporary misdirection film comes close to its $160 million production budget and its estimated $100 million marketing expenditures (Fritz). Prior to *Inception*, *The Sixth Sense* was the template for the successful misdirection film, earning $293 million at the box office during its domestic theatrical run, which made it the seventh highest grossing film ever in the United States at the time (imdb.com). Unlike *Inception* and many other contemporary films that reap enormous profits, though, *The Sixth Sense* was an unanticipated sensation because it was not packaged as blockbuster fare. Similar to *Inception*, however, it was well-received by critics and arthouse audiences, suggesting that its particular narrative structure was the primary appeal for many viewers. Its changeover was so memorable that its high artistic reputation appears to be secure in a number of circles because the American Film Institute included it on its revised 2007 list of the Top 100 films ever made, and imdb.com voters ranked it as the 159th best film of all time on the Top 250 list, as of August 2015.

Although such theatrical profits are impressive, a film's financial performance in theaters only reveals so much about its cultural and economic worth. The domestic box-office take is now often just an indicator of the effectiveness of exorbitant marketing campaigns. More importantly, a Hollywood film's profitability and cultural legacy extend well beyond its run in U.S. theaters. The imdb.com rankings and other similar lists, likewise, have limited value in relation to what they express about the value that a culture places on a particular film. The results of the Top 250 list have probably been skewed by a number of factors, including the influence of preexisting critical discourses on voters and the relatively homogeneous demographic characteristics of participants on the site. However, even though lists such as these are not precise barometers of cultural tastes, they can reveal a great deal about what is considered superior by a particular interpretive community. For voters on imbd.com, films that provoke retrospective reinterpretations of narrative causality are among those deemed to have the greatest artistic merit. Many other recent films appearing on the imdb.com Top 250 list as of August, 2015, including *Pulp Fiction* (7th), *The Usual Suspects* (24th), *Memento* (44th), *The Prestige* (51st), *A Beautiful Mind* (148th), *Shutter Island* (2010, 192nd), and *12 Monkeys* (1995, 205th), provide further support for this observation. The existence of this potentially lucrative niche audience begins to indicate why industry executives were increasingly willing to produce so many misdirection films during the period under study in spite of their often shaky box-office performances.

The unexpected commercial and critical success of *The Sixth Sense* played a key role in making misdirection films a big part of Hollywood's creative plans. However, the film's remarkably strong box-office performance and six Academy Award nominations were surprises even to industry insiders. The circumstances surrounding the film's release suggest that it was neither intended to be a cash cow nor a prestige product because it was modestly budgeted at $40 million and hit theaters on August 6, 1999, the tail end of the summer blockbuster season and before the beginning of the release period typically reserved for Oscar fare (imdb.com). Disney's lack of confidence in *The Sixth Sense* was perhaps best exemplified by the fact that the media conglomerate sold the rights to distribute the film to Spyglass Entertainment and kept only a small distribution fee for itself (Stewart 302). The unanticipated positive reception of *The Sixth Sense* contributed to Hollywood's subsequent greenlighting of many misdirection films, some of which were specifically designed to garner cultural and industrial cachet. *A Beautiful Mind*, for example, an adaptation of Sylvia Nasar's 1998 Pulitzer Prize-nominated novel of the same name, was up for eight Academy Awards and scored four of the most celebrated statues at the 2002 ceremony, including the only Best Picture win for a contemporary misdirection film. *A Beautiful Mind* was not an anomaly because *Atonement*, which similarly was adapted from a critically acclaimed novel, Ian McEwan's 2001 book of the same name, was nominated for seven Academy Awards in 2008, including Best Picture, Best Supporting Actress, and Best Adapted Screenplay (imdb.com). Misdirection films clearly became crucial components of the media conglomerates' portfolios in the 2000s, as best evidenced by blockbusters like *Inception* and prestige films like *Shutter Island*, directed by Martin Scorsese, arguably Hollywood's foremost auteur. Such production strategies suggest that they were not just unexpected hits by that time, as they were throughout the 1990s, thanks to the surprise success of films, like *The Crying Game*, *Pulp Fiction*, *The Sixth Sense*, and *The Usual Suspects*.

Perhaps nothing more effectively displays the growing faith that industry executives had in the economic potential of misdirection films than their increasing willingness to attach established A-list stars, such as Halle Berry (*Perfect Stranger* [2007]), Pierce Brosnan (*Shattered* [2007]), Nicholas Cage (*Adaptation* [2002]), Russell Crowe (*A Beautiful Mind*), Tom Cruise (*Magnolia* and *Vanilla Sky*), John Cusack (*Identity* [2003]), Robert De Niro (*Hide and Seek* [2005]), Leonardo DiCaprio (*Inception* and *Shutter Island*), Michael Douglas (*The Game* [1997]), Richard Gere (*Primal Fear* [1996]), Anthony Hopkins (*The Human Stain* [2003]), Nicole Kidman (*The Others* [2001] and *The Human Stain*), Ben Kingsley (*Shutter Island*), Sean Penn (*The Game*), Meryl Streep (*Adaptation*), Denzel Washington (*Fallen* [1998]), and Bruce Willis (*Pulp Fiction*, *12 Monkeys*, *The Sixth Sense*, *Unbreakable* [2000], *Lucky Number Slevin* [2006], and *Perfect Stranger*), to these projects throughout the period. Misdirection films have also been produced with such regularity of late because they have provided Hollywood with many of its newest, bankable leading men and women. Actors, such as Christian Bale (*American Psycho* [2000], *The Machinist* [2004], and *The Prestige*), Edward Norton (*Primal Fear*, *Fight Club*, and *The Illusionist* [2006]), Guy Pearce (*Memento*), Brad Pitt (*12 Monkeys* and *Fight Club*), Kevin Spacey (*The Usual Suspects*), and Naomi Watts (*Mulholland Dr.*), established their esteemed critical reputations in large part by starring in one or more misdirection films early in their careers. Finally, a number of Hollywood's hottest young filmmakers during the period, including David Fincher (*The Game* and *Fight Club*), Gregory Hoblit (*Primal Fear* and *Fallen*), Nolan (*Memento*, *The Prestige*, and *Inception*), and Shyamalan (*The Sixth Sense*, *Unbreakable*, and *The Village* [2004]), helped to develop their authorial standing by directing multiple misdirection films. The genre, then, was on the minds of the majors and ultimately resonated with many viewers starting in the 1990s because shifting cultural, industrial, and technological circumstances made them more attractive to producers and some audiences.

Chapter Outline

In subsequent chapters, I first differentiate misdirection films more thoroughly from affiliated classifications and further chart evidence to support the claim that these films constitute a verifiable genre. Consequently, I employ the discursive approach to genre to theorize and provide historical evidence to back my assertion that the misdirection film is a distinct category. As my discussion of the master key film already suggests, though, there are potential issues associated with using the discursive approach to genre because it can take years for the alternative interpretations of narrative information to originate, circulate, and calcify. Chapter 1, therefore, grapples with both the benefits and shortcomings of the discursive approach to genre. After distinguishing the misdirection film from some of its closest cinematic relatives, I examine the utterances associated with it to show that although the discursive approach is more culturally and historically attuned than traditional forms of genre study, dogmatic reliance on it can negatively impact how the genre's constituents are subsequently interpreted and evaluated.

I begin to forge, in greater detail, the connections between contemporary misdirection films and their cultural contexts in chapter 2. I determine the reasons why two overlapping narrative forms—misdirection films and conspiracy theories—have appeared with such regularity in the United States since the early 1990s. Irrespective of their subject matter, misdirection films prompt spectators to engage in interpretive behaviors that align with those employed by conspiracy theorists. Like misdirection films, conspiracy theories counter "official" explanations with an alternative account that is more satisfying than what was initially provided. Although conspiracy theorizing seems to challenge traditional ways of comprehending history, it also resembles misdirection films by relying on the same kind of causal reasoning as the narratives to which it is opposed by suggesting that everything can be understood according to a totalizing causal logic that can be traced back to the specific actions of historical agents. Not coincidentally, this ever-popular, American cultural pastime has flourished in the United States during a neoliberal-era characterized by the consolidation of corporate power and the diminishing agency of non-elites. Misdirection films frequently articulate these concerns about dwindling individual autonomy. This tendency is typified by the chapter's case studies—*Jacob's Ladder* and *Arlington Road*—which portray protagonists as victims of devious plots against them and also encourage viewers to reinterpret their meanings conspiratorially.

Chapter 3 continues to link the misdirection film to its cultural contexts and paranoid thinking by examining how its depictions of gender illustrate how it frequently relies on and upholds classical standards to work its deceptive magic as well as maintain the existing social order. Although the revelations in contemporary misdirection films typically show that seemingly feminized primary male characters are unexpectedly more powerful than their conventionally masculine protagonists, they usually do not suggest that multiple masculinities are a reality. Rather than demonstrating the progressive potential of the decoupling of masculinity from other aspects of identity, *Unbreakable* and *The Usual Suspects* exemplify how misdirection films often portray manhood regressively to uphold dominant ideologies about gender. The chapter details how these two films present disturbing fantasies of male masquerade in which men covertly maintain their authority by flaunting their purported fragilities. Even though their duplicitous narratives are well-suited to display masculinity as a construction, misdirection films like these instead confirm that gender performance is a skill men master to hide the male essence that "really" lies beneath the surface.

The narrative logic of these films begins to indicate why they are attractive to Hollywood's most coveted market: young, white, male viewers. Many core fans identify with the struggle and eventual triumph of seemingly disempowered male characters who surprisingly turn out to be primary causal agents. Chapter 4 explores the ways in which the online reception of misdirection films demonstrates how the industry successfully generates profit by catering to audiences that most commonly interact with its products obsessively in the digital age. I examine how *Mulholland Dr.* and *Memento* were produced and promoted to capitalize on this lucrative target market's propensity to engage in repeated, post-theatrical viewings, particularly on DVD, and discuss their meanings online. Their atypical complexities inspired an inordinate amount of interpretive work devoted to figuring out their "true" meanings in virtual communities. Interestingly, fans often cite the intentions of their almost always male creators to support their interpretations. In the end, these films are successful in the aftermarket largely because they satisfy a desire for mastery, a yearning often associated with young, tech-savvy, male film collectors who also consider themselves discerning Hollywood cinephiles.

As with any genre, certain creative personnel have become inextricably linked to it. Chapter 5 extends my industrial analysis by documenting the sharply contrasting career trajectories of the two filmmakers most closely connected to the contemporary Hollywood misdirection film: Shyamalan and Nolan. While Shyamalan's branding efforts in relation to the genre have, at least for the time being, derailed his once promising career, Nolan's connections to the misdirection film have helped make him into one of the industry's most valuable auteur commodities. In the wake of *The Sixth Sense*, Shyamalan jumped at the chance to market himself almost exclusively as the genre's preeminent director, a ploy that began to backfire with successive films and has now been abandoned, perhaps only temporarily, to reconstruct his floundering image. In contrast, Nolan's success as a marketable property is largely a consequence of promotional strategies that dovetail better with New Hollywood's industrial logic. Importantly, his ascent to the top of the misdirection film genre has not been ignored in advertising, but it never became the primary emphasis of marketing campaigns. This approach has proven much more effective for weathering the vicissitudes of taste and box-office volatility than the myopically focused one associated to Shyamalan. The comparative assessment of the two directors' changing reputations, then, expresses some of the perils of packaging misdirection films for consumption as well as the connections between authorship, genre, and industrial conditions in contemporary Hollywood cinema.

Although the industry's consistent willingness to attach A-list stars and up-and-coming directors to misdirection films since the 1990s illustrates Hollywood's continued faith in the genre, it was not until 2010 that it briefly reached fully elite status. Prior to this time, only a handful of misdirection films had been prestige products granted relatively large budgets. In 2010, however, the industry released two misdirection films—*Inception* and *Shutter Island*—that demonstrate its confidence in the genre had soared to new heights. Chapter 6 outlines how the creation and promotion of these two films highlight the importance of the misdirection film to the industry's larger strategies at the time. Interestingly, DiCaprio starred in both films, making his portrayal of the reconstruction of the broken man key to their success. The final chapter, therefore, ties the book's major arguments together by providing case studies that show how the genre had become optimal by this time for its cultural, industrial, and technological contexts.

Surprisingly, the misdirection film seems to have fizzled out temporarily after reaching its apotheosis in 2010. The Conclusion briefly explores the reasons for and results of this sudden and unexpected decline in generic output. Technological advancements are at the root of many of the most plausible culprits and explanations, as changes in home-video greatly impacted the industry's revenue streams. In the preceding years, the supremacy of the DVD was already being challenged seriously by other nontheatrical platforms, including Blu-ray, on-demand, and streaming video online. These developments paved the way for moving-image texts that employ the narrative mode to begin migrating more frequently to other media. The television industry, for instance, was able to replicate Hollywood's formula with DVD by adopting a viable publishing model for the first time in its history. As the success of shows, like *Lost* (2004–2010) and *Heroes* (2006–2010), reveals, these technological advancements enabled television producers to cash in on products that similarly respond to the same cultural anxieties and desires as the misdirection film. Such a tendency begins to suggest how and why the narrative mode has endured even though it has virtually disappeared, at least for now, from the silver screen.

The chapters that follow this introduction map the historical trajectory of the contemporary Hollywood misdirection film—from its high point, beginning in the early 1990s to its current downturn—by situating the genre in its cultural, industrial, and technological surround. My exploration ultimately demonstrates how, on one hand, these films have been fashioned in response to certain conditions that have remained stable in Hollywood, while, on the other hand, the ways they are constructed are a consequence of new circumstances that made their production and reception more favorable than ever before in the industry.

1

Retrospective Issues

The Discursive Approach to Genre and the Misdirection Film

A lot of recent films seem unsatisfied unless they can add final scenes that redefine the reality of everything that has gone before; call it the Keyser Söze syndrome.

Roger Ebert, from his review of *Fight Club*

Nothing prepared me for *Magnolia*'s conclusion, and for that I am grateful . . . *Magnolia* is admittedly not for everyone, but those who "get" the film are in for something that ranks as more of a cinematic experience than a mere movie.

James Berardinelli, from his review of *Magnolia*

During the studio era, it was standard for the "A" picture to be part of a program that played on a continuous loop. Consequently, viewers were unaccustomed both to getting to theaters by precise start times and to experiencing the feature film uninterrupted from beginning to end. Historically specific promotional strategies were required to market the misdirection film effectively in that context because it was not well positioned for dominant movie-going practices at the time. As

Joan Hawkins documents, to coincide with the release of *Psycho* (1960), Alfred Hitchcock virtually copied tactics from the marketing campaign for *Les diaboliques* (1955) by creating advertisements that instructed spectators to arrive before the film began and urged them not to spoil the ending (378). Thanks in part to Hitchcock's marketing ploys, exhibition practices grew more favorable for optimizing the misdirection film's narrative pleasures. It subsequently became routine for exhibitors to screen feature films at advertised start times. In spite of these new conditions, Hollywood did not back many misdirection films until the 1990s when cultural, industrial, and technological conditions all became more favorable for their production and reception. Not coincidentally, at the same time when these films exploded in popularity, the term "spoiler warning" became part of the common parlance to discourage viewers from ruining the primary pleasures associated with them in online forums or elsewhere.

This is the kind of discursive evidence that begins to demonstrate that misdirection films do, in fact, constitute a genre with a rich history that has changed over time. In this chapter, I chart the discourses associated with *Fight Club* (1999) and *Magnolia* (1999) to reveal how the particular ways in which various groups engage with misdirection films render them distinct from other Hollywood fare. *Fight Club*'s critical reputation has grown immensely since its theatrical release largely because of its complex narrative structure; however, its changeover was typically cited as a weakness initially. As a result, it was identified as a constituent of the genre immediately and suffered commercially and critically as a result of being characterized as a clear-cut misdirection film that employed the changeover unsuccessfully. *Fight Club*'s changeover, however, transformed into an asset in the post-theatrical market, vaulting it into the contemporary canon. Yet, much debate remains about the film's merits because its changeover's full significance is difficult to interpret definitively. In contrast, whereas *Magnolia* was initially received more favorably by some critics, it took some time for its status as a misdirection film to calcify because its master key first had to be unearthed and understood. This delayed discovery and reinterpretation of the film, likewise, ultimately improved its reputation. Similar to *Fight Club*, though, there is no consensus about the master key's impact on the film's gender commentary, making it challenging to determine *Magnolia*'s cultural politics. Put simply, there is still extensive disagreement about both films' takes on gender because of how the meaning of all narrative information potentially changes dramatically in light of the revelation's significance.

Drastic reconsiderations of misdirection films' cultural relevance are common, particularly in relation to markers of identity, because of both the atypical ways they are constructed and viewers interact with them. Such deferred classifications and assessments reveal that reception can depend heavily on how these films are classified, discussed, and comprehended at distinct moments in time, suggesting why generic groupings and interpretations can enormously influence a film's reputation. The following analysis of both films, then, shows why the creation and persistence of generic classifications shape how constituent films are subsequently understood and evaluated.

Theoretical Gag Order: The Drawbacks of the Discursive Approach to Genre

While terms associated with narrative surprise, like spoiler warnings, are frequently deployed in relation to misdirection films, they are not the only kinds of media texts that inspire groups to utter them. Such alerts are perhaps now most commonly used by television viewers, especially in a digital era in which shows are increasingly watched repeatedly via timeshifting technologies and discussed zealously in virtual communities. The advent of new devices and platforms, like DVD, DVR, and social media, has played a huge role in prompting the "forensic fandom" that Jason Mittell identifies as characterizing the reception of the narratively complex fictional programming that now pervades increasingly serialized American television ("Forensic"). As the success of shows, such as *Alfred Hitchcock Presents* (1955–1965) and *The Twilight Zone* (1959–1964), suggests, television has perhaps always been the ideal moving-image medium for misdirection narratives since its relatively short, episodic nature usually misleads audiences for far less time during a single viewing than the standard Hollywood film. In fact, Hitchcock once memorably quipped in *TV Guide* in 1957 that the audience acts "like grown-ups when they get something for free in their own homes" but "become children again when they have to pay" (qtd. in Kapsis 38). Although television has never actually been free, the perception that audiences do not pay for it can help foster greater acceptance of narrative experimentation on the medium. As Mittell and Jonathan Gray point out in their discussion of the reception of *Lost* (2004–2010), television fans are often willing to "give themselves over to creators to be manipulated and controlled through the storytelling process" and that, contrary to conventional wisdom, spoiling does not ruin the fun, but instead "make[s] a show that they love even more enjoyable." Conversely, discursive evidence indicates that most misdirection film fans agree with *USA Today*'s Mike Clark who, in a review of *The Sixth Sense* (1999), claims its changeover should be preserved because "anybody who would divulge that deserves the kind of fate that would permit young Cole to see him walking around in blood" (10E).

Even though there may be similarities in how misdirection narratives are structured on film and television, the differences in the ways they are typically received begins to illustrate why it is appropriate to conceive of these films as constituting a distinct genre. Of course, spoiler warnings are also used for many other types of Hollywood films that do not fall in the misdirection genre, particularly those that are also loaded with narrative surprises or complexities. This suggests some of the drawbacks of solely relying on discursive evidence from user groups to determine generic categorizations because many films that do not inspire retrospective reinterpretations of all that has come before also are associated with these utterances. Like other humanistic methods, the discursive approach to genre is inexact and subjective because it has a strong qualitative dimension that cannot be precisely quantified. There is, for instance, no minimum threshold of utterances that determines if a given film should be classified in a genre. More importantly, the existence of such evidence is often a matter of happenstance to begin with, which leads to unsystematic results that can leave generic creation in the hands of those whose motives for executing the groupings vary widely.

Despite these methodological shortcomings, there are numerous reasons why the discursive approach is useful to theorists who strive to avoid traditional genre study's ahistorical pitfalls. Rick Altman's *Film/Genre* seminally illustrates how the discursive approach's culturally and historically attuned method considers film genres to be "defined by multiple codes, corresponding to the multiple groups who, by helping to define the genre, may be said to 'speak' the genre" (208). This summary shows how the discursive approach can free genre study from its static and reductive trappings by perceiving of genres as cultural categories always subject to reconstitution based on how user groups define them at distinct moments. Thus, I rely on Altman's semantic/syntactic/pragmatic model to highlight how the misdirection films' textual properties (semantics) and meanings (syntax) prompt groups of people to engage with them (pragmatics) in ways that separate them from other Hollywood fare.

Many scholars recently attempting to rescue genre theory from its ahistorical leanings also incorporate pragmatics to highlight how user groups, such as audiences, critics, exhibitors, and producers, contribute to perpetually fluctuating categorizations. James Naremore posits in *More Than Night*, for example, that film noir is best conceived of as "a loose, evolving system of arguments and readings that helps to shape commercial strategies and aesthetic ideologies" (11). Film noir is a touchstone category for genre theorists precisely because the term was coined *ex post facto* by French critics. Even though no one set out to make a film noir during its classical period since the genre had not been created yet, constituent films were distinct to those who classified them in the group retroactively. Regardless of how capricious or accurate any of these originating critics' categorizations are, their ramifications have been significant. The genre's conventions have been frequently mobilized by filmmakers since at least the late 1960s often to challenge some Hollywood standards and certain dominant ideologies. I grant that such accounts of film noir's history and legacy may overstate the genre's unconventionality and its ideological uniformity; however, its atypical characteristics were recognizable to those who initially identified it and their definitions of the genre have since influenced many producers. Genres, in short, are both out there and not out there. Definitive elements are always arbitrary and subject to change, but those very conceptions can instrumentally shape production trends for years to come.

Unfortunately, the way that the discursive approach to genre has developed discourages this critical intervention because it dissuades scholars from birthing new categories. According to most accounts, the discursive approach in Film Studies can be traced back to Andrew Tudor, who, in the 1970s, presciently argued that genre study is predicated on a self-fulfilling prophecy that adheres to a circular logic, whereby constituent texts are cherry-picked to exemplify the attributes already thought to distinguish a category. To counter this methodological shortcoming, Tudor instead views genres as "sets of cultural conventions" defined by what groups of people "collectively believe them to be" at given historical moments (139). This is the key principle that guides Mittell's influential, yet misguided, application of the discursive approach in *Genre and Television*, in which he urges scholars to "examine the cultural processes of generic discourse *prior* to examining the generic texts that have been traditionally viewed as identical to the genre itself" (emphasis in original, 16). Discovering utterances that reveal a film's generic identity *first* indeed mitigates Tudor's empiricist dilemma. This approach, though, is contingent on luck that becomes more likely with the luxury of retrospect. To avoid succumbing to ahistorical methods, scholars have to wait for others to make the generic connections to get the hard proof to group constituents accordingly. More disconcertingly, the self-fulfilling prophecy is still possible, as the majority of discursive evidence can be ignored in favor of atypical utterances, such as Ebert's pejorative account of *Fight Club* cited in this chapter's epigraph.

Although Mittell urges critics to attend to the extratextual universe first, he admits that categories "run through texts," raising the specters of textual analysis and intertextuality in discursive genre study (*Genre* 13). Yet, he also critiques Altman for adding pragmatics to account for the discursive surround as a mere addendum to his formative semantic/syntactic theory of genre, which, respectively, examines both a genre's recurrent textual elements and how those attributes are repeatedly deployed. Specifically, Mittell contends that "despite Altman's foregrounding of cultural processes, textual structure remains the centerpiece" rendering it incompatible with a focus on how "categories operate outside the bounds of the text" (*Genre* 16). Mittell, therefore, encourages a turn to textual evidence *only after* the requisite extratextual utterances are discovered, regardless of how random the rationale is for their inclusion in the first place. To take *Fight Club* as an example, according to this logic, I could mention the self-aware references to its duplicitous narrative as confirmers of its status as a misdirection film only because Ebert luckily connected it already to *The Usual Suspects* (1995). Consequently, the unnamed narrator's (Edward Norton) voiceover after discovering that Tyler Durden (Brad Pitt) is a product of his dissociative identity disorder, in which he says it is "a changeover, the movie goes on and nobody in the audience has any idea" now becomes harmonious with Mittell's conception of the discursive approach.

The potential pitfalls of Mittell's application of discursive genre theory are more clearly evinced by a master key film, like *Magnolia*, which was not immediately classifiable in the misdirection film genre because it only became one thanks to belated utterances by critics and fans. Unsurprisingly, I have discovered no initial reviews and promotional materials that definitively categorize it as such. This is because the reasons for and meanings of writer/director Paul Thomas Anderson's inclusion of a climactic rain of frogs were designed to mystify, at least initially.

Figure 1.1. The unnamed narrator faints during *Fight Club*'s changeover upon discovering that Tyler Durden is a manifestation of his dissociative identity disorder.

As with Berardinelli's review of *Magnolia* referenced in the epigraph, Ebert's review, which comes close to putting it in the misdirection genre, claims that the film's "threads converge, in one way or another, upon an event there is no way for the audience to anticipate. This event is not 'cheating,' as some critics have argued, because the prologue fully prepares the way for it, as do some subtle references to Exodus." Yet, he subsequently advises audiences to "Leave logic at the door" to appreciate the film fully. At best, then, reviewers could only speculate that *Magnolia* might be narratively coherent after repeated viewings, a critical trope that persists in reviews of some of Anderson's subsequent films also filled with seemingly eternal narrative ambiguities, especially *The Master* (2012). In his review of *The Master*, for instance, Colin Covert of the *Minneapolis Star-Tribune* epitomizes these suppositions by noting "Anderson's audacious films defy facile interpretation. Having seen it just once, I'm not sure I grasp it . . . I'm uncertain if the film's final scenes should be interpreted as dreams or reality." This discursive evidence merely suggests there *could* be a master key that unlocks the meaning of the film's many ambiguities, making it a stretch to call it a misdirection film only based on such speculation.

There are conceivably many instances for which no corroborating extratextual evidence exists for misdirection films prior to the publication of textual analysis that unearths their secrets. This presents a substantial challenge to identify potential constituents by using only pragmatics, which is why I adopt Altman's semantic/syntactic/pragmatic approach rather than heed Mittell's call for scholars to turn to textual properties only after first identifying the requisite extratextual evidence. This is partly because producers can and do initiate intertextual connections, which can be accounted for by semantics and syntax, that help to situate films in generic categories. Another key shortcoming of Mittell's approach is that the chances of discovering discursive affirmations of generic identity are more remote for many films released before new technologies democratized both film criticism and repeat viewings in post-theatrical settings. This comparative dearth of available evidence makes critical discourse the most likely repository of these generic utterances because, as Altman theorizes, "critics' desires to use regenrification as part of their critical arsenal" are "unpreventable" (82). If such a critical tendency is inevitable, I contend that it should be embraced rather than avoided in spite of its ahistorical drawbacks. As Altman notes, critics' generic inventions can have positive outcomes. Decades ago, for example, numerous feminist-inspired scholars reclassified some melodramas into the non-industrially recognized woman's film genre. Although this regrouping is unverifiable using the discursive approach, as existing utterances did not categorize them accordingly, the interventions of these scholars encouraged productive reconsiderations of these films in relation to patriarchy, Hollywood conventions, prevailing evaluations, and so on.

Historical distance, then, is the frill that permits theorists to map the discursive roots of critically generated genres, like the woman's film and film noir. Crucially, such originating utterances only exist in the first place because innovative scholars and critics created the labels and associated groupings based on semantic and syntactic evidence without waiting for others, like industry professionals, to do it for them. As Altman's rigorous historical research illustrates, these stories of generic initiation are not the exception because categories always calcify retroactively, regardless of who prompts the grouping. Now taken-for-granted monikers, such as the western and the musical, moved from first being adjectives associated with established categories to the nouns that ultimately denoted the genres themselves in industrial discourse (Altman 50–53). It is impossible to know, therefore, if or when a term will transform from being a modifier into the stable generic label itself. Although few media scholars have theorized how and why their own generic creations come into fruition, literary theorist Tzvetan Todorov tried to justify his origination efforts by distinguishing between "theoretical" and "historical" genres in his book, *The Fantastic*, a genre he invented that is characterized by the reader's hesitation between the uncanny and the marvelous, two related genres he also birthed. Fifteen years later, though, Todorov retracted his position by arguing that while it is "always possible" for individual critics to identify "a property common to two texts, and to put them together in a category," genre becomes "useful and operative" when "we agree to call genres only the classes of texts that have been historically perceived as such" (*Genres* 17). To salvage Todorov's useful differentiation, Steve Neale contends that media scholars should "distinguish theoretical genres from genres proper by renaming the former 'theoretical categories' " (43). In contrast, I argue that the term "theoretical genres" is appropriate because it's impossible to know if or when new terms and groupings will redraw previously agreed-upon boundaries.

Despite all of its problems, it is misguided to abandon the notion of genre entirely because it remains the primary way that groups, such as critics, exhibitors, producers, and spectators, relate Hollywood films to one another and differentiate them from each other. Marketing strategies for misdirection films begin to reveal why it is valuable to use Todorov's notion of theoretical genres rather than completely jettison the concept of genre. In particular, it shows how producers have capitalized on a growing awareness of these films as distinct in the minds of audiences, while, at the same time, accentuating their historical generic identities. These practices were exemplified by taglines associated with *The Sixth Sense.* Although one of the film's taglines, "Not every gift is a blessing," highlights its status as a supernatural thriller, other taglines, such as "Discover the secret of *The Sixth Sense*" and "Can you keep a secret?," foreground its memorable changeover (imdb.com). Similarly, *The Usual Suspects* was marketed as a crime drama with the tagline "Five Criminals. One Line Up. No Coincidence." Additional taglines, including "The truth is always in the last place you look" and "In a world where nothing is as it seems you have to look beyond . . . ," though, more directly alert viewers that there will be significant narrative surprises (imdb.com). The impetus for this seemingly contradictory marketing strategy is twofold. On one hand, it maintains the secret by securing expectations in the conventions of historical genres that may not inspire retrospective reinterpretations of narrative information. On the other hand, it allows producers to advertise the films in a hybrid fashion, as belonging to historical genres as well as to a theoretical genre renowned for narrative unreliability that has not yet been industrially codified as such.

Theatrical trailers and television spots for misdirection films demonstrate a similar dual marketing approach. An advertisement that aired shortly after the release of *The Usual Suspects* clearly positions the film according to its historical and theoretical generic identities. The ad displays scenes from the film, as favorable excerpts from reviews are superimposed over the images. The first anecdote to appear is taken from Jack Kroll's *Newsweek* review, proclaiming it to be "The best crime movie of the 90s." This reaffirmation of the film's status in a historical genre is followed by an omniscient narrator's voiceover and snippets from other reviews that emphasize the presence of the changeover. The words "Twist . . . Twist . . . Twist," are extracted from Tom Christie's *Details* review and coupled with the narrator's statement that the film has a "twist and a twist and a twist." Immediately thereafter, the narrator announces that the film has "a whopper of an ending," as the same phrase from Janet Maslin's *New York Times* review concurrently appears onscreen. In short, even though the commercial begins by situating the film as a crime drama, it subsequently accentuates its status as a misdirection film.

A cursory examination of film reviews also indicates that critics use language to describe these films as part of a theoretical genre by discussing them in ways that differ from their historical generic identities. Ebert's aforementioned reference to *The Usual Suspects* and aversion to its legion of imitators undoubtedly connects films officially categorized in other genres according to a new criterion that identifies their unique narrative structures as the semantic element that binds them together. Critic Rob McKenzie makes similar observations in response to the same upcropping of films:

> Nowadays, though, what used to be a surprise is like the toy at the bottom of the Cracker Jack Box; it's a surprise that is not a surprise, but if we don't get it, we feel ripped off. Not only are these twist endings almost inevitable, they've gotten a lot more twisted. What used to be a denouement—literally the untying of the knot—is now just as often a renouement. We can suspend our suspension of disbelief for the first 95% of the show because everything we need to believe is at the end. These films are like Enron's double bookkeeping: one story going on at the surface, the awful truth percolating unseen beneath. (SP 7)

These kinds of reactions exemplify how critics attempt to place labels, such as "Keyser Söze syndrome," "twist endings," and "renouement," on films that are industrially classified in other ways. Clearly, critics have written about these seemingly unrelated films in a manner that groups them together and distinguishes them from other Hollywood fare. The discourses surrounding these films demonstrate that various groups of people cluster otherwise unrelated Hollywood films together because of the particular narrative engagement that they demand from spectators.

Yet, as the spoiler warning issue suggests, discursive evidence alone is often not enough to distinguish misdirection films from others in closely affiliated genres that do not encourage the exact same viewer activities. Many other types of films have dramatic surprises at the end, but very few of these revelations also inspire spectators to reinterpret the meaning of virtually everything that has come before. If the discursive approach is coupled with more conventional genre analysis, then such issues can be redressed. Altman's semantic/syntactic/pragmatic model is thus appropriate because it combines discursive analysis with an examination of the films' textual properties and recurrent meanings. Continued attention to semantics and syntax offers the possibility of including otherwise neglected films in the genre, in turn, creating the requisite discursive evidence for subsequent scholars to justify sustained groupings in a historically sound fashion. The value of this approach can be best demonstrated by a brief discussion of how misdirection films are related to other genres with similar semantic and syntactic elements, but also have unique enough textual properties to distinguish them from these affiliated films.

If You've Seen One, You Haven't Seen Them All: Differentiating the Misdirection Film

Hollywood has long depended on genre to niche market a relatively undifferentiated product line that largely adheres to classical storytelling and representational conventions. That is not to say that the industry's strategy is to promote generic purity. As Altman's historical analysis reveals, Hollywood usually downplays generic specificity in favor of hybridity in marketing campaigns. After all, the classical film's dual plot structure—the primary quest narrative and the heterosexual romance subplot—is engineered partly to appeal, respectively, to perceived masculine desires for action and to purportedly feminine wishes to see characters overcome romantic relationship struggles. Yet, a film's semantic genre elements, particularly when they are explicitly foreground from the outset, as they are in most classical films, can modify viewer expectations. For David Bordwell, generic motivation always has a potential bearing on the kinds of hypothesis forming activities that the spectator conducts when viewing classical Hollywood films. He contends that genre cues and constrains interpretive activities further than the classical film already does by limiting the narrative outcomes most likely to occur. For instance, he argues that most Hollywood films are clearly positioned as constituents of genres that, unlike the misdirection film, do not purposely mislead spectators about the meaning of most narrative information. Instead, viewer guesses about narrative causality are typically met in a highly predictable fashion because a majority of Hollywood films end when the protagonist's clearly defined goals are satisfactorily attained or denied, fulfilling expectations raised at the start and leaving no primary causal lines of action dangling permanently.

Bordwell acknowledges that some Hollywood genres contain narratives that intentionally fool spectators about the meaning of information. The whodunit film is just one prominent example of a genre in which spectators expect that crucial narrative information will be withheld. In the whodunit, a primary player is usually revealed to possess seemingly secure character traits that unexpectedly prove to be unstable by the conclusion. The genre conventions, therefore, encourage spectators to determine who is misleading them before he or she is unmasked as the culprit. In an attempt to explain why virtually all films of this ilk should still be considered classical in spite of these tendencies, he theorizes that the expectations raised by genre are what keep them from being non-classical. Bordwell maintains that the whodunit film is classical because its "overt play of narration and hypothesis forming is generically motivated," meaning that "we want uncertainty, we expect both characters and narration to try and deceive us, and we therefore erect specific sorts of first impressions, cautious provisional ones, based as much upon generic conventions as upon what we actually learn" (*Classical* 40). The con artist film is another prime example of a genre that is difficult to label as non-classical even though it induces both diegetic characters and viewers to interpret narrative information in a manner that ultimately proves to be incorrect, usually because of the exposure of a late revelation. I do not, therefore, include contemporaneous Hollywood con artist films, such as *Catch Me if You Can* (2002) and *Matchstick Men* (2003), or any of David Mamet's similarly themed films, like *The Spanish Prisoner* (1997) and *Redbelt* (2008), in the misdirection film genre precisely because, following Bordwell's logic, their narrative revelations expose elaborate ruses in accordance with the expectations raised from the beginning.

Misdirection films, by contrast, are often packaged as constituents of historical genres that do not alert audiences that they will be narratively unreliable: *A Beautiful Mind* (2001) is a biopic, *Unbreakable* (2000) is a superhero film, *Atonement* (2007) is a romantic drama, and so on. Of course, not all misdirection films are marketed in a manner that disguises the presence of a likely duplicitous narrative. However, misdirection films packaged as constituents of historical genres that are designed to mislead spectators, such as the mystery, detective, and thriller, also provoke them to reinterpret narrative information in a patently non-classical fashion. Misdirection films advertised as detective films, for example, typically do not abide by the same rules that traditionally govern the classical detective film. Like the whodunit, Bordwell argues that even though the Hollywood detective film often misleads viewers about the veracity of character motivation to prevent them from guessing its unexpected revelation, it still ultimately adheres to the rules that govern the classical film. Again, he relies on generic motivation as his primary defense for this argument. Bordwell claims that Hollywood detective films abide by the tenets of "fair play," a set of rules that became codified in detective literature, which imply that "the reader has as good a chance to discover the solution as the detective does" (*Narration* 67). As long as the viewer is made aware that there is a puzzle to solve and has a legitimate chance to figure it out before the explanation occurs, the detective film should still be considered classical because generic conventions compensate for its apparent departures from Hollywood's narrative and formal principles.

As David Richter's analysis of *Fallen* (1998) demonstrates, however, misdirection films packaged in the detective genre typically fool audiences precisely because they violate the tenet of fair play. *Fallen* centers on detective John Hobbes's (Denzel Washington) effort to hunt down and kill a murderous demon named Azazel, who has possessed a series of human hosts. The film begins *in media res*, as Hobbes explains, in voiceover, that what is being depicted is his brush with death. The reasons that he describes the event as such, though, do not become apparent until the end of the film. When the film returns to the opening scene at the conclusion, it finally starts to become clear that Hobbes previously described this moment as his near-death experience because it portrays the detective's attempt to destroy the demon. Specifically, he has concocted a plan to lure it to a deserted location to trick it into possessing him after he kills its current host and then ingests fast-acting poison to kill himself. Importantly, it already has been established that Azazel can only possess a new victim if its current host comes into direct contact with another living person, meaning that the demon should die after Hobbes commits suicide. Even though there are no other potential human hosts present, the demon does not perish after it enters Hobbes's rapidly dying body. Instead, it possesses a stray cat that inspects Hobbes as the poison takes effect. The revelation scene, as Richter explains, thus, invalidates the spectator's expectations of both "story logic and conventions of representation" (15). In terms of narrative, the established rules made it seem as though the demon could only possess human beings. As it relates to form, the presence of Hobbes's voice in the opening narration made it virtually impossible to guess that it was actually the demon describing its near death experience as it possessed the detective momentarily before it moved to its feline host. Although the film's genre immediately signals its narrative unreliability, it cannot be comprehended according to habitual standards because the revelation violates the spectator's expectations in such a way that it is almost impossible that anyone could have predicted the resolution before its exposure.

These examples reveal why an exploration of semantics, most notably, how the revelation transforms the meaning of information in ways that distinguish these films from similar genres, is a good starting point for identifying constituents that have not been discursively labeled accordingly, or for providing the corroborating evidence for films that have been already grouped as such by random utterances. According to Altman and other genre theorists, though, semantics should be combined with syntax partly to compensate for taxonomic genre theory's tendency to downplay film's relation to culture. Syntax attends to how semantic elements are recurrently deployed in connection to relevant cultural conditions by examining their thematic significance. This kind of genre study has been often referred to as the myth or ritual approach, which is exemplified by Thomas Schatz's *Hollywood Genres*. In that book, he theorizes that film genres remain salient as long as they provide satisfactory, imaginary resolutions to irreconcilable ideological oppositions in the broader cultural sphere. Hence the reason that the continued, formulaic deployment of semantic elements that characterize genres consistently appeals to audiences. The misdirection film, therefore, leverages its fundamental semantic element—the changeover and the master key—in relation, at least in part, to the spectator's desire to access the "truth" during an age in which its very existence has been increasingly challenged.

In subsequent years, Schatz and other adherents of the myth and ritual approach have been rightly criticized for relying on the method to achieve ahistorical ends. Although such a perspective can yield historically sound connections between films and their contexts, it has been typically deployed to show that genres always resolve underlying cultural tensions in the same fashion and evolve toward increasing self-consciousness, as they supposedly move from a nascent developmental phase to a self-referential stage of maturity. It is inaccurate, then, to contend that all contemporary misdirection films express the same ideological agenda in relation to the status of the "truth." Even though most misdirection films contain revelations that assuage fears about relativity, there are some that seem to revel in perpetual uncertainty. I also do not want to imply that the interpretations of any of the misdirection films presented in this book are absolute. My readings and the ones offered by fans that I rearticulate are often persuasively countered by alternative comprehensions because elements contained in many of these films, like eternal ambiguities, provoke a plurality of viable interpretations. Additionally, it is a mistake to claim that the genre has become increasingly self-reflexive over time, as there have always been varying degrees of intertextual references in the genre. In *Arlington Road* (1999), for instance, Oliver Lang (Tim Robbins) exclaims "I guess we're not in Kansas anymore, eh, Toto." Such an explicit reference to a highly recognizable misdirection antecedent—*The Wizard of Oz* (1939)—is significant because 1999 is the very year that these films began flooding the market and became culturally ubiquitous. Producers of *Arlington Road* had no idea that, just one month later, the release of *The Sixth Sense* would dominate the box office for weeks, spawn a legion of imitators, and contain dialogue that would become inescapable in popular culture. Self-reflexivity occurs at any point in a genre's development, especially because various groups, including scholars, can retroactively identify semantic and syntactic generic links, irrespective of filmmaker motives.

The impossibility of determining authorial intent begins to suggest why semantics and syntax are best combined with a pragmatic approach to genre. Since accessing the minds of filmmakers directly is a fantasy, an examination of discourses that circulate around and run through these films, including textual evidence itself, reveals how genres operate culturally. In *American Film Cycles*, Amanda Ann Klein provides a foundation for privileging pragmatics by arguing that "while film genres are primarily defined by the repetition of key images (their semantics) and themes (their syntax), film cycles are primarily defined by how they are used (their pragmatics)" (4). Although I agree with her that pragmatics should be paramount, I do not share her view that this applies only to cycles and not to genres. As Klein correctly notes, existing genre theory typically treats cycles "as messy structures in flux, poised either to become stable genres or to disappear quickly" (6). Herein lies the rub with the notion of the cycle. Since genres are a retroactive phenomenon, cycles are always on the precipice of turning into a genre. Labeling a set of films as a cycle is a precarious endeavor if the premise is based on the fact that it suddenly becomes a genre when groups of people notice that it reappears. Such logic renders the occasionally used term "transhistorical cycle" contradictory or nonsensical because once a set of films with similar semantic and syntactic properties, like misdirection films, returns and is discursively identified, it can be characterized as a genre. An examination of the discourses circulating within and outside of the text demonstrates how semantics and syntax are interpreted and activated by various groups to construct generic parameters at various historical moments.

Despite her insistence on emphasizing the unique properties of the cycle, many of Klein's central notions are applicable to my exploration of the misdirection film genre. In addition to foregrounding the importance of pragmatics, her work indicates how studying particular moments in a genre's history can yield precise findings about its relationship to its specific contexts. She contends that it is possible to "view film cycles as a mold placed over the zeitgeist, which, when pulled away reveals the contours, fissures, and complicated patterns of the contemporary moment" (Klein 20). A small slice of a genre's history can indeed reveal more micro-level information than an exhaustive genre study does about a set of films' relationships not only to concrete cultural circumstances, but also to more exact industrial and technological conditions. I focus only on contemporary misdirection films, then, because I intend to show how they have been constructed in direct response to particular cultural, industrial, and technological changes that impacted commercial film producers and audiences during a specific period in time. As Klein's study also highlights, such claims about the links between genres and their contexts are further strengthened by grounding them historically within the discursive surround. Consequently, the following examples epitomize how utterances related to this group of films circulate as well as how and why such discourses can significantly alter the ways in which constituents of the genre are discussed, evaluated, and understood for years to come.

Obliterating the "Ideal" Man: *Fight Club*'s Misunderstood Changeover

The story of the belated appreciation of *Fight Club* is already a legendary illustration of this phenomenon. It is correctly identified as a key moment in the history of post-theatrical exhibition because it was one of the first films to be completely reassessed as a consequence of its tremendously effective DVD release. Its delayed success in the aftermarket is partially attributable to the way that the film's two-disc collector's edition DVD (2000) was packaged for consumption more strategically than its theatrical release. *Fight Club*'s theatrical marketing campaign told spectators little about the film itself. The promotional materials, for instance, centered as heavily on a pink bar of soap as they did the actors in the drama. *Fight Club*'s taglines were also intentionally ambiguous. One positioned the film as being about "mischief, mayhem, and soap" and another claimed that it "works great even on bloodstains" (imdb.com). Although these advertisements subtly allude to the film's commentary on consumerism and masculinity in the United States, they most clearly obfuscate its narrative content. Such tactics were employed for two primary reasons. First, they functioned not to alienate *Fight Club*'s intended audience—young, white, heterosexual men—by making the film's explicit critique of their behaviors implicit. Second, they cloaked the changeover entirely, a tactic that departs from conventional misdirection film advertising because it generally at least alludes to the presence of an alternate way to interpret the narrative.

By contrast, in addition to promoting its then virtually unprecedented array of special features, the back cover of the two-disc collector's edition DVD alerts audiences that the *New York Times* claims that *Fight Club* "just might require another viewing," blatantly signaling the presence of its changeover. Moreover, many of the excerpted quotations that pepper the booklet accompanying the DVD foreground the film's critiques of conventional masculinity. The final quote listed in the insert, for instance, is from Bret Easton Ellis, author of *American Psycho*, another renowned novel from the period that similarly critiques hegemonic masculinity and was adapted into a misdirection film, who claims that *Fight Club* both "rages against the hypocrisy of a society that continually promises us the impossible: fame, beauty, immorality, life without pain" and is a "dizzying take on the male fear of losing power." In sum, the film only found a core audience after both its duplicitous narrative and depiction of contemporary white, heterosexual, American male paranoia were featured prominently in its advertising.

The importance of the changeover in the film's aftermarket resurrection cannot be overstated. Fan discourse illustrates the impact of its narrative structure on its now lofty, but still controversial, reputation. Spectators have consistently expressed uncertainty about *Fight Club*'s gender politics in the years since its theatrical release, spawning great disagreement online about the film's cultural merits, or lack thereof. A fan who posted on the film's "User Comments" page on the *Internet Movie Database* in April 2008, for instance, calls *Fight Club* "the greatest movie ever made" and declares that it provides "great insight into the universal male psychology" (imdb.com). Unfortunately, it is impossible to guess exactly what this contributor believes the film has to say about men because, as other participants on the site demonstrate, there is substantial disagreement about its final message in light of the changeover's meaning. For example, a presumably male viewer's response, accessed at the same time as the one above, reports that after seeing the film he "wanted to move into a broken house and get in touch with the primordial nature that has been silenced in men everywhere by years of materialism bullshit" (www.imdb.com). Conversely, another contemporaneous viewer's comment speculates that "the solution Tyler offers is horrible, but he's so charismatic that you'll hardly notice it" (www.imdb.com). On one hand, then, for some spectators, Tyler's character represents the remedy for dispossessed American men. On the other hand, some spectators interpret the film as ultimately lambasting the narrator's hyper-masculine alter-ego.

Reviewers were similarly divided about *Fight Club*'s commentary on gender. Peter Rainer of *New York* magazine blasts the film for depicting "the squall of an essentially white-male generation that feels ruined by the privileges of women and a booming economy." *Entertainment Weekly*'s Lisa Schwarzbaum similarly complains that the film "floats the idiotic premise that a modern-day onslaught of girly pop-cultural destinations (including IKEA and support groups) has resulted in a generation of spongy young men unable to express themselves as fully erect males." In contrast, Michael Wilmington of the *Chicago Tribune* claims that the film "satirizes and examines violence far more than exploiting it" because it is a "hilarious ride into the twisted recesses of the modern male psyche, with an amazing knife-twist surprise ending that some may compare to the ending of *The Sixth Sense*." In addition to praising the film's gender politics, Wilmington also champions its changeover, which, like Ebert, he connects directly to another prominent misdirection film. This is significant not only because it provides further discursive evidence of *Fight Club*'s placement in the misdirection film genre. It also showcases the connections between how the changeover is interpreted and the way in which the film's larger take on masculinity is understood. Ebert's negative discussion of the film's changeover, for instance, bleeds into an unfavorable discussion of its portrayal of gender by characterizing it as "macho porn" that women "will instinctively see through" even though "men may get off on the testosterone rush." The discrepancy about the film's gender politics often hinges on how viewers comprehend the changeover's significance and its retroactive domino effect on the film's entire meaning, suggesting why there is a lot at stake in how it has been read in relation to genre and other constituents of the misdirection film category.

As these responses to the film indicate, *Fight Club* contains a complex narrative that is challenging to decipher initially and remains confounding on repeated viewings despite the fact that it has a changeover that ostensibly reveals its secrets unambiguously. The narrative centers on the reasons for and proposed remedies to the unnamed narrator's (who often refers to himself as "Jack," one of the pseudonyms he uses at support groups) malaise. The main cause for the film's polarized reception is the vastly different interpretations that persist even after the exposure of the changeover about what the film identifies as the culprits for and antidotes to the narrator's problems. Determining the film's takes on gender and sexuality, then, depend on how the changeover's significance is understood retrospectively. Most notably, considerable debate remains in virtual communities about the extent of the unnamed narrator's dissociative identity disorder, which Tyler is revealed to be a manifestation of during the film's memorable changeover sequence. Some fans speculate that, like the characters introduced and incorrectly presumed to be real in similarly themed misdirection films, such as *A Beautiful Mind* and *Identity* (2003), that a number of *Fight Club*'s other characters, most prominently, Marla Singer (Helena Bonham Carter), may also be imagined, alternate personas. Such discussions are epitomized by the forum on the website, *Movie & TV Stack Exchange.com*, entitled "In *Fight Club* is Marla Singer a second figment of Jack's imagination?". Obviously, if Marla—the film's sole, primary female character—is only a fabricated product of the narrator's disorder, then interpretations of how she and the other characters are represented are likely to shift drastically.

Fight Club's narrator is initially depicted as a cubicle-inhabiting, corporate drone who works as a product recall cost appraiser for a large automaker and takes orders from a male boss who is infatuated with traditionally feminine concerns, like the color cornflower blue. The narrator's emasculating role demands that he help the company make huge profits by concealing the dangers associated with their vehicles. As the sequence in which the narrator's condo breathtakingly transforms into the pages of a furniture catalog illustrates, he seems to put up with the job to feed his insatiable hunger for consumer products. When his condo unexpectedly explodes and all of his possessions are incinerated, however, his values begin to change. The narrator's metamorphosis is guided by his decision to reach out for help to a mysterious acquaintance, named Tyler Durden, instead of Marla, the woman he loves to hate, after his condo is destroyed. When Tyler and the narrator subsequently meet at Lou's Tavern, it becomes apparent that the charismatic Tyler is trying to shepherd the narrator's masculine transformation by spewing cliché-ridden rants about the feminizing forces he deems responsible for their problems, such as the influences of consumer culture on traditional manhood.

Upon leaving the bar, Tyler alludes to a budding sexual tension between the two by asking the narrator to "cut the foreplay and just ask" if he can stay at his place. After the narrator finally makes the request, Tyler invites him to squat at his dilapidated house until he gets his life back together. In return for the favor, Tyler demands that the narrator "hit him as hard as he can," leading to their first fight. Surprisingly, the uptight narrator finds the sadomasochistic activity to be pleasurable because during their almost post-coital exchange, the narrator informs Tyler that "they should do this again sometime." When the two finally arrive at Tyler's house, however, it becomes clear that they will not be consummating their relationship with homosexual activity. As Melissa Iocco theorizes, the film's heterosexist tendencies are evident when Tyler shows him around the house because he only points out the location of the bathroom and stresses that they will stay in separate bedrooms. She keenly notes that his tour of the place reveals that "now that they are in a different and more personal environment and situation, their bodies and fluids should not mingle" (Iocco 52). A strictly homosocial relationship then develops between the two, eventually encouraging the narrator to emulate Tyler by giving up all of his possessions. The friends end up founding a bare-knuckled boxing organization, called "Fight Club," which meets in the basement of Lou's Tavern, to help other emasculated men reclaim their lost manhood. In this restricted setting, these seemingly feminized men also regain their virility by attaining sadomasochistic satisfaction, albeit in a violent and patently non-sexualized fashion.

Under Tyler's direction, Fight Club eventually "leaves the basement" and turns into a full-fledged rebellion, referred to as "Project Mayhem." Juxtaposed with the comparatively diverse Fight Club, Project Mayhem is comprised almost exclusively of young, white, and presumably heterosexual men, who are bent on annihilating the feminizing forces that they perceive to be the causes of their predicament. As Iocco contends, by taking this turn, the film ultimately seems to promote "homosocial and male bonding through violence and destruction" (50). Importantly, the film also shuts down the possibility that a homosexual relationship will ever develop between Tyler and the narrator. During their most sexually tinged scene in the house's bathroom, a naked Tyler tells the narrator what he believes is at the root of their problems. While taking a bath, he and the narrator share stories about how they were abandoned by their fathers, leading Tyler to speculate that "we're a generation of men raised by women, I'm wondering if another woman is really the answer to our problem." Thus, it seems that the burgeoning revolution should potentially strengthen the latent sexual bond between Tyler and the narrator by removing women from the picture, but it ultimately has the opposite effect.

For many critics and scholars, the presence of this kind of troubling dialogue that scapegoats women and fantasizes about eliminating them is a testament to *Fight Club*'s misogynistic sensibility. In fact, the film has been condemned by a number of scholars, such as Terrell Carver, who disavows it for its purportedly reprehensible treatment of Marla Singer, whom he interprets as a metaphor for " 'woman,' very enigmatic and 'other' " who is "dangerous and unpredictable, sexually voracious in a totally ludicrous way and in sum the object in the most basic and stereotypical kind of male fantasy" (130). In relation to the film's complicated takes on capitalism and patriarchy, Henry Giroux also reads the film as having reactionary tendencies. He theorizes that *Fight Club* "is less interested in attacking the broader material relations of power and strategies of domination and exploitation associated with neoliberal capitalism than it is in rebelling against a consumerist culture that dissolves the bonds of male sociality and puts into place an enervating notion of male identity and agency" (henryagiroux.com). For Giroux, the film only draws attention to the ways that late capitalism and the associated triumph of consumerism have purportedly feminized many white, heterosexual, middle- and working-class men, meaning that it fails to demonstrate how neoliberalist economic policies have consolidated the power of elites and made it more difficult for traditionally subjugated groups to attain equality in economic, political, and social arenas.

Although Giroux's reading is admirable, it does not jibe with the ways in which *Fight Club*'s ending encourages viewers ascribing to the "Marla is just another persona" explanation to reinterpret narrative information much differently. Like Carver, Giroux claims that Marla functions as a metonymical stand-in for the kind of women who some men would like to believe "exist to simultaneously make men unhappy and to service their sexual needs." Such a portrayal, Giroux argues, "reinscribes white heterosexuality within a dominant logic of stylized brutality and male bonding that appears predicated on the need to denigrate and wage war against all that is feminine." I grant that the film depicts how white, heterosexual, American men can overcome their emasculation; however, I contend that it does not urge them to accomplish this goal by blaming women for their problems and also laudably exposes the absurdity of hegemonic masculine gender performance in the process.

To ascribe a blatantly chauvinistic logic to *Fight Club*, critics have to ignore the full implications of the changeover, which is key to one of the most compelling retrospective reinterpretations of the film's meaning circulating in virtual communities: the "Marla is not real" explanation. *Fight Club* unexpectedly ends in classical Hollywood fashion with the romantic coupling of Marla and the narrator. Yet, this happy Hollywood ending, which seems incongruous with what has come before, is immediately thrown into question by the demolition of the offices of the major credit card companies that were the targets of Project Mayhem, which, in anti-capitalist fashion, erases the debt record. Additionally, shortly after the couple holds hands, the film cuts to an almost subliminal insertion of a close-up of a penis, an image that Tyler would typically splice into family films while working as a projectionist. These seemingly contradictory images strongly encourage viewers to scrutinize the film's positions on gender and sexuality by interrogating the veracity and meaning of the compulsory heterosexual coupling.

In addition to these yoked visual contradictions, the film's ending is rendered more ambiguous by the Pixies' "Where is my Mind?," which plays on the soundtrack as the towers collapse and the end credits roll. This music choice suggests that although it may seem that the protago-

Figure 1.2. Marla Singer and the unnamed narrator hold hands, as they watch the Project Mayhem-inspired demolition of credit card companies at the end of *Fight Club*.

nist's psychological state has become unequivocally clear because of the extended battle just depicted with an imaginary Tyler, it is important to remember that the narrative has been focalized through the perspective of an unreliable narrator throughout most of the film. Indeed, the film's final sequence, in which the action finally catches up with the narrator's opening voiceover, is the only time that narrative information is not filtered directly through the narrator. After all, the very first frame makes it clear that viewers are receiving narrative information through the mind of the unnamed narrator, as the creative opening credit sequence literally takes place inside of his brain. Once the opening credits end, the camera zooms out of the brain to showcase the character whose skull the camera was just inside. The narrator's voiceover then begins the film's prolonged flashback structure by hinting at the real relationship between Tyler and him. His narration informs spectators that he is constantly asked if he "knows Tyler Durden," "how that old saying of you only hurt the one you love works both ways," and that "[he] knows" about the details of Project Mayhem "because Tyler knows" about them. After a virtuosic, digitally enhanced tour of the foundations of multiple office buildings visually confirms Project Mayhem's destructive potential, the narrator concludes the opening voiceover by claiming that he "realizes that all of this, the gun, the bombs, the revolution, has got something to do with a girl named Marla Singer." Rather than interpret this statement as an expression of the film's misogyny, it is possible to read it as a commentary on the war occurring inside the narrator's mind because it is difficult to accept Marla as being any more real than Tyler.

The virtual impossibility of Marla's existence is suggested immediately by her character introduction. The narrator first encounters Marla at a meeting of a support group for testicular cancer survivors, a quintessential depiction of literal emasculation that would not likely accept a female member. Not coincidentally, the theme of castration recurs throughout *Fight Club*, as many male characters are threatened with having their balls cut off by others. Although the narrator never had testicular cancer, he decides to join the group because it provides him with a cathartic release that helps him cope with his insomnia. Marla, like the narrator, is a faker who visits the groups in order to ease her own maladies. Her obvious status as an imposter in this and other similar groups, such as the one composed of people suffering from tuberculosis in which she reports her chain "smoking doesn't go over at all," begins to signal the low probability of her physical existence.

The narrator then claims, in voiceover, that Marla is a problem because her presence in the groups ruins his ability to release his emotions, meaning that he again cannot sleep. When he follows Marla out the door presumably to confront her, the first visual clue that she might be simply a figment of his imagination appears. As the camera takes his point of view, an almost subliminal shot of Tyler, his other primary alter-ego, which reappears throughout the opening scenes, is superimposed on the image of her walking down the alley. The film then cuts to a fantasy scene from the narrator's perspective in which he challenges Marla about being a fraud. Her presence in his mind is subsequently reconfirmed when the narrator participates in a guided meditation seminar for cancer patients for a second time. As his voiceover informs viewers if he "had a tumor he would name it Marla," the camera cuts to what was previously depicted as his imagined place of serenity: a frozen cave inhabited by a talking penguin. When he enters the cave this time, though, he shockingly discovers that a smoking Marla has replaced the penguin.

Once the session ends, the angry narrator finally seeks out Marla to threaten her. When the two begin to exchange dialogue for the first time, it becomes clear that they at least think very similarly because they complete each other's sentences. After the narrator threatens to expose her, Marla surprisingly responds by claiming that she "saw him practicing telling her off," alluding to her privileged access to his mind because it can only reference the fantasy confrontation sequence that was depicted moments ago. To compromise, the two characters then begrudgingly attempt to split up the support group meeting schedule so that their paths never cross. Their discussion escalates into a disagreement because Marla claims to want to attend the meetings of both "the brain parasites" and "the organic brain dementia" groups, to which the unnamed narrator retorts she "*can't have the whole brain!*" The double-entendre-laden sequence ends with Marla standing in the middle of a busy city street in which, mysteriously, no cars have to swerve out of her way; this moment also hints at the revelation a final time, as their dialogue reminds viewers that the narrator's real name still has not been mentioned because he has gone by so many different aliases in support group meetings.

The alternate identity that initially becomes dominant in the narrator's mind, of course, is Tyler and not Marla. Tyler, like Marla, is a chain-smoking caricature; it is difficult to imagine he could be real as well because he is such an exaggeration of the masculine ideal. In spite of there being fleeting glimpses of Tyler early in the film, most explicitly as he passes the narrator on a moving walkway at the same time that the narrator's voiceover ruminates about the possibility of awakening "in a different time and a different place as a different person," his character is not formally introduced until the two serendipitously meet on an airplane. As with Marla, the actual relationship between the two characters is hinted at when the narrator tells Tyler that they "have the

Figure 1.3. *Fight Club*'s unnamed narrator fantasizes about confronting Marla Singer to demand that she stop attending the same support groups.

exact same briefcase." Their subsequent exchange reveals Tyler's self-assurance, sexual ambiguity, and anarchistic tendencies. After informing the narrator that he knows how to make explosives out of household materials, he complicates his masculinity and sexuality by deliberating about whether to give the narrator "the ass or the crotch" before exiting the row, suggesting both his traditional confidence and the budding sexual tension between the two.

Fight Club's memorable changeover sequence, the inspiration for my use of the term to describe the narrative tendency, leaves no doubt that Tyler's character should be interpreted as how the narrator initially imagines he would be if he was the ideal man. The narrator's growing awareness of his real relationship to Tyler prompts him to call Marla to ask if they have ever had sex, which the film previously revealed to be satisfying, but cartoonish and degrading to Marla. In fact, she informs the narrator in a subsequent conversation that this is one of Tyler's greatest talents. But, if both Tyler and Marla are not real, these ridiculous sex scenes become little more than the stuff of masturbatory fantasies. Marla's response on the phone sparks the apparitional appearance of Tyler, who chastises the narrator for violating their code of silence. Their exchange finally initiates the narrator's realization that he and Tyler are actually the same person. In classic changeover fashion, the film hammers viewers over the head with the revelatory information by presenting flashbacks of Tyler's previous acts of mischief and mayhem, only this time with the narrator in Tyler's place or with Tyler erased from the image entirely. To confirm his real identity further, Tyler then explains that he represents "all the ways" that the unnamed narrator "wishes he could be." Speaking not only to the narrator, but also to men in the audience, Tyler exclaims that he "looks like you want to look," "fuck[s] like you want to fuck," is "smart, capable, and, most importantly am free in all the ways that you are not." There was perhaps no better choice for this role than Brad Pitt, who had already won *People* magazine's "Sexiest Man Alive" award in 1995 and would be the first to be crowned with the solo title a second time in 2000 thanks largely to his chiseled appearance in *Fight Club*, to play the character who possesses the attributes that are the envy of many men. In comparison to the comparatively soft-bodied and plain-looking Edward Norton, there is little question which character spectators are supposed to identify as the ostensibly ideal man.

In contrast to critics who deem *Fight Club* as misogynistic for these reasons, however, the film can be read as progressive in relation to gender because of how what transpires after the changeover ultimately critiques Tyler's ideal masculinity, especially if Marla is also interpreted not to be real. Just moments before Marla and the narrator hold hands, the narrator destroys his hyper-masculine alter-ego with a self-inflicted gunshot that literally lobotomizes the Tyler portion of his brain to make room for the Marla persona. This act is necessary, as Tyler insinuates during the changeover sequence, because Marla knows too much about his real identity as a similar manifestation of the narrator's dissociative identity disorder. Consequently, the narrator's decision to obliterate his hyper-masculine persona in order to save Marla suggests that the film's gender politics are more radical than scholars like Carver and Giroux acknowledge. I grant that the narrator's decision to shoot himself is understood by the members of Project Mayhem, who may also be just a figment of his imagination, as a quintessential act of masculine strength. Yet, his decision to destroy Tyler and not Marla reveals that, as he tells Tyler, he does not "need [him] anymore" because his "eyes are open" to the destructive nature of his masculine violence and aggression. Put simply, he finally realizes that he has to allow his more feminine alter-ego to become the dominant persona to put an end to his discontent.

Although the narrator's choice to kill Tyler clearly expresses the unacceptability of this traditional form of masculinity, his act also allows him to pursue a conventional heterosexual romance with Marla, albeit perhaps only in his mind, which, in turn, demonstrates why critics are correct to claim that the film's cultural politics are contradictory and somewhat conservative, even if Marla is not real. His decision to be with Marla reiterates the film's heterosexism because the sexual tension between Tyler and the narrator posed such a threat to the patriarchal order that it needed to be destroyed and replaced with a more traditional romantic relationship. As the narrator assures Marla in the film's last line, although she met him "at a very strange time," the happy ending indicates that everything is now "going to be fine." In sum, *Fight Club* ultimately conveys mixed messages to viewers subscribing to virtually any reading, including the provocative "Marla is not real" interpretation, by rewarding its white, male protagonist with the literal woman of his dreams for abandoning his aberrant masculine identity in favor of a kinder and gentler, yet unquestionably heterosexual, masculine persona. The film's cultural status, therefore, is contingent on how groups interpret and judge the impact that the ambiguous changeover has on the rest of its meaning. What people make of the film, in the end, is overwhelmingly linked to the ways in which it is evaluated and discussed as a misdirection film and its relationships to other films in the genre.

Atoning for the Sins of the Father: Unlocking the Meaning of *Magnolia's* Master Key

Like *Fight Club*, *Magnolia*'s convoluted narrative is challenging to interpret definitively, even in retrospect, making it difficult to decipher its cultural messages. *Magnolia*'s narrative ostensibly centers on a loosely connected series of events that depict the individual crises an array of characters—none of whom can be clearly identified as the protagonist—inhabiting suburban Los Angeles experience. Many of these characters interact little with each other and even though their lives sometimes intersect, they all seem to follow relatively distinct narrative trajectories—that is, until the film's climactic moment in which a rain of frogs affects them simultaneously and brings many of them into direct contact. Although the rain of frogs provides closure to all of the characters' predicaments, its meaning is never formally explained. Instead, the film's characters and spectators are seemingly left to ponder its causes and effects eternally.

Magnolia's three-hour-long and apparently non-classical narrative is largely a product of the atypical circumstances under which it was made. In an unusual move for the industry, New Line Cinema, a subsidiary of Time Warner, gave director Paul Thomas Anderson an almost unprecedented degree of artistic freedom on the project. Specifically, production head Michael De Luca famously told Anderson that he would have final cut on the film before the studio even knew anything about the script (Hirschberg SM 55). The uncharacteristic decision to give Anderson such authorial power was motivated by the critical and commercial success of *Boogie Nights* (1997), the director's second feature film and his first project for New Line, which was nominated for three of the most celebrated Academy Awards and won Golden Globes for Best Supporting Actor (Burt Reynolds) and Best Supporting Actress (Julianne Moore). However, although the film was ultimately profitable, it only brought in $26 million on its $15 million budget during its run in U.S. theaters (imdb.com). This is not a profit margin that typically warrants the decision to give a relatively unproven commodity such artistic latitude. New Line's gamble on Anderson's follow-up effort proved to be unsuccessful at the box office. *Magnolia* did not even make back its production costs during its domestic theatrical run, reaping only $22 million on its $37 million budget (imdb.com). As with its predecessor, though, the film was a hit with critics and garnered a number of prestigious accolades, including three Academy Award nominations and the Best Supporting Actor Golden Globe for Tom Cruise (imdb.com).

Like many other contemporary misdirection films that performed poorly in theaters, *Magnolia*'s reputation has been bolstered by its run in post-theatrical markets. Upon its theatrical release, reviewers typically lauded the film's ambition, but chastised its narrative ineffectiveness. *New York Times* reviewer Janet Maslin typifies this reception by writing "It's astonishing to see a film begin this brilliantly only to torpedo itself in its final hour . . . as the desperate reach for some larger meaning begins, the sheer arbitrariness of [Anderson's] approach is laid bare." Although the seemingly incoherent rain of frogs was generally perceived to be the biggest narrative problem initially, the film's belated appreciation is largely attributable to a reinterpretation subsequently popularized by fans, which claims that the calamity is the key to understanding the film's meaning intelligibly. Importantly, a semantic/syntactic/pragmatic examination of the discourses associated with the film demonstrates that this reinterpretation of narrative information is not the sort that can be easily dismissed as baseless. In addition to reviewer and fan discourse, an analysis of textual properties, particularly the film's *mise-en-scène* (semantics), its display of Anderson's thematic preoccupations (syntax), and the way it was marketed (pragmatics), provides corroborating evidence to illustrate that it is a misdirection film because it suggests that the alternative meaning was deliberately buried for viewers and not just created out of thin air by overzealous fans.

The film's trailer is a logical start point for this analysis because even though it primarily advertises it as a melodrama by presenting many of the film's characters in emotionally over-wrought scenes, it also hints that it might be a misdirection film. After the preview depicts the last of its primary characters—police officer Jim Kurring (John C. Reilly)—kneeling in front of a cross, it inexplicably ends by cutting to an enigmatic shot of a frog, which is coupled with a voiceover narration that states, "And this will all make sense in the end." However, the preview may seem to be just disingenuous on first blush due to the film's ostensible narrative incoherence. In classical fashion, though, many of *Magnolia*'s ardent fans claim that the catastrophe can be understood as being narratively related to the film's other events. One of the reasons that the film's reputation has grown considerably, then, is because, like most misdirection films, it can be reinterpreted retrospectively in a rather conventional manner by those in the know. Rather than understanding its "truth" as being unknowable or its events as being dictated by the random forces of chaos, according to this fan logic, those who "correctly" read between *Magnolia*'s lines are able to determine what "actually" happened and why its most baffling events "really" occurred.

Although the rain of frogs literally comes out of the blue and appears to be completely unmotivated, many fans argue that it can be logically explained by the film's master key—the number 82. As Ebert speculates in his aforementioned review, events from the film's outset, especially in the seemingly unrelated prologue, consistently foreshadow its appearance. This reassessment of the film's meaning was ultimately buttressed by other critics' interpretations and Anderson's self-promotional tactics. Just a month after its December 1999 theatrical release and associated flurry of perplexed reviews, Mark Caro published an article in the *Chicago Tribune* in which he discussed with Anderson the many 82s and the direct references to Exodus scattered throughout the film's *mise-en-scène*, strongly suggesting that the number and its corresponding bible verse are somehow important to comprehending the narrative coherently. Perhaps most notable among these instances in the *mise-en-scène* occurs immediately before Kurring's windshield is about to be hit by the first of the falling frogs. He fleetingly passes a bus stop that contains a barely legible advertisement, which simply reads "Exodus 8:2." This subtle clue is only discernable on digital technologies, such as the DVD player, that allow viewers to pause the image pristinely and has become easier to distribute to other fans with the advent of the World Wide Web, particularly with the use of Web 2.0 platforms. The presence of this kind of explicit semantic detail indicates that the number references the Old Testament passage that tells of God's infliction of the ten plagues on the Egyptians as punishment for their persecution of the Jews. Exodus 8:1 reads "And the Lord spake unto Moses, Go unto Pharaoh, and say unto him, Thus saith the Lord, Let my people go, that they may serve me." Exodus 8:2 then reads "And if thou refuse to let them go, behold, I will smite all thy borders with frogs." Consequently, this evidence begins to offer spectators a way to interpret the strange catastrophe and all of the film's other ambiguous moments as actually being narratively relevant.

The film's extended prologue, for instance, seems to make little narrative sense until the master key is decoded. At first, it appears to

Figure 1.4. A fleetingly observable advertisement that reveals the details of *Magnolia*'s master key, which appears directly before Jim Kurring's car is hit by the first of the frogs.

be, at best, indirectly related to the rest of the film because it is only referenced again briefly at the conclusion and its meaning is never explicitly explained by subsequent events. A close analysis of the prologue's *mise-en-scène*, however, suggests that the scenes are about more than just a meditation on chance versus grand design. During the prologue's first scene, one of the men of Greenberry Hill, coincidentally either Joseph Green, Stanley Berry, or Daniel Hill, is hanged with the number 82 affixed to his shirt for the murder of *family man* Sir Edmund William Godfrey. In its second scene, Craig Hansen (Brad Hunt), the *estranged father of four* and the firefighting pilot who accidentally kills scuba diver, Delmer Derian (Patton Oswalt), flies a plane numbered 82 and is seen in a casino attacking a blackjack dealer, who is coincidentally Delmer, when he is upset by receiving an 8 instead of the 2 that he needs. The magnitude of the guilt from the act prompts Hansen to commit suicide. Finally, the bizarre shooting of 17-year-old Sydney Barringer (Chris O'Hara) is told during the 8:20 p.m. meeting of the American Association of Forensic Science. Sydney jumps from a rooftop ledge adorned with ropes coiled to form the number 82, only to be accidentally shot in the stomach by his mother as he passes his family's apartment #682 window just before he lands on a safety net that would have saved his life. As a result, Sydney's parents are arrested for turning the attempted suicide into a homicide. In short, the prologue is relevant to the rest of the film because it links the number 82 to divine punishments inflicted on people who destroy families.

If the number 82 is connected to the biblical passage, then the rain of frogs can indeed be understood as a modern-day punishment

Figure 1.5. Craig Hansen's plane is emblazoned with one of the many explicit references to 82 in *Magnolia*'s prologue.

enacted by a vengeful God on the film's subsequent two primary father figures—Earl Partridge (Jason Robards) and Jimmy Gator (Phillip Baker Hall)—for ruining their families. Divine intervention disciplines these two animally named men for mistreating their children, as Partridge abandoned his son, Frank (Tom Cruise), and Gator sexually abused his daughter, Claudia (Melora Waters). Specifically, during the rain, a frog knocks a gun out of Gator's hand as he tries to commit suicide to escape facing the slow death of cancer alone and Partridge dies with Frank at his side when the frogs begin to fall before he can get a word out to fulfill his dying wish of reconciling with his son.

The post-frog sequence ultimately reveals that the film's second generation of men, guys like Frank, need to embrace a new form of masculinity if they are ever to improve the situation their fathers created for subsequent generations. The sequence does this by focusing on the two characters from that cohort most closely linked to the film's two dying patriarchs: Frank is Earl's offspring and Jim shares more than just a name with Jimmy since he has become romantically involved with Claudia. Importantly, these two characters initially represented polar opposite masculinities, as Frank was a hyper-sexual misogynist and Jim was a lonely divorcee in search of a fulfilling heterosexual relationship. During the rain of frogs, however, Frank becomes the type of man that Jim is—a sensitive man who is not ashamed to reveal his emotions and care for women—as opposed to being like the destructive patriarchs represented by Partridge and Gator. Indeed, he cries uncontrollably at Earl's deathbed and is able to reconcile with his father even though Earl is unable to return the favor. He is then shown nurturing Linda Partridge (Julianne Moore), the stepmother he previously despised, in the hospital. Additionally, the catastrophic event encourages the film's only third-generation male character—wunderkind Stanley Spector (Jeremy Blackman)—to plead with his verbally abusive father to start "being nicer" to him. Finally, to confirm that Jim's behavior is what the film promotes as ideal, the once-wrathful God explicitly rewards the officer. As the frog aftermath scene concludes, Jim's gun, which he previously cried over losing, and which, as Joanne Clarke Dillman accurately contends, is "the phallic signifier par excellence," miraculously falls from the sky (144).

Significantly, such a reinterpretation of narrative meaning is plausible, at least in part, because fans can support it by making recourse to authorship. In addition to Anderson's own publicity efforts that began shortly after the film's release, a review of his oeuvre augments this reading's credibility. Each of Anderson's first six feature-length films, from *Hard Eight* (1996) to *The Master* (2012), centers on the terrible consequences that result when father figures desert their biological or adopted sons. Of course, this particular reassessment of *Magnolia*'s meaning is anything but immediately evident because, instead of presenting a formal explanation for the rain of frogs, the film simply cuts to an intertitle that reads, "So Now Then." This intertitle is followed by a cut that briefly returns to the prologue, subtly alluding to its relationship to the master key. After highlights from the prologue replay, the voice-of-God narration then explains, "There are stories of coincidence and chance and intersections and strange things told . . . And it is in the humble opinion of this narrator that strange things happen all the time . . . And *the book says* we may be through with the past, but the past isn't through with us" (emphasis added). This offhanded reference to the Bible, which has been previously uttered by a number of the film's characters, potentially connects the rain of frogs to a divine plan. This insinuation, however, is not a blatant exposure of the hidden truth, as are the explanations provided by the changeover. In contrast, it is the kind of clue that signals that there might be a way to connect the events of the narrative according to a new master thread that attributes the events of the narrative to a specific causal agent, whom viewers never expected to be actually behind it all.

The film's open-ended conclusion, therefore, creates not only a likely response of frustration and befuddlement from viewers. It also has potential to inspire interpretations that contradict the master key reading outlined above. In fact, those who do not categorize it as a misdirection film often interpret the film to be, like *Fight Club*, ideologically conservative as it relates to gender. Dillman, for instance, observes that it is inaccurate and easy to think that the film places blame for the emasculation of most of the film's second-generation, white-male characters on familiar culprits. Initially, these men indeed appear to have been feminized by a number of developments, such as the intrusion of marginalized groups, like women and other minorities, into the workforce, the elimination of men from the reproductive realm, and the cultural acceptance of homosexuality. For starters, Phil Parma (Phillip Seymour Hoffman) is a male nurse who reveals in a conversation with Earl that, even though he is desperately trying, he does not have a girlfriend. Additionally, "Quiz Kid" Donnie Smith (William H. Macy) is openly gay, cannot find a partner with whom to share his love, and is fired from his job at an electronics store by his immigrant bosses. Finally, Jim has not been on a date since his divorce and garners less respect as a police officer than a female colleague who commandeers a crime scene investigation from him.

Not all of the younger male characters in the film, though, are as explicitly emasculated by contemporary cultural conditions as Phil, Donnie, and Jim. Frank is the mastermind behind "Search and Destroy," a workshop he devised to help men reclaim their lost traditional manhood. Frank's disconcertingly misogynistic performances at his seminars leave no doubt that he holds women accountable for the issues that men face. His frightening self-help sessions urge his followers to conquer their problems by copying his disgusting womanizing exploits. The circumstances leading to Frank's eventual character transformation, however, reveal that it is Earl (and not women, as he himself asserts and as some critics claim) who can be read as being most responsible for his predicament. Frank is hesitant to meet with his terminally ill father even after he learns that his death is imminent. He has justifiable hatred for Earl because he left Frank to tend to his dying mother by himself at a young age. Although it is odd that Frank eventually agrees to meet with Earl in the end, the rain of frogs rewards the act because his hated father dies before he can make peace with his son. According to this revised causal logic, it is men like Earl, and not the more traditionally identified scapegoats initially proffered by the film and by Frank himself, such as women, gays, and other minorities, who should be punished for the problems that *Magnolia*'s second-generation, white-male characters experience.

Without knowledge of the meaning of the master key, it is easy to interpret the film's female characters, as Frank initially does, to be the ones largely responsible for the male struggle. The film's three primary, white, female characters—Linda, Rose Gator (Melinda Dillon), and Claudia—each indeed appear to stand in the way of the intergenerational maintenance of masculine authority. *Magnolia*'s system of rewards and punishments, however, reveals that these women and the film's other female characters should not be held accountable. Instead, they too are ultimately depicted as the unfortunate victims of the outmoded, destructive behaviors of the film's traditional patriarchal oppressors. The characters who most blatantly expose the ways in which conventionally masculinist behaviors of men are no longer tenable are two African-American women: the disobedient apartment tenant, Marcie (Cleo King), and the journalist, Gwenovier (April Grace). Each of these women is strategically paired with Jim and Frank, respectively. As Dillman argues, the responses of both women to these men reveal how Jim and Frank's attempts to enact hegemonic masculinity are unsuccessful (149).

Early in the film, Jim is called to investigate a domestic disturbance in the apartment of Marcie, an imposing and unruly African-American woman, who practically disappears from the film after her memorable and extended introduction. Despite his best effort to assert his authority as a police officer, Marcie refuses to comply with Jim's demands. After tiring of her uncooperative antics, he attempts to handcuff her to a massive sofa in order to search her apartment. As he tries to administer the cuffs, Marcie defiantly slaps Jim numerous times. Once the cuffs are secured, she comically drags the sofa across the room in pursuit of him. Jim is obviously incapable of controlling this woman with his traditionally masculine performance. As Dillman summarizes, the film treats Marcie as a woman who "wreaks havoc on the social order" and "is an enigma that Jim and the film refuse to solve" (149). Marcie's uncontainable and inexplicable character shows how conventional strategies that white men employ to express their authority over women and other minorities are now ineffective.

Similarly, Gwenovier, who, unlike Marcie, is a professional career woman, brazenly challenges Frank's masculine power during an interview that he assumes is going to be a puff-piece. She confrontationally asks searing questions about concealed aspects of Frank's personal history. In response, Frank tries to evade her inquiries by heightening his hyper-masculinity. His tactics, though, do not faze the tenacious reporter. Like Jim, Frank cannot manage the situation that quickly escalates out of his control. All he can do in response, as Dillman claims, is to "stop speaking" (149). Gwenovier, who reveals that Frank's *über*-masculinity is a façade that has been fashioned to cover up his childhood emasculation, renders him impotent. In the end, *Magnolia*'s African-American women are among the most powerful characters in the film because they are the ones who expose how white, heterosexual men can no longer rely on antiquated gender performances to maintain their authority.

The film's primary, white, female characters are also ultimately revealed not to blame for the men's problems, according to the reinterpretation inspired by the master key. Linda is a golddigger who married a much older man because she hoped to inherit his empire. Her intrusion into the Partridge family thus prevents the transfer of resources from

Earl to Frank that would have sustained masculine authority. Indeed, she is initially so focused on keeping the money from Frank that she even assaults the passive Phil for attempting to fulfill Earl's dying wish to reunite with his son; however, Linda eventually falls in love with Earl and declares that she wants to renounce the inheritance. A number of powerful men, most notably Earl's attorney (Michael Murphy), stand in the way of her wishes. The guilt associated with her inability to remedy her selfish actions provokes Linda to try to take her own life, but unlike Craig Hansen from the prologue, whom God punishes by letting him kill himself, or Jimmy Gator, who is unable to escape his terminal cancer by committing suicide because of divine interference, she is saved by God. She is rescued by another narratively ambiguous African-American character—Dixon (Emmanuel Johnson)—a child rapper who refers to himself as a prophet in one of his verses. As a result of this divine intervention, she gets a new lease on life and forms the bond with her stepson, Frank, that her husband never got the chance to reestablish before his death.

The depiction of Rose, likewise, is easy to perceive as disturbing because she is portrayed as a dutiful wife to a man undeserving of that kind of support; however, she ultimately decides to leave Jimmy in the final stages of his cancer. Although her decision is warranted because she abandons her husband after he openly admits that he cheated on her with many women and practically confesses to molesting Claudia, her choice is surprising because she seems like she would stand by her man. Her characterization is further complicated by the fact that she neglected to care for her daughter's welfare by not stopping her husband's sexual abuse. Yet, Rose is not punished for her complicity and disloyalty because, like the other women in the film, there is little that she could have done to thwart the patriarch. Instead, she gets into a car accident during the rain of frogs, but is not hurt by the crash and is able to reach Claudia's apartment in time to comfort her during the event. Unlike Jimmy, then, God does not punish her for her transgressions. She ultimately comes out of the rain stronger because she is finally free from her husband and can help Claudia cope with the trauma inflicted by her monstrous father.

Jimmy's sexual abuse has provided Claudia with an inability to maintain a healthy, romantic relationship. As a result, she numbs her pain with a severe cocaine addiction. In fact, a strung-out Claudia tells Officer Jim on their first date that they should never talk to one another again even though they seem to be enjoying each other's company. By the end of the film, though, her character is also turned around by the rain of frogs. In the film's final scene, Claudia is in her bed as Aimee Mann's "Save Me" plays on the soundtrack. Barely audible under Mann's lyrics of "Come on and save me from the ranks of the freaks who suspect they could never love anyone," Jim can be heard attempting to convince Claudia that he will be a good companion. Instead of punishing her, then, the rain of frogs finally inspires her mother to recognize Jimmy's incest and rewards her with a relationship with Officer Jim, a compassionate man who is the exact opposite of her abusive father, perhaps putting a halt to her self-destructive habits. Surprisingly, the scene then concludes abruptly, with Claudia staring into the camera, breaking the fourth wall. After three harrowing hours, *Magnolia*'s seemingly open narrative simply ends with Claudia's return of the gaze, challenging spectators to figure out how the film's narrative ambiguities might be able to be reinterpreted into a message about how the destructive actions of men threaten the future of humanity. Without knowledge of the way the master key changes the rest of the film's meaning and, therefore, of *Magnolia*'s status as a misdirection film, such an interpretation is not possible. For those who lack that understanding or do not buy the associated reading, it is likely perceived as an indulgent and narratively incoherent film that contains troubling depictions of gender, instead of being an incendiary commentary on patriarchy and the negative consequences of traditional masculinity.

Magnolia and *Fight Club* exemplify what is at stake when user groups actively create and sustain genres. Identifying or failing to label constituents correctly can dramatically impact how films are interpreted and understood for years to come. Even when misdirection films are defined as such, determining their meanings, especially those that contain complicated narrative structures that resist being definitively reinterpreted with ease, can be a challenging endeavor. This phenomenon makes them

Figure 1.6. Claudia Wilson Gator breaks the fourth wall by staring directly into the camera in *Magnolia*'s final shot.

particularly susceptible to formal and ideological critiques that may not hold up to closer scrutiny. Indeed, although it is easy to read both *Fight Club* and *Magnolia* as being narratively lazy or incoherent, a semantic/syntactic/pragmatic approach to genre reveals that their duplicitous narratives were strategically constructed to be byzantine, but perhaps ultimately decipherable. Consequently, whereas both films are often accused of being destructive to women and sending dangerous messages to men, a more careful analysis of the discourses running through and associated to them indicates that they may instead contain comparatively progressive representations of gender. Importantly, these retrospective reassessments are only possible after the full significance of the changeover or master key is understood. Comprehensions of their cultural politics change dramatically, in other words, once they become identified as constituents of the misdirection film genre and are read accordingly. In the end, it is imprudent to leave it to other groups of people, such as industry professionals, to create genres and classify films, as many who champion the discursive approach would have it, because such classifications can impact the way a film is evaluated for decades. Instead, scholars need to stop denying the inevitable genrefication impulse and embrace the power to birth potentially enduring and meaningful categories, regardless of the ahistorical drawbacks.

2

The Truth Is Out There

Manufacturing Conspiratorial Narrative Coherence

> A new partnership of nations has begun, and we stand today at a unique and extraordinary moment. The crisis in the Persian Gulf, as grave as it is, also offers a rare opportunity to move toward an historic period of cooperation. Out of these troubled times, our fifth objective—a New World Order—can emerge: A new era—freer from the threat of terror, stronger in the pursuit of justice and more secure in the quest for peace. An era in which the nations of the world, east and west, north and south, can prosper and live in harmony.
>
> —George H. W. Bush, to a joint session of Congress on September 11, 1991

> This is a cover story, right?
>
> —Martin Vail [Richard Gere] in *Primal Fear* [1996]

In 1991, shortly after the first U.S.-led invasion of Iraq, President George H. W. Bush delivered a series of speeches in which he memorably called for the formation of a New World Order (NWO). The crisis in the Persian Gulf, he claimed, created a chance for the United

States to lead a global power regime characterized by collective policing of international interests. As the first of the epigraphs above reveals, he once articulated his vision to a joint session of Congress on *September 11*, 1991, exactly ten years before the infamous al-Qaeda attacks on the World Trade Center and the Pentagon. Although Bush hoped that his NWO addresses would make it clear that he was directing a coalition of nations to ensure that principles such as freedom, justice, and the rule of law would reign supreme, his rhetoric was largely not received as he intended. As Harry West and Todd Sanders summarize, many instead believed that it outlined a conspiratorial plan to "subordinate the will of the American people to that of an unelected transnational bureaucracy and an international elite that might dictate its governing objectives" (3).

The paranoid reaction to Bush's addresses is incongruous, considering the drastic changes occurring around the globe at the time. The fall of the Berlin Wall in 1989 and the imminent crumbling of the Soviet Union meant that U.S. economic and military supremacy were now virtually unchallenged. The negative reaction to Bush's call for a New World Order is especially telling, then, because it exemplifies a kind of conspiracy theorizing that has been increasingly directed at the U.S. government of late. The dissemination of conspiracies about the government's suspected involvement in and motives for a number of events in recent years, ranging from the crash of TWA flight 800 and the unsolved murders of Tupac Shakur and the Notorious B.I.G. to the two invasions of Iraq and the targeted killing of Osama bin Laden, have been inescapable. Yet, the shockingly sinister and spectacularly catastrophic simultaneous hijacking of four commercial airliners by al-Qaeda operatives on September 11, 2001, was conspiracy theory's defining moment in the United States. In addition to paranoid accounts of the events of 9/11 that claim it was actually an inside job, the official explanation, as Ray Pratt argues, made it "the preeminent historical example of a *real* terrorist conspiracy theory" because it demonstrated beyond a doubt that "what we previously thought was paranoia just might have turned out to be a form of heightened awareness" ("Theorizing" 256). The massive death toll of 9/11 unquestionably made conspiracy theory all-too-real for many Americans who had the privilege of living in a nation that had never been subjected to a terrorist attack resulting in civilian casualties anywhere near that magnitude. The almost unbelievable details of the hijacking plot indeed gave credence to the proverb that "just because you're paranoid, doesn't mean they're not out to get you."

This chapter focuses on exploring why two overlapping discourses—misdirection films and conspiracy theories—have recently appeared with such regularity in the U.S. for many of the same reasons. According to

Paul Silverstein, conspiracy theorizing is an interpretive practice that "prioritizes agency and fetishizes causality in making sense of everyday incoherence" (647). The misdirection film similarly ties up all potential loose ends by giving spectators an alternative account that, in retrospect, typically adheres to a classical narrative logic driven by individual character agency. Like many conspiracy theories, misdirection films provide viewers with a more attractive explanation of narrative information than what is initially supplied because they reveal that there is actually a more spectacular, yet still highly familiar way, to understand the relationship of events. Consumers of conspiracy theory and misdirection films alike derive pleasure from order being made out of chaos by those who see past the surface to draw the "correct" conclusions.

The Popularization of a Great American Tradition: Agency Panic and Contemporary Conspiracy Theorizing

Conspiracy theory is a topic that has been ubiquitous in contemporary mass media representations and has long been popular in Hollywood. On television, for example, the Fox series, *The X-Files* (1993–2002), was hugely successful, grabbing "16 percent of all television viewers" at its peak in 1997 (qtd. in Hellinger 218). A number of recent conspiracy-themed documentary films also received significant media coverage. The most notable among these was Michael Moore's attempt to chronicle the "real" motives behind the second invasion of Iraq in *Fahrenheit 9/11* (2004). Similarly, Nick Broomfield's *Kurt and Courtney* (1998) and *Biggie and Tupac* (2002) provided more sensational explanations for the mysterious deaths of three of the most recognizable popular musicians of the 1990s than what had been presented in mainstream news media. In addition, *Loose Change* (2007, 3rd Ed.), one of the most successful documentary films ever distributed primarily on the web at the time, suggests that 9/11 was an inside job. In mass-market literature, Dan Brown made the Catholic Church and the story of Jesus the subject of a grand conspiracy in *The Da Vinci Code* (2003). The book rapidly became an international sensation and was eventually adapted into a 2006 Hollywood film. Prior to the 1990s, Hollywood's conspiracy-themed film peak was in the 1970s, when it released films such as *The Conversation* (1974), *The Parallax View* (1974), and *All the President's Men* (1976) at the same time that the details of the Watergate scandal dominated the news headlines.

During the period under study, though, there has been a comparative explosion of conspiracy films that did not fall into the misdirection genre, such as *JFK* (1991), *Bob Roberts* (1992), *Nixon* (1995), *Men in Black* (1997), *Wag the Dog* (1998), *Enemy of the State* (1998), *The X-Files* (1998),

Primary Colors (1999), *The Contender* (2000), *The Manchurian Candidate* (2004), *Shooter* (2007), *The X-Files: I Want to Believe* (2008), *W.* (2008), and the aptly titled *Conspiracy Theory* (1997). Yet, I focus this chapter exclusively on misdirection films for a couple of primary reasons. First, although recent conspiratorial-themed Hollywood films may similarly articulate a growing concern about the status of the "truth," they do not inspire viewers to reread the relationship of events in a paranoid fashion in the same way as misdirection films. Second, Pratt's *Projecting Paranoia* already does an admirable job of forging connections between the rise of conspiratorial-themed Hollywood films and changes in post-WWII U.S. culture. Pratt does not consider, however, how misdirection films, irrespective of whether or not they explicitly dramatize conspiracy, tap into similar fears and desires that have made conspiratorial-themed films appealing to some audiences since the early 1990s.

Just as conspiracy-themed films are hardly new, conspiracy theorizing is not solely a product of the contemporary moment. Consequently, a brief examination of its historical legacy in the U.S. will be useful for explaining why it has been both a persistent American cultural practice and the reasons that it recently has flourished in particular ways. Such an account also lays the foundation for revealing how the misdirection film's specific narrative structures assuage anxieties and fulfill desires in a manner that resembles conspiracy theorizing. As numerous critics point out, conspiratorial thinking has always been prevalent in the United States because the interpretive practice is endemic to American political culture. Of course, conspiracy theorizing is not uniquely American. As West and Sanders note, conspiracy theorizing "proliferates around the globe" and "may take on vastly different forms in different locales" (5). Yet, the manner in which it often materializes in the U.S. is connected to cultural, political, and historical circumstances. The United States, for starters, was founded on a healthy skepticism of centralized power because its democratic system of governance was created in direct response to the tyranny of British monarchical rule. A perpetual state of paranoia about the government should be expected, therefore, as U.S. citizens are supposed to question the motives of those in power to ensure that they do not become the unwitting subjects of an authoritarian regime. In spite of this civic responsibility, theorists, like Richard Hofstadter, have famously considered conspiracy theorizing to be a negative aspect of American political culture by arguing that it amounts to little more than "collective paranoid delusions" (5).

Some scholars have rightly taken issue with this aspect of Hofstadter's pejorative conception of conspiracy theorizing. Critics, like Fredric Jameson and Mark Fenster, counter that some contemporary iterations of the practice are anything but pathological because they reveal the limited options for most U.S. citizens to negotiate their relationship to authority in a neoliberal age. Fenster contends that conspiracy theories "ideologically address real structural inequities, constituting a response to a withering civil society and concentration in the ownership of means of production, which together leave the political subject without the ability to be recognized or achieve representation in the public realm" (67). For Fenster, the prevalence of conspiracy theorizing suggests that most U.S. citizens now have few plausible choices for opposing power. Such a perspective is similar to Jameson's notion of conspiracy theorizing as the "poor person's cognitive mapping," which he describes as the means on which the disenfranchised subject relies to cope with the overwhelmingly bureaucratic cultural logic of late capitalism ("Cognitive" 356). These scholars, then, contend that conspiracy theorizing is a justified response to the neoliberal economic and political policies dominant in the West since the Reagan-Thatcher revolution. In a neoliberal era dominated by corporate deregulation and consolidation, the gap between social classes has widened, the influence of big business has expanded both domestically and internationally, the power of labor unions has eroded, and so on. As a result, some paranoid sentiments, like those contemporary conspiracy theories often express, are appropriate in a milieu in which an increasingly small group of elites has gone to great lengths to secure power and resources.

Although these scholars posit that conspiracy theorizing can be a reasonable response to contemporary circumstances, they also criticize it for ultimately being apolitical. Fenster worries that conspiracy theory fails "to inform us how to move from the end of an uncovered plot to the beginning of a political movement" in which "we can begin to organize people in a world organized by complex divisions based on class, race, gender, sexuality, and other social antagonisms" (226). Conspiracy theory, at least as Fenster understands it, offers subscribers the opportunity neither to become politically engaged nor to change structural inequities. In contrast, Clare Birchall argues that an examination of conspiracy theorizing can be instructive to those who hope to conduct the kind of politically engaged scholarship that is fundamental to Cultural Studies. In particular, Birchall theorizes that Cultural Studies has "always involved itself in the nature of specialist and everyday knowledge and how we use them to produce, consume, and interpret the culture around us" (16). According to her conception, the Cultural Studies project, especially as it has been influenced by Michel Foucault, explores how dominant epistemologies are socially constructed. She depends on this perspective to theorize how certain interpretive practices, like conspiracy theorizing, are positioned as illegitimate in relation to more established ways of knowing. Before the findings of Copernicus, Galileo, and Kepler were accepted, for example, those who denied that the earth was the center of the universe were labeled heretics. Now, those who believe in a geocentric model are considered fanatics who refuse to acknowledge the more legitimate discourses of science. As Birchall argues, such examples show that "all knowledge is only ever 'theory' " and that "any transcendental truth claims rely on contingent strategies of legitimation" (73). As with the counter histories that Cultural Studies scholars often produce, conspiracy theorists discredit widely accepted accounts by challenging the veracity of those very explanations. Birchall, therefore, posits that conspiracy theorizing can ultimately be read as "affirming the cultural studies 'project'—as being endemic of cultural studies' openness to the question of what legitimate knowledge is" (85).

Accounts that contradict "official" narratives often concern those in power precisely because they potentially expose how those explanations are also highly constructed. As Daniel Hellinger and Dennis Judd document, America's ruling class, like "elites in every society," have always striven to "preserve their economic privilege and political power, and often engage in conspiracies for this purpose" (4). To support this bold statement, they contend that the flexibility of the U.S.'s democratic political system and the modernist rhetoric that it espouses are what have long served as both the cover story and means for the implementation of the agenda of those in power. According to Hellinger and Judd, for instance, the U.S. Constitution was not drafted by the people because a powerful group of elites instead conspired "in secret" and "beyond their legal mandate" to create a document much less democratic than alternatives that were actually drafted by the people at the time (4). Importantly, the often empty promises of equality and participation in government that the Constitution offers are still key factors in the dominance of elites. Throughout U.S. history, the decentralization of power the document purports has neither leveled the playing field nor provided the populace with clear explanations for the government's motives and actions. In fact, elites in the United States have consistently gone to extreme lengths to marginalize groups of people from the democratic process and have continually concealed the reasons for their tactics. Groups such as the illiterate, the poor, non-landowners, women, and African-Americans have been denied the right to vote in the U.S. precisely because of the threat that they posed to power. Similarly, with each passing year, evidence mounts that many politicians are more concerned with pleasing the benefactors who helped them get elected than they are with serving their constituents. Finally, since the Cold War, the instances in which those in power have blatantly violated the rights promised to U.S. citizens out of concern for "national security," exemplified by McCarthyism, the PATRIOT Act, as well as the NSA spying scandal, have become more frequent and spectacular.

For those in power, then, conspiracy theory can threaten one of the most important ways that authority is maintained. As Hellinger writes, conspiracy theories "cast suspicion on the transparency and legitimacy claims of actions undertaken by the police, military, and intelligence agencies, whose missions include actually undertaking conspiracies" (205). In contemporary democratic societies, institutions that serve and protect the people are often believed to operate in an open and honest fashion because they are designed to uphold fundamentally modernist ideals like truth, justice, freedom, and equality. As a result, when the supposedly irrational and paranoid claims of conspiracy theorists prove accurate, it can shake the very core of democratic society. In the aftermath of the Watergate scandal, for instance, it became impossible to deny that the government employs unauthorized surveillance techniques and creates elaborate cover-ups to maintain authority. Yet, as many scholars theorize, conspiracy theory's ultimate power lays not in its ability to reveal the "truth." Instead, it is a threat because it raises doubts about the veracity of official explanations. West and Sanders contend that conspiracy theories create "discourses that are constructed in contradistinction to the (also constructed) truths of transparency" (15). Silverstein, likewise, conceives of conspiracy theorizing as "a form of 'vernacular' knowledge production contrasting with overlapping 'official' modes of knowledge production that outlines an alternative 'truth regime'" (646). In short, conspiracy theories create oppositional accounts, which often suggest the likelihood that those constructing authoritative discourses also rely heavily on conspiratorial means to accomplish their objectives.

Clearly, it benefits those in power to make it seem as though the alternative explanations of conspiracy theorists are unfounded by referring to them as kooks, or other such derogatory labels, which can be accurate descriptions for some of its subscribers in certain instances. However, the real threat that conspiracy theorizing poses explains why, as West and Sanders argue, those "bound up with the notion of transparency expend a great deal of energy in attempts to paint Other ways of seeing with the brush of 'ignorance,' 'irrationality,' or 'superstition'" (12). Many conspiracy theorists are demeaned because it seems unreasonable to rely on the logic at a time in which power supposedly operates in the open and in the best interests of the people. Although conspiracy theorists have long been labeled as paranoiacs on the fringe, West and Sanders correctly contend that nonetheless "evidence suggests that a broad cross section of Americans today—traversing ethnic, gender, education, occupation, and other divides—give credence to at least some conspiracy theories" (4). In light of the recent wake of high-profile scandals that have exposed the reprehensible dealings of upper-echelon U.S. government and corporate officials, such as those involving executives at Enron, WorldCom, Tyco, and some of the world's preeminent financial service companies, it is understandable why such paranoid thinking is becoming more commonplace.

Virtually all discussions of contemporary conspiracy theorizing in the United States point to the assassination of President John F. Kennedy as a marker of a new period in its history. As Pratt argues, it was "an epistemological break" that caused "both the general populace and a significant subgroup of intellectuals to question their ability to *know* the truth rather than merely believe or sense it" (*Projecting* 221). Paradoxically, the more evidence that the Zapruder film revealed, the less the public was able to determine what "really" happened. The "truth" of the JFK assassination was also compounded by the mountain of information compiled by the Warren Commission in support of its unconvincing lone gunman theory, which, as Marita Sturken notes, most believed "constituted a cover-up and was at least part fiction" (72). The lack of closure to the assassination created, in Benedict Anderson's language, an "imagined community" of U.S. citizens, united by their simultaneous consumption of the same narratives that unsatisfactorily explained events. Significantly, for Anderson, this virtual camaraderie only became possible after the onset of modernity and the requisite development of print-capitalism. The newspaper, Anderson contends, was crucial to making a cohesive group out of disparate individuals because in the act of reading, the reader becomes "aware that the ceremony that he performs is being replicated simultaneously by thousands (or millions) of others of whose existence he is confident, yet of whose identity he has not the slightest notion" (35). Although Anderson fails to consider how oral traditions made this phenomenon possible in pre-modern societies, his thesis demonstrates that such practices have been amplified by the advent of subsequent mass media and communication technologies. Indeed, it is cliché for those old enough to remember the Kennedy assassination to report where they were when they learned about it on broadcast media. Similarly, many in that cohort would likely share their dissatisfaction with the "official" account after seeing the Zapruder film, Lee Harvey Oswald's murder on live television, and so on.

Television's development into the dominant mass medium has played a large role in the proliferation of similarly themed conspiracy theories in post-WWII U.S. culture. Since at least JFK's assassination in 1963, a number of seminal events in American history that received significant television news coverage, including the Vietnam War and subsequent misguided U.S.-led invasions, the Watergate scandal, as well as the similarly suspicious assassinations of Robert F. Kennedy, Martin Luther King, Jr., and Malcolm X, have either not been satisfyingly explained by official accounts or blatantly exposed the conspiratorial activities of those in power. Pratt theorizes that such events have conditioned American citizens to believe that "agencies of the U.S. government have the right—perhaps even the duty—to lie to protect national security" and that "even though they vote and pay taxes to support it, they do not have the right to know all the government's secrets" (*Projecting* 21–22). Unsurprisingly, not all U.S. citizens have taken kindly to this infantilization, which begins to explain why conspiracy theorizing spread widely in U.S. culture during the 1960s and 1970s and has only escalated since that time.

A casual search for conspiracy theories on the web indicates that conspiracy theorizing is not something that is only done by extremists. The Internet, like many technologies before it, has unquestionably made the distribution of conspiracy theories easier. Yet, the Internet is not solely responsible for the recent proliferation of conspiracy theories. During the 1980s and early 1990s, the distribution of conspiracy theories, as Birchall documents, was greatly "facilitated by technological developments that made personal computers, laser printers, and desktop publishing software more available" (35). These new technologies provided conspiracy theorists with a cost-effective way to disseminate messages through publications, such as zines, which have become easier to replicate on the web. Put simply, the Internet has dramatically intensified tendencies that predated its existence. The development of this new communication technology, in conjunction with the practice's omnipresence in popular culture, has, as Birchall claims, "ensured conspiracy theory a stable presence on the cultural scene" (38).

The persistence of the liberal democratic myth in the United States is the primary reason why conspiracy theory has always been and will likely continue to be central to American political culture. As Timothy Melley posits in *Empire of Conspiracy*, Americans are reared on the modernist principles of liberalism, which promotes free will, individual rights, and restrictions of government power. These discourses have long been the primary means by which most U.S. citizens conceive of their agency, revealing why there is strong suspicion of centralized government. The belief that the select few in power do not control the will of the people, however, has been strongly challenged recently by the exposure of the aforementioned conspiracies undertaken by the government and its conduits in big business as well as in surveillance and law enforcement. This nervous concern over the loss of individual sovereignty underpins much of the conspiratorial expression that has become more popular of late. Melley labels such paranoia as "agency panic," which he defines as "an intense anxiety about an apparent loss of autonomy or self-control—the conviction that one's actions are being controlled by someone else, that one has been 'constructed' by powerful external agents" (12). Many contemporary American conspiracy theorists, therefore, question the veracity of authoritative narratives by attributing what "really" happened to actual historical individuals and/or organizations with the power to dictate their actions. According to Melley, most post-WWII conspiracy theorizing is thus "a fundamentally conservative response—'conservative' in the sense that it conserves a traditional model of the self in spite of the obvious challenges that postwar technologies of communication and social organization pose to that model" (15).

Postmodern Disguise: Misdirection Films and Hollywood Modernism

The premise that individual identity is most appropriately conceived of as a construct is often linked to the broader cultural logic of postmodernism because it contradicts the established notion that an "authentic" persona actually exists. Whereas modernist-inspired agency panic maintains that it is possible for those with the requisite interpretive acumen to locate a bounded self, postmodernist-inspired thought posits that it is a fantasy to identify a genuine persona. Scholars inspired by Jameson's writings on postmodernism, for instance, claim that schizophrenia is a prototypical condition of a mass-mediated era dominated by television and characterized by associated socially and culturally constructed identities. The much disputed, polysemic term "postmodernism" has been typically employed, as Robert Stam observes, to describe anything ranging from "a discursive/conceptual grid, a corpus of texts, a style or aesthetic, a paradigm shift, a prevailing sensibility" to "an epoch" (754). Crucially, these potential uses of the term are not mutually exclusive. As Stam points out, Jameson takes a "multidimensional approach which sees postmodernism as *simultaneously* a style, a discourse, and an epoch" (emphasis in original, 754). If postmodernism is deployed to name an indisputable change in multiple arenas, then I am hesitant to refer to the post-WWII period in the United States as the postmodern since neither contemporary American conspiracy theorizing nor recent Hollywood misdirection films constitute significant aesthetic, epistemological, or historical breaks from the conventional forms of expression with which they are most closely contrasted.

The ubiquity of the term "postmodernism" in scholarly and popular discourse, though, makes it difficult to ignore the concept completely. Consequently, I argue that postmodernism is, in Raymond Williams's terms, most appropriately conceived of as being "emergent" because it classifies "the new meanings and values, new practices, new relationships and kinds of relationships" that "are continually being created" by social formations at times in which existing dominant epistemologies and cultural practices still reign supreme (123). The tenets most commonly associated with postmodernism, such as relativity, multiculturalism, and the rejection of metanarratives, are not principal in a culture still characterized by well-established artistic canons, the competing discourses of religion and science, as well as firmly entrenched hierarchies of ability, class, gender, race, sexuality, and so on. Following Douglas Kellner's lead, I thus employ postmodernism, "as a placeholder, or semiotic marker, that indicates that there are new phenomena that require mapping or theorizing" (46). Postmodernism, therefore, describes emergent contextual shifts that have not yet superseded dominant ways of thinking. Although these forces have exerted some influence on aesthetics and culture, their impact is not substantial enough to signal that there has been an unequivocal transition into a new epoch.

My position on the postmodernist debate is influenced by scholars, like M. Keith Booker, who speculate that the post-WWII period in the U.S. represents a late phase of modernity rather than the start of the postmodern era. As with Booker, I grant that it is imprudent to ignore how a number of conditions resulting from and subsequent to WWII, including the ravaging of European lands, the dropping of atomic bombs on Hiroshima and Nagasaki, the eventual fall of the U.S.S.R., as well as the consequent international economic and military dominance of the United States, have all contributed to virtually unchallenged American power and the unfettered spread of global capitalism, which theorists like Jameson claim to be the defining characteristics of postmodernism. Booker persuasively theorizes, however, that these changes pale in comparison to "the radical transition from medieval Catholic hegemony to the emergent capitalism of early modernity" (30). Since the fall of feudalism and church rule in the West, in other words, there have been few, if any, economic, political, and cultural shifts that have altered the inexorable progress of modernity and its requisite industrialization, technological development, and establishment of liberalist governments that purport to serve the interests of the people.

The post-WWII period in the U.S., then, is best understood as a late phase of modernity that is still largely governed by its guiding principles. Hollywood misdirection films can be considered a product of this period because they also often seem to interrogate modern epistemologies on first blush; however, in the end, they rarely undermine that very way of comprehending the world completely. Yet, some scholars contend that these are precisely the kinds of films that demonstrate that Hollywood's production strategies have changed dramatically in response to postmodernity. In *A World in Chaos*, Tom Pollard and Carl Boggs argue that contemporary Hollywood films routinely challenge the modernist narrative and formal practices that dominate earlier periods. Interestingly, the authors offer a definition for modernist cinema that is similar to David Bordwell's notion of the classical film. They theorize that the ethos of "cinematic modernism" was "tied to the emergent studio system" and "set out to depict historic struggles between good and evil in a world where (typically white male) protagonists stood for a coherent, progressive set of values" in which "the hero (however flawed or tragic) was invested with the power to influence or transform society" (5–6). As with Bordwell, Boggs and Pollard contend that the portrayal of the protagonist's struggle to overcome seemingly insurmountable obstacles propels the typical golden age Hollywood film. They take this conception further, though, and theorize that in a majority of studio-era Hollywood films, the protagonist's objectives have strong ideological implications because they are typically tied to modernist notions of truth, justice, economic expansion, industrialization, nationalism, and so on.

Although Boggs and Pollard maintain that these kinds of narratives were dominant during the studio era, they admit that a few Hollywood films, such as misdirection films directed by Hitchcock, Lang, and Welles, challenged the principles of modernity at the time. However, they subsequently argue that the cultural and industrial changes precipitated by the U.S. victory in WWII and the ensuing breakup of the studio system have resulted in a sustained assault on the project of modernity. This cinematic shift is what many scholars identify as a tangible change in world cinema, a claim made perhaps most influentially by Gilles Deleuze in *Cinema II*, in which he argues that the classical Hollywood movement-image film has been supplanted by the time-image film in some non-U.S. cinemas after WWII. Boggs and Pollard, though, offer an important caveat to this conception because they note that although "postmodern" Hollywood films "build on a revulsion against tightly structured, formulaic, narrowly commercialized methods linked to the studio system," their ability to be made entirely "independently of corporate production has never been fully resolved or even confronted" (7). The latter half of this statement is particularly relevant to this book. Even though misdirection films encourage viewers to engage with them distinctly, they exist in a system in which a few media conglomerates still tightly control the industry. Boggs and Pollard thus theorize that this tension epitomizes an "age where the restless search for new epistemological and aesthetic paradigms—a search often taking its architects in the direction of chaos and even apocalypse—has infused the spirit of much contemporary filmmaking" and "entails a profound critique and rejection (but never full transcendence) of modernity" (7–9). Contemporary misdirection films similarly want to have it both ways. Although misdirection films appear to interrogate some of the classical film's basic narrative, formal, and ideological principles, I argue more strongly than Boggs and Pollard that they are not as radical as they initially appear. In retrospect, they instead can be read as usually remaining within the classical paradigm and often upholding dominant American ideologies.

Such a tendency aligns misdirection films culturally with recent explicitly conspiratorially themed Hollywood films. In *Projecting Paranoia*, Pratt relies heavily on Melley's conception of agency panic to argue that the films he studies often express a nervous concern that powerful forces behind the scenes nefariously dictate people's actions. As a result, Pratt claims that the films he analyzes "may be seen as unconscious reflections of state-supported repression of movements for human emancipation, or the belief among significant sectors of the public that their lives are no longer under their own control" (*Projecting* 2). Such a hypotheses is echoed by Patrick O'Donnell, who similarly posits that the presence of many conspiratorial-themed literary narratives during the brief historical period reveals that, "one knows that she is part of a series of orchestrated events over which she has no control, but knowing it confers a kind of legitimacy upon the knower; she can be manipulated, but she can't be fooled about being manipulated" (190). Hollywood's recent production trends demonstrate that films that depict powerful agents who conduct covert operations that go undetected by most U.S. citizens, such as the now iconic men in black, appeal to audiences. The popularity of these representations is noteworthy because even though they suggest that many spectators willingly admit that such agencies exist, they also indicate that most citizens acknowledge they are powerless to fight them. The contemporary misdirection film's success also reveals that many Hollywood spectators acknowledge that the classical film is a particular construction despite the fact that it still sutures them into its protagonist-driven narrative logic so effectively.

Importantly, then, Melley's notion of agency panic also accurately describes the existential plight of many of the misdirection film's protagonists. The heroes of these films often suffer from afflictions, such as dissociative identity disorder (*Adaptation* [2002], *A Beautiful Mind* [2001], *Fight Club* [1999], *Identity* [2003], and *Shutter Island* [2010]), that enable their actions to be controlled by other characters who know about and exploit their conditions to fulfill their own objectives. Moreover, even primary characters in misdirection films who do not have mental illnesses are often at the mercy of someone else's bidding, like those revealed to be the unwilling pawns in an evil mastermind's plot (*Arlington Road* [1999], *Unbreakable* [2000], *The Usual Suspects* [1995], etc.). Indeed, the revelatory information in almost every misdirection film exposes the fact that someone (*Lucky Number Slevin* [2006], *The Village* [2004], etc.) or something (whether it be ghosts in *The Others* [2001] and *The Sixth Sense* [1999], dreams in *Jacob's Ladder* [1990], *Mulholland Dr.* [2001], and *Vanilla Sky* [2001], or even deities in *Magnolia* [1999] and *Pulp Fiction* [1994]) has been controlling a main character's actions unbeknownst to both him or her and the audience. The epiphanies of these films clearly articulate a nervous concern over the authenticity of individual autonomy. As I demonstrate below, many misdirection films can thus be understood according to a hyper-classical narrative logic because they ultimately prioritize agency and fetishize causality—the key components of the definition that I use to understand conspiracy theorizing—in their alternative explanations of the "actual" reasons for and the "real" culprits behind otherwise unsatisfactorily explained events.

Just Because You're Paranoid Doesn't Mean You Can Do Anything About It: *Arlington Road* and Agency Panic

Arlington Road offers perhaps the clearest example of why it is appropriate to examine contemporary misdirection films in relation to a specific kind of cultural paranoia; it depicts memorable conspiratorial plots in recent U.S. history and encourages audiences to reinterpret narrative information retrospectively in a conspiratorial fashion. The explicit combination of this theme and narrative structure in this particular film, though, was not entirely successful with audiences or critics. In comparison to other misdirection films released in 1999 (e.g., *The Sixth Sense*, *Fight Club*, and *Magnolia*), *Arlington Road* received little publicity, was completely ignored by the Academy of Motion Picture Arts and Sciences, and made little splash at the domestic box office. In fact, it netted approximately $24 million during its run in U.S. theaters, barely recuperating its modest $21.5 million budget (imdb.com). The film's narrative centers on Michael Faraday (Jeff Bridges), a George Washington University Political Science professor, who is experiencing difficulty coping with the tragic death of his FBI-agent wife, Leah Faraday (Laura Poe). Michael holds the Bureau responsible for her murder because she was killed during a mission based on faulty information. The film also depicts the struggle that develops between Faraday and his new neighbor, Oliver Lang (Tim Robbins), who initially seems to be little more than a prototypical suburban husband and father, but turns out to be a key member of a conspiratorial plot against the U.S. government that Michael tries to foil.

The casting of Robbins in one of the film's lead roles is noteworthy because it can be understood as one of the first moments in which a recognizable Hollywood star was unofficially typecast as a misdirection actor. He was likely considered for the part because of his performances in *Jacob's Ladder* and *The Shawshank Redemption* (1994), which although it is not a misdirection film, contains a major plot twist that Robbins helps to conceal with his performance. It is also significant that Spencer Treat Clark, who subsequently stars in *Unbreakable*, plays Michael's son, Grant Faraday, and that the film was scored by Angelo Badalamenti, who would later compose a similar eerie soundtrack for *Mulholland Dr.* The cast and crew, therefore, are peppered with names that demonstrate an increased industrial awareness that the misdirection film constitutes a genre replete with its own associated creative personnel.

The way that the film was marketed also suggests one of the reasons why misdirection films are often considered a genre in the popular imagination. Misdirection films contain narrative structures that inspire interpretive activities that both express paranoia about the concealment of the "truth" and a yearning to unearth it from its hiding place. Few contemporary misdirection films, though, make these shared cultural anxieties and desires explicit thematic concerns. As an exception to this trend, *Arlington Road* was promoted with taglines, such as "Your paranoia is real," "How well do you know your neighbor?," and "On July 9, terror hits home," prepping the audience to be on high alert. It is purely coincidental, of course, that the film was advertised in the rhetorical style of the George W. Bush administration and its War on Terror; however, such promotional ploys are noteworthy because they suggest that marketers recognized that recent events in U.S. history had made it such that many were willing to believe that, in the years leading up to September 11, 2001, it was plausible that they could be living amongst well-camouflaged terrorists.

Unlike many of Hollywood's post-9/11 terrorist-themed films released during the period under study, such as *The Sum of All Fears* (2002), *Munich* (2005), *Syriana* (2005), *United 93* (2006), and *World Trade Center* (2006), though, *Arlington Road*'s narrative was not inspired by the actions of international, radical extremist factions. Instead, its narrative was based largely on the tragic events associated with a number of domestic, right-wing militia groups, including those related to both

Ruby Ridge's Randy Weaver and Timothy McVeigh, whose bombing of Oklahoma City's Murrah Federal Building was the deadliest terrorist attack in the United States prior to September 11, 2001. Significantly, as West and Sanders observe, in the aftermaths of both tragedies, Weaver and McVeigh publicly professed a "deep suspicion of power in the New World Order" (3). That is, the two were domestic terrorists in the 1990s whose behaviors were believed to be provoked partly by their profound distrust of the motives behind the U.S. government's recent actions.

Arlington Road presents thinly veiled fictional accounts of these significant events in 1990s U.S. history most explicitly during scenes that portray Faraday's course on American Terrorism. In classical fashion, Faraday's lectures are not narratively tangential because they provide key information about the protagonist's primary struggles. The scenes impart information about the circumstances of his wife's death and showcase his difficulty dealing with the loss. However, the scenes serve another important purpose: they reveal that Faraday is suspicious about the actions of the U.S. government and encourages viewers to identify with his justifiable paranoia. The first classroom scene opens with Faraday's assertion that the U.S. government has not lived up to the promises set forth in the Declaration of Independence and the Constitution. He informs his American Terrorism class that "Two hundred years ago a revolution was fought for certain beliefs like liberty, self-rule, self-reliance, and justice for all, and there are many in this country who feel we have not yet won that war." His lecture thus teaches his students that the modernist principles on which the country was founded are a charade. He subsequently points out that various groups have resorted to terrorism to protest the government's restrictions of their individual freedoms throughout U.S. history. Faraday then raises a series of questions about why such anti-government, terrorist acts have recently been on the rise. Echoing the sentiments of those puzzled by the paradoxical response to Bush's NWO speech, he asks "why, at a moment of social prosperity is the anti-government movement at its peak?" In response, Faraday articulates the growing sense of disenfranchisement in the U.S. by noting that "fewer and fewer of us are voting" and "more of us are joining the resistance." In short, the first classroom scene unfavorably portrays the U.S. government for limiting individual sovereignty and suggests that the growing opposition to its authority is understandable.

In the second classroom scene, Faraday offers a specific example of this anti-government resistance by presenting the tragic details associated with the demolition of the fictional Roosevelt Federal Building in St. Louis, Missouri, which are clearly based on the McVeigh bombing. Faraday begins by documenting what he deems to be the unconvincing "official" account. He reports that authorities concluded that a man, named Dean Scobee, acted alone in the attack. In particular, they claim that he committed the crime solely because he owed approximately $10,000 in back taxes to the IRS, whose offices were housed in the building. As Faraday challenges the veracity of these findings, a perturbed student interrupts the lecture by shouting, "Come on professor, the Feds did this whole investigation." An unimpressed Faraday counters that the "investigation didn't satisfy" him. He then puts another student on the spot by asking her to tell the class how she felt once the authorities identified Scobee. As Faraday surmises, her initial feelings of fear and her ultimate sense of security reveal why the "official" explanation can easily be dismissed as a cover story designed to provide the paranoid masses with a convenient scapegoat to pacify them. Faraday's second lecture articulates a compelling alternative account of the traumatic event fashioned in contradistinction to the "official" report, which he and many others believe to be completely unsatisfying.

For the final lecture scene, Faraday and his students are depicted outside of the classroom, at a field at Copper Creek, the location where Leah was killed. As Faraday begins recounting the details of the tragedy to his students, the film cuts to images of the event that are clearly coded as a flashback. In contrast to his description of the Scobee incident, it is significant that this event is presented in such a manner because classically trained spectators tend to expect flashbacks to be accurate. As Bordwell acknowledges in his discussion of Hitchcock's *Stage Fright* (1950), the director's first, unsuccessful attempt to make a misdirection film, it "is probably the canonic case of unreliable narration in classical cinema" because its opening flashback "turns out to have been the visual and auditory representation of a lie" (*Narration* 61). For Bordwell, that film failed with classical viewers because unless flashbacks are explicitly marked as potentially unreliable, convention dictates that they contain dependable information. Unlike his controversial account of the Scobee bombing, then, the Ruby Ridge inspired story depicted in the flashback is likely assumed to be factual. Of course, this is the case even though Faraday seems to be experiencing extreme psychological distress since his wife's death and harboring hatred for the FBI. It is subsequently revealed that the FBI mistakenly flagged Randy Weaver stand-in, Seaver Parsons, as a potentially dangerous domestic terrorist, who they believed was stockpiling weapons for a future act of violence. Specifically, during a surveillance mission at the Parsons' home, Leah and her colleagues are spotted by one of Parsons' sons, triggering a series of unfortunate events that end in a slaughter. As Faraday explains to his class, although it was true that Parsons was a renowned right-wing extremist, the FBI failed to realize that he "was a separatist, but not a terrorist," who was likely just legally trying to obtain merchandise to open a gun shop. In this scene, therefore, spectators become privy both to the kinds of covert operations that U.S. government agencies regularly conduct and the terrible consequences that can occur when incorrect causal connections are made as a result.

Arlington Road, however, is not a film that portrays conspiratorial acts as committed only by those in power. As the film's shocking changeover reveals, those who oppose the U.S. government's restriction of individual freedoms also regularly participate in conspiracies. The film's surprise conclusion shows, like other contemporary conspiratorial-themed Hollywood films, such as *Conspiracy Theory*, the remake of *The Manchurian Candidate*, and *Shooter*, that the consistent and seemingly unfathomable lone gunman theories produced by "official" accounts are fabrications. In *Arlington Road*, though, these theories are revealed as erroneous not because they have been manufactured by those in power to ease the anxieties of the public, as Faraday speculates in class in relation to the Scobee incident. Instead, they have been produced by those aiming to sabotage the government as a means to hoodwink the authorities. The film eventually exposes the fact that Faraday's seemingly perfect suburban neighbors—the Lang family—are actually key members of a militant, anti-government terrorist group that has played a crucial role in a number of horrific acts that have been incorrectly pinned on lone, rogue attackers. It is revealed, for instance, that the Langs lived in St. Louis at the time of the Roosevelt Federal Building bombing and that their son, Brady (Mason Gamble), was a member of the same Discovery Scout troop at which Dean Scobee volunteered. Unfortunately, by the time Faraday unearths the truth, it is too late because unbeknownst to both him and the audience, he has become the next unwitting participant in a new plot to destroy U.S. government agencies.

Most of the narrative thus focuses on Faraday's attempt to confirm his suspicions about his neighbors and convince others that his paranoia is justified. He constructs a conspiratorial account in which Oliver Lang is actually an alias for a convicted teenage pipe-bomber, named William Fenimore, who Faraday theorizes has sought revenge against the government since it unfairly seized his family's farm water source when he was a boy. Although no one else believes him for most of film, it is ultimately revealed that paranoia indeed can be a sense of heightened awareness because virtually all of Faraday's hypotheses eventually prove correct.

Oliver explicitly confirms many of Faraday's theories during the film's climactic chase sequence. When the two get into a physical altercation as Michael pursues a van (aptly emblazoned with the company name, Liberty), which he believes both contains Grant and is packed with explosives, Lang chastises Faraday for his obsessive desire to discover the truth by yelling, "You had to know, you couldn't leave your neighbor alone." It seems, then, that Faraday has become a legitimate threat to the terrorist organization because his conspiratorial account of Oliver's real identity may jeopardize the mission. He subsequently further validates Faraday's hypothesis by confessing that he is just "a messenger" and that "there's millions" like him "ready to take up arms" to make the government "pay for their sins." The dramatic confrontation between the film's protagonist and antagonist, therefore, appears to put an end to almost all of the film's primary causal lines of action. Now that Faraday has been proven right about his neighbor's involvement in a terrorist conspiracy, all that needs to happen for the film to conclude with a happy, Hollywood ending is both for him to stop the bombing and to save his son.

The film's ending, however, does anything but resolve the narrative in anticipated fashion. His dogged pursuit of the van ultimately takes him to the basement garage of the J. Edgar Hoover FBI building. Upon arrival, he convinces a group of skeptical FBI agents, led by Leah's ex-partner, Whitt Carver (Robert Gossett), to search the van. Shockingly, the van is empty and the trunk of Faraday's rental car is instead revealed to be packed with explosives. Consequently, it appears that the bomb was placed in the rental car when Michael was out of the vehicle for a brief period during his fight with Oliver, suggesting that their confrontation was staged by Lang's terrorist organization as part of the conspiratorial plan. The explosives are then detonated from a remote location by other members of Lang's team, destroying the offices of the FBI. Next, the film abruptly cuts to a television news report from the rubble in which a newscaster explains that "preliminary reports indicate the bombing was the working of" Faraday alone and that it has not yet been confirmed "if the bombing had anything to do with Faraday's wife, who was an FBI agent." The conspiratorial nature of the erroneous "official" account, then, is already being established by the initial media coverage of the event.

These inaccuracies are further codified in the news report by a series of anecdotes delivered by Faraday's former students, who claim that the professor was deeply disturbed by the circumstances surrounding his wife's death. Importantly, the final one of these statements is uttered by an ex-student of Faraday's, who was revealed during the bomb detonation sequence to belong to the same anti-government terrorist organization as the Langs. In the interview, she notes, "All I know is what he told me in his office after class—sweetheart, one day those men are going to pay, one day those men are going to burn." The news montage that explains the traumatic event indicates how supposedly transparent "authoritative"

Figure 2.1. A television newscaster presents an inaccurate report that attributes the bombing of the J. Edgar Hoover FBI building solely to Michael Faraday in *Arlington Road.*

accounts are often just as constructed as conspiracy theories. It reveals how the "truth" is concealed by the organization behind the conspiratorial plot and its conduits in the media through a fetishization of causality and a prioritization of agency. Indeed, although spectators are now aware of what "actually" happened and who is "really" responsible for the traumatic event, the uninformed characters of the diegetic world are doomed to believe that one man acted alone to destroy the government institution that he blamed for his wife's unfortunate death.

The way that *Arlington Road* asks the audience to reread narrative causality in relation to how it is misunderstood by diegetic characters is especially relevant because it ultimately encourages viewers to engage in conspiratorial interpretive activities. Although it is true that most spectators likely never suspected that such an alternative explanation for narrative causality was possible, it is safe to assume that a majority of them are able to understand how the meaning of what has come before changes in light of the revelation. This is largely because the revised explanation of the causal relationship of events, like most conspiratorial accounts, adheres to a familiar narrative logic. Fenster even uses Bordwell's notion of the classical Hollywood film to conceptualize how those who engage in conspiracy theorizing routinely rely on many of the storytelling principles that are fundamental to its highly recognizable mode of narration. Citing one of Bordwell's sections of *The Classical Hollywood Cinema* he notes:

> The "classical" conspiracy narrative attempts to unify seemingly disparate, globally significant elements and events within a singular plot, doing so through the traditional logic of conventional popular narratives, including "causality, consequence, psychological motivations, the drive toward overcoming obstacles and achieving goals. Character centered—i.e., personal or psychological—causality is the armature of the story." (Fenster 108)

The conspiratorial narrative, therefore, typically employs the same techniques as the classical film to explain narrative causality. In both cases, the events of the narrative can be fully understood as the workings of a single person or a group of individuals who, despite the many obstacles that arise, triumphantly attain the goals that were initially set forth.

Although the conventions of the classical narrative encourage spectators to believe that *Arlington Road* centers on Faraday's attempts to unmask the architects of the terrorist plot, the surprise conclusion, in hyper-classical fashion, reveals that the film only ends satisfactorily when the Langs are shown to accomplish their objectives. This is why the film concludes with scenes that depict both Oliver burning his files on Faraday and the Langs speculating about the details of their next mission. The existence of this surveillance evidence, in fact, indicates that Faraday had been explicitly selected for the gambit long before the Langs ever moved into the neighborhood. He was targeted as the perfect man to bomb the Hoover building because of the circumstances surrounding his wife's murder. Moreover, his scholarly fascination with radical extremist groups made him the ideal candidate to discover Oliver's secret identity, enabling them to trick Faraday into unknowingly delivering the bomb to the FBI's headquarters.

This logic only begins to suggest the deviousness and complexity of the Langs' plot. Faraday first meets his new neighbors, for instance, when he drives Brady to the emergency room after a purported fireworks accident. However, it is questionable whether he is even the Langs' son because during the changeover Grant is shown being cared for by other members of the conspiratorial cabal, suggesting that Brady could be an orphaned child of another victim from a prior plot. This seemingly outlandish explanation becomes even more plausible because Oliver is portrayed as an explosives expert, who will go to virtually any length, including severely injuring children, to lure Faraday into participating in the scheme. During his physical confrontation with Faraday, he even alludes to his willingness to harm kids if it will help him in the fight against the U.S. government by noting, "this is war Michael . . . in war children get killed." Admittedly, it seems far-fetched that such an intricate plot could ever really work. Viewers have to suspend disbelief to think that any group could arrange it so that a badly injured child wandering in the middle of a suburban neighborhood would be spotted by no one other than a lone passerby. Of course, *Arlington Road* was released shortly before the exposure of the revelations that al-Qaeda operatives took flight lessons in which they blatantly expressed no interest in learning how to land, were able to overtake four commercial airliners with little more than box-cutters, crashed planes into both towers of the World Trade Center and the Pentagon over the course of a one hour period without being stopped by the U.S. military, and so on. The existence of these kinds of overlapping discourses suggests why conspiracy theorizing has gained such cultural currency in the United States of late. Although the Langs' murderous scheme seems implausible, even for a Hollywood movie, a more diabolical, intricate, and horrifying conspiratorial plot dramatically unfolded in the U.S. just two years later.

It is the Langs, then, and not Faraday, who are ultimately *Arlington Road*'s primary causal agents because they are revealed to be responsible for orchestrating the film's events. Such an epiphany clearly articulates the kind of agency panic that Melley argues underpins much contemporary conspiracy theorizing, as Faraday's actions are depicted as being completely manipulated by powerful forces beyond his control, even though he is an expert on the historical existence and practices of such terrorist organizations. In the end, the film's changeover leaves little doubt that, despite the fact Faraday was well aware of the Langs' nefarious objectives long before the destruction of the Hoover building ever occurred, he was incapable of stopping them from turning him into the perfect suicide bomber, making it a representation of contemporary conspiracy theorizing *par excellence*.

Here Come the Men in Black: *Jacob's Ladder* and Paranoia as Heightened Awareness

Like *Arlington Road*, *Jacob's Ladder* is one of the few misdirection films to make justifiable paranoia an explicit thematic concern. Whereas *Arlington Road* foregrounds its focus on conspiratorial activities early and often, the presence of a devious plot orchestrated by the U.S. government does not become fully evident until the end of *Jacob's Ladder*. Specifically, the changeover reveals that narrative events have been a representation of the dying dream that a soldier, Jacob Singer (Tim Robbins), the film's protagonist, experiences while he unsuccessfully fights to stay alive after apparently suffering a mortal combat wound to his abdomen. During the film's ostensible climactic explanation before the changeover, a mysterious man, Michael Newman (Matt Craven), who trails Jacob throughout the dream, explains that he is a chemist who was forced by the military to manufacture an experimental, aggression-enhancing drug, nicknamed "The Ladder," to amplify soldiers' performance. Newman then notes that Jacob's platoon served as guinea pigs for the drug, which caused the soldiers to slaughter each other. This revelation is shocking because Jacob and viewers have been led to believe, since the film's opening bloody battle scene that a superimposed title classically indicates takes place in the "Mekong Delta" on "6 Oct. 1971," that the platoon was brutally ambushed by the Viet Cong. Although the changeover calls into question all that the dream shows, as it exposes how preceding events have been focalized through the mind of the comatose protagonist, a title card appears before the end credits roll, asserting that the U.S. military used a drug, colloquially referred to as BZ (quinuclidinyl benzilate), on test subjects during the Vietnam War, even though "The Pentagon denied the story." This epilogue suggests that many conspiratorial elements of the dream, such as the lawyer, Geary's (Jason Alexander) declaration that Jacob's platoon never served in Vietnam because they were "discharged on psychological grounds" after the military instead had them participate in clandestine "war games in Thailand," might, in fact, be true.

Jacob's Ladder's anti-Vietnam War message was part of a spate of Hollywood films, including more acclaimed titles, like *Apocalypse Now* (1979), *Full Metal Jacket* (1987), and *Platoon* (1986), that belatedly critiqued the controversial invasion. The popularity of the Vietnam War film cycle suggests that *Jacob's Ladder*'s focus on the conflict had little to do with the filmmakers' struggles to get Hollywood backing. Instead, it was likely its duplicitous narrative structure that most made it seem potentially unprofitable because it took a decade until screenwriter and co-producer Bruce Joel Rubin's screenplay was finally released (Hartl). It was not until the now defunct Carolco, a fleetingly successful independent studio that also released another, more economically successful misdirection film that same year, *Total Recall* (1990), and collapsed as rapidly as it surprisingly rose to prominence, backed the project after the majors passed on it, that the film even went into production. Unlike some of Carolco's incredible successes in the early 1990s, most notably *Terminator 2: Judgment Day* (1991), *Jacob's Ladder* barely made back its production costs, earning approximately $26 million in U.S. theaters on its $25 million budget, where it was ultimately distributed by Sony subsidiary, TriStar Pictures (imdb.com). As with other misdirection films, then, it can be considered a Hollywood film from an industrial perspective because it was eventually distributed domestically by a media conglomerate even though it was produced independently.

These atypical production circumstances help to explain why the film epitomizes the textual properties of the contemporary misdirection film by mixing classical tendencies with non-classical elements. Aside from the aforementioned postscript, the only things that the viewer can accept as fact in light of the changeover is that a man named Jacob Singer died in a military infirmary tent after putting up a valiant struggle to stay alive while doctors tried to save him. The veracity of everything that precedes this moment, therefore, is uncharacteristically thrown into question by the changeover. In contrast to most misdirection films with a clear-cut changeover, *Jacob's Ladder*'s revelation further complicates, rather than clarifies, what "actually" happened. Yet, director Adrian Lyne's decision to include the afterward about the military's purported experimental use of BZ strongly suggests the possibility that the dream narrative's explanatory sequence—Newman's admission that he concocted the drug surreptitiously administered to Jacob's platoon under duress—"really" occurred. Like *Arlington Road*, in retrospect, *Jacob's Ladder* is a film that quintessentially links the overlapping discourses of the misdirection narrative and conspiracy theorizing explicitly together by portraying a paranoid story of a protagonist who has been unwittingly manipulated by powerful forces beyond his control. In particular, even though Jacob, who is affectionately dubbed "the professor" by his platoon because he completed a PhD prior to going to Vietnam, is highly intelligent and is the only one of the crew who refuses to stop investigating the military's role in the incident after the other war veterans are coerced to drop the lawsuit, he is ultimately shown as being powerless to do anything about it. Viewers similarly realize at the end that they likely have been fooled despite the fact that the film uncharacteristically encourages them to interrogate the veracity of information consistently prior to the exposure of the changeover.

The lingering ambiguity after the changeover, then, is not the only aspect that renders *Jacob's Ladder* more non-classical than most other contemporary misdirection films. In comparison to many changeover films, which do not call the validity of events into question until the revelation, *Jacob's Ladder* constantly forces the viewer into a cognitive crisis by making it difficult to delineate between fantasy and reality. Such uncharacteristic ontological blurring transpires throughout the film, first occurring immediately after the opening battle scene in which spectators are led to believe that the strong marijuana that the group smokes before the attack is the reason they seem to go crazy during the bloodbath. Upon being bayonetted in the stomach by an unidentified attacker at the end of the opening combat scene, the film abruptly cuts to Jacob, now garbed in an U.S. Postal Service uniform, awakening on a New York City subway train with Albert Camus's classic, existential novel *The Stranger* in his hands. The edit initially appears to be a prototypical classical cut because Jacob grabs his abdomen as he wakes up startled, which helps orient the viewer in time and space by framing the preceding war scene as a dream. In retrospect, however, this dream's relationship to reality is complicated by the ways in which the changeover renders everything that comes before it functionally polyvalent.

Although the radical changes in Jacob's location and costume are initially jarring to the viewer, it subsequently becomes clear that the majority of the film is set in New York City after his discharge, ostensibly situating it in the "coming home" Vietnam War film subgenre. Constituent films, such as *Coming Home* (1978), *The Deer Hunter* (1978), *First Blood* (1982), and *Born on the Fourth of July* (1989), feature the trials and tribulations of returning veterans. *Jacob's Ladder*, likewise, appears to center on the post-traumatic stress that Jacob experiences after the war. Jacob's precarious mental state is the primary reason why the events that unfold throughout the New York City scenes are not initially understood to be the product of his dying dream. Viewers are instead led to believe that disturbing images may actually haunt him in his waking life in spite of his efforts to forget about the war. In fact, he tells his chiropractor, Louis (Danny Aiello), that he became a letter carrier rather than pursuing a faculty job upon returning from his service because "after 'Nam [he] didn't want to think anymore." Rather than interpret the entire New York City narrative as part of the dying dream, spectators are tricked into trying to determine if his terrifying visions are genuine or imaginings induced by postwar paranoia.

Yet, after Jacob awakes on the subway, the film slyly hints at the real explanation by focusing on subtle clues in the *mise-en-scène* that reference the dying dream. When Jacob comes to, the camera switches to his point of view as he gazes at two seemingly innocuous, but retrospectively narratively significant, advertisements. The first one claims that "New York may be a crazy town, but you'll never die of boredom," subtly alluding to the fact that Jacob is actually about to pass away at the end of the New York City dream. The second advertisement more cleverly reveals the film's big secrets, as it reads: "Hell. That's what life can be, doing drugs. But it doesn't have to be that way. Help is available, day or night." This ad is retroactively relevant because Jacob's

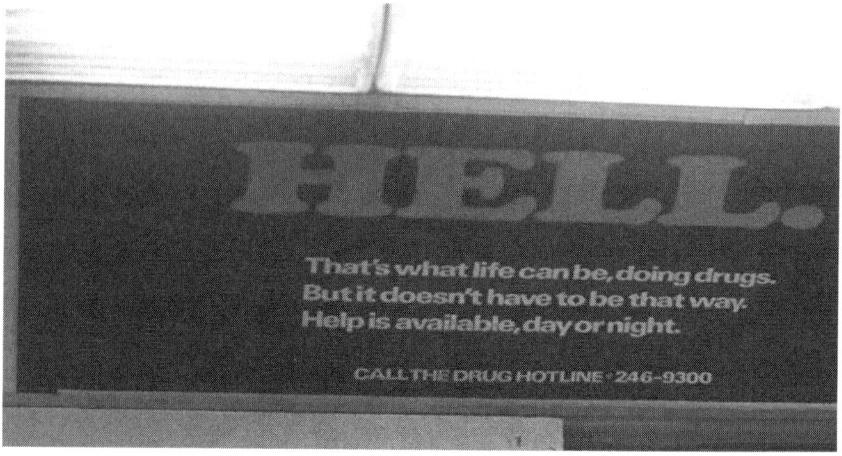

Figure 2.2. An advertisement in *Jacob's Ladder* alludes to its changeover that reveals Jacob Singer is having a drug-themed, dying dream in which demons try to drag him to hell.

dying dream about The Ladder centers on his visions of the demons that he thinks are trying to drag him and most of his fellow soldiers to hell even though no one, aside from most of his platoon-mates, believes they are real. Jacob's co-worker girlfriend in the dream, Jezebel (Elizabeth Peña), for instance, insists that the demons are actually just "winos and bag ladies" that populate the streets of New York City. Similarly, Rod (Anthony Alessandro), the only ex-platoon mate who is not haunted by the visions, asserts that his fellow vets are "all fucking paranoid" because "it was bad grass, that's all" and "there's no such things as fucking demons." Without knowledge of the changeover, both viewers and diegetic characters are encouraged to spend the dying dream narrative trying to determine if Jacob's visions are authentic or just delusions. As a result, the film's biggest clues about the presence of the changeover, such as when a palm reader tells Jacob that his lifeline indicates he is "already dead" and the many similar instances that hint that he is actually dying, are likely interpreted initially as potential manifestations of his post-traumatic stress-inspired hallucinations, instead of being read as evidence of the fact that he is about to pass away.

The truth of the coming home narrative seems to be resolved when it is eventually revealed that Jacob both must acknowledge his impending death and stop holding onto his life's regrets for the demons to cease pursuing him. This finally happens after Newman's explanation about The Ladder in the dream, when Jacob returns to the Brooklyn apartment he shared with his family and realizes that Louis's Meister Eckhart-inspired advice of letting go of his earthly concerns will make the demons go away. In addition to lines of dialogue, like when Jacob asks Louis if "anyone has ever told him" that he looks like "an overgrown cherub," and formal choices, such as the heavy back-lighting that consistently makes Louis resemble a guardian angel, the narrative importance of the chiropractor and his advice are reiterated immediately prior to the changeover. Specifically, his earlier Eckhart-laden dialogue replays on the soundtrack right before the film cuts to a flashback, shot in home-video style, displaying key moments from what appears to be Jacob's actual family life. This formal choice is significant because it is not the first time that the aesthetic is used. The most notable time it was employed prior to this moment is during an earlier flashback within the dying dream, which reveals the tragic accident that killed Jacob's youngest son, Gabe (Macauly Culkin). Consequently, the stylistic change is significant because it is likely deployed to delineate these non-Vietnam scenes retroactively to signal their truth value in relation to the rest of the dying dream. After Jacob's life literally flashes in front of the viewer's eyes, he finally reunites with Gabe, who leads him up a staircase, symbolically indicating

Figure 2.3. Jacob Singer's chiropractor, Louis, is depicted angelically largely because of heavy backlighting in *Jacob's Ladder*.

that his soul is ascending to heaven. Such a reading is reiterated formally, as the film cuts to a bright, white screen immediately before the shocking changeover occurs. In sum, the use of the home-video clips is designed to help spectators retrospectively distinguish fact from fiction in the dying dream narrative.

Throughout the rest of the pre-changeover sequences, the constant classically edited oscillations in and out of the dream make for often maddening transitions from what seems to be the subconscious imagination to waking life, but they also function consistently to fool the viewer by seemingly delineating fantasy from reality in clear-cut fashion. Retrospectively, though, it becomes virtually impossible to figure out what actually happened in Jacob's life because the changeover throws into question almost all that the dying dream depicts. As with the home-video footage, this is why the inclusion of the BZ postscript could be crucial to reinterpreting the film's meaning in a potentially coherent fashion. Indeed, its appearance at the film's conclusion after the changeover occurs suggests that Newman's revelation about the government's experimental use of BZ on Jacob's platoon has at least some merit. As a result, the film's most paranoid scenes, particularly those featuring U.S. government agents, become more believable, in retrospect, than many of the other elements of the dying dream. Most notably, it is Jacob's encounters with these mysterious men in black that potentially haunt spectators as being plausible after the changeover is revealed. Before he is able to escape, these intimidating, secret agents brutally kidnap Jacob, beat him, and attempt to kill him to

Figure 2.4. *Jacob's Ladder*'s men in black, government agents abduct Jacob Singer.

stop him from investigating the military's actions. The now ubiquitous men in black in Hollywood cinema suggest that their actual existence has recently become highly plausible to U.S. audiences. Their important role in *Jacob's Ladder*'s dying dream is thus a testament to the justifiable paranoia that pervades the viewing experience of the misdirection film. The popularity of such images illustrates that spectators and citizens alike readily acknowledge that they know they are now being controlled by powerful forces, such as men in black and Hollywood filmmakers, even though they are powerless to stop them. This awareness demonstrates why the retrospective reinterpretations the misdirection film inspires and much contemporary conspiracy theorizing about the abuses of formidable institutions, like the U.S. government, have resonated strongly with many people during the same historical moment.

Contemporary misdirection films and some recent conspiracy theories are interrelated discourses that offer similar responses to their particular contexts. They are both narrative forms that have become popular of late because they appeal to a population that has grown increasingly skeptical of the project of modernity, but is not yet willing to abandon its foundational principles. Many contemporary conspiracy theories and misdirection films resonate with some audiences because they ultimately reveal, in accordance with the discourses of liberalism, that a select few individuals are really still in control of their lives. Although such alternative accounts should be applauded for exposing the constructedness of purportedly transparent "official" explanations, they paradoxically also usually adhere to the very narrative logic to which they are opposed. Most misdirection films indeed can be retrospectively reread in a hyper-classical fashion even though they initially seem to challenge some of Hollywood's most basic narrative and formal conventions. This tendency has strong cultural implications because many of these films, like the conspiracy theories they resemble, appeal to some viewers by transforming everyday incoherence into narratives that are both ultimately more conventional and supportive of dominant ideologies than they initially appear to be.

3

Constructing the (Im)perfect Cover

Masculine Masquerade and Narrative Agency

Successful misdirection film actors, like Tim Robbins, perform in ways that capitalize on the spectator's tendency to comprehend the causal relationship of narrative events as being attributable to the actions of a prototypical goal-oriented, male protagonist. Misdirection films prey on the spectator's propensity to associate narrative causal agency with men who behave in ways that are coded as authoritative and in control in relation to other characters. Such interpretations suggest that many audiences are inclined to consider some forms of manhood as ideal and active. It also demonstrates that many spectators are quick to judge other kinds of masculine performances as aberrant and passive. Gender performance, therefore, can function in a similar way that the classical Hollywood narrative does in the misdirection film. Indeed, although misdirection films challenge viewers to reconsider initial interpretations drastically, they also both rely on classical conventions to encourage audiences to draw incorrect causal suppositions and often can be reinterpreted according to a character-centered, causal logic that renders them hyper-classical, in retrospect. Similarly, gender performance in misdirection films generally leads audiences to believe that they understand the true personas of primary characters even though it is ultimately revealed that they jumped to incorrect conclusions about their real identities and narrative power.

The potential for misinterpretations of the links between gender performance and agency, of course, extend into the broader cultural sphere. Perhaps nothing demonstrates this phenomenon better than the aftermath of Osama bin Laden's targeted killing on May 2, 2011. His death raised serious concerns about the U.S. government's suppression of information related to the event, including photographic evidence confirming his death. It was peculiar, then, that among the first artifacts made public were videos showcasing the al-Qaeda leader studying and managing his media image. Even more bizarre was the subsequent decision to announce that a stash of heterosexual pornography was confiscated from his expensive Abottabad compound. These efforts were clearly an attempt to demystify bin Laden's legend as the pious, cave-dwelling commander of al-Qaeda. Such revelations suggest that government officials hoped his public persona would be reinterpreted as an intricate performance that concealed an "authentic" gendered identity aligned with hegemonic Western masculinity, characterized by a voracious appetite for wealth, fame, power, and women.

The event's fallout was also highlighted by news media accounts comparing it to a Hollywood film. This link was verified when Seal Team 6's successful raid became the climax of *Zero Dark Thirty* (2012). The escapade, though, appeals to Hollywood for reasons that extend beyond just the chance to reenact the operation. *Zero Dark Thirty*'s central focus—its dogged heroine Maya's (Jessica Chastain) triumphant hunt for bin Laden—illustrates how Hollywood routinely distorts history by overemphasizing tales of exceptional individuals attaining lofty objectives. Such a tendency is unsurprising because whereas other cinematic traditions often do not present protagonist-driven quest narratives, Hollywood films have mass appeal largely because formal decisions are almost always subservient to its recognizable storytelling formula. In addition to the financial rewards linked to this canonical narrative and its associated invisible style, Hollywood benefits from it by mitigating political divisiveness. Its obsession with remarkable people overcoming seemingly insurmountable obstacles oversimplifies complex situations by boiling them down to Manichean battles between good protagonists and evil antagonists. Although this helps the industry avoid taking unambiguous stands on controversial issues, its recurrent practices have cultural ramifications. Classical protagonists, for instance, are disproportionately white, heterosexual men. *Zero Dark Thirty* thus notably features a female lead in a traditionally male role. How far it deviates from dominant ideology is debatable, however, as professional dedication results in alienation for Maya, who is denied even the joy of the compulsory heterosexual romance.

These examples show how mass media functions as an ideological state apparatus by engaging in the process of hegemonic negotiation. Media conglomerates do not portray culture monolithically because they both express and produce historically situated notions of identity. Yet, to maximize profits, producers generally play it safe by ultimately supporting conventional conceptions of cultural categories, like gender. In this chapter, I examine how a similar representation of masculinity in *Unbreakable* (2000) and *The Usual Suspects* (1995) epitomizes both how reactionary gender politics persist in Hollywood and the ways in which the misdirection film is particularly well-suited for surreptitiously maintaining male dominance. My argument thus extends the connections between misdirection films and conspiracy theorizing forged in the previous chapter by focusing specifically on how the genre's particular narrative machinations can effectively dovetail with expressions of contemporary white-male paranoia about the loss of cultural authority. *Unbreakable* seems to center on the role that African-American comic book dealer, Elijah Price (Samuel L. Jackson), who has a severe brittle bone disease, plays in the remasculinization of real-life superhero, David Dunn (Bruce Willis). Likewise, in *The Usual Suspects*, Verbal Kint (Kevin Spacey), an allegedly small-time crook purportedly afflicted with cerebral palsy, recounts how he helps reformed criminal legend, Dean Keaton (Gabriel Byrne), resurrect his outlaw glory. Both films' changeovers, however, show that their ostensible helper characters are actually archvillains who exploit their protagonist buddies. The following analysis of these two films illustrates how the misdirection film enables Hollywood to sustain traditional conceptions of manhood at a time when explicit mediations of hegemonic masculinity are received skeptically. Specifically, even though the changeovers reveal that seemingly feminized primary male characters are more powerful than conventionally masculine protagonists, they do not suggest that multiple masculinities are a reality. I ultimately contend that their apparent defiance of established male hierarchies instead supports dominant ideology by imagining that men's primal spirit endures behind a façade of aberrant masculinity.

Masquerade Required: Preserving Male Essence in the Misdirection Film

Depictions of primary male characters concealing an authentic male identity under an emasculated cover represent a significant change in ideal manhood in Hollywood. These men are a far cry from the muscle-bound heroes, played by Arnold Schwarzenegger, Sylvester Stallone, and

Bruce Willis, that characterized Hollywood in the 1980s. For Susan Jeffords, such "decisive, tough, aggressive, strong, and domineering" male protagonists were products of the times, as they intersected with Ronald Reagan's agenda to undo the policies of Jimmy Carter's administration, which were deemed "weak, defeatist, inactive, and feminine" (11). When Reagan's excessive masculine posturing no longer seemed as necessary in the immediate post-Cold War moment, she notes, sensitive family men began replacing hyper-masculine protagonists. This shift was typified by Schwarzenegger, who appeared in films blending his action hero persona with a domestic facet, including *Kindergarten Cop* (1990), *True Lies* (1992), and *Junior* (1994). Although such developments seem to embody vastly different masculine standards, Jeffords contends that they are actually "overlapping components of the Reagan Revolution," encompassing both "a strong militaristic foreign-policy position" and "a set of social values dependent on the centrality of fatherhood" (13). Her reading exemplifies how apparent transformations in gender representation back the same ideological project. How, then, do misdirection films, like *Unbreakable* and *The Usual Suspects*, extend this trend by articulating fantasies of continued male dominance that are appropriate for their contexts?

Discerning the gender politics of these two films is tricky partly because their atypical narrative structures effectively encourage spectators to draw incorrect conclusions, which can allow them to conceal their ideological messages more effectively and render their cultural expressions more ambiguous. The misdirection film's typical depiction of gender exemplifies how it frequently relies on classical standards to work its deceptive magic. As *Psycho* (1960 and 1998) and *The Crying Game* (1992) have famously shown, the misdirection film is perhaps more adept than any Hollywood genre at making audiences aware that it is easy to misconstrue markers of identity, such as gender and sexuality, exposing how viewers draw hasty conclusions about characters' relative narrative agency. Although most misdirection films do not prompt spectators to reevaluate a primary character's identity this drastically, many encourage audiences to understand gender as being unstable. This is especially true in relation to masculinity because numerous contemporary misdirection films stunningly reveal that male protagonists are victims of a fantasy or at the mercy of seemingly weaker male characters.

Even though these films contain surprise endings that illustrate that gender is constructed, they generally do not ultimately show, as Judith Butler seminally theorizes in *Gender Trouble*, that masculinity is entirely performative because "what we take to be an internal essence of gender is manufactured through a set of acts, posited through the gendered stylization of the body" (xv). Similarly, they do not demonstrate, as Jack

Halberstam does in *Female Masculinity*, that "masculinity becomes legible where and when it leaves the white male middle-class body" since it can be mobilized by anyone, irrespective of ability, class, race, sex, and sexuality (2). Instead of demonstrating the progressive potential of decoupling gender from other markers of identity, *Unbreakable* and *The Usual Suspects* typify how misdirection films regressively depict gender performance as a way to conceal an antiquated male core that remains intact.

Although it is usually deployed in relation to women and femininity, the concept of masquerade relates to the kind of gendered deception male characters undertake in these two films. Like Steven Cohan in *Masked Men*, I thus use masquerade for its "theatrical rather than phallocentric implications," which is "in accordance with Butler's theorization of gender as 'performative' " (26). Masquerade is appropriate for analyzing mediated masculinity, as he contends, not because of Joan Riviere's psychoanalytically inspired conception of femininity as a way "to conceal a secreted theft of the phallus" (qtd. in Cohan 26). Instead, masquerade's theatrical dimension reveals how portrayals of masculine artifice can disrupt rigid notions of biologically determined gendered identity. Yet, as Jackie Stacey suggests in her analysis of *Gattaca* (1997), masquerade can be difficult to apply to representations of manhood since the "impossibility of masculinity" highlights "the more general façade of 'authentic' masculinity" (1862). I grant that such logic applies to a film, like *Gattaca*, in which an inauthentic perfect masculinity is the disguise because ideal masculinity is indeed shown to be unattainable when the copy and the original are both exposed as fabrications. *Unbreakable* and *The Usual Suspects*, by contrast, unveil a male essence behind an *imperfect* masculine cover. Masquerade, therefore, as Chris Holmlund notes, accounts for how films that reveal that an authentic masculinity exists below the surface "reinforce hegemonic power relations" by exhibiting "that there may be something underneath which is 'real' and/or 'normal' " (224).

The narrative fantasy of cloaked male quintessence appeals to a culture in which media representations of masculinity in crisis have become practically inescapable. Since the early 1990s, numerous Hollywood films have focused on the difficulties that white, heterosexual, American men, who perform their gender traditionally, are having maintaining authority. In 1999 and 2000 alone, for instance, as Philippa Gates observes, many films "centered on male protagonists in crisis," appearing "to indicate a broader social concern that at the turn of the new millennium masculinity was, indeed, in crisis" (46). Interestingly, of the films she cites—*American Beauty* (1999), *Fight Club* (1999), *Magnolia* (1999), *The Sixth Sense* (1999), *American Psycho* (2000), *The Beach* (2000), *Memento* (2000), and *Unbreakable*—all but *American Beauty* and *The Beach* are misdirection films, reiterating the narrative mode's suitability for expressing cultural fears and desires related to manhood. Of course, patriarchy is always in crisis because of perpetual threats to its supremacy. It is still valuable, though, according to Michael Kimmel, to analyze "the times when dominant masculinity is widely perceived to be under threat because there is a search for the timeless and eternal when old definitions no longer work and the new definitions are yet to be established" (3). Similarly, Nicola Rehling writes that "masculinity in crisis" troublingly "postulates a once stable, coherent, unified masculinity," making it valuable to identify "which particular forms of male insecurity are made manifest at specific historical junctures" (2–3).

Instead of abandoning the "crisis model" for examining masculinity, an exploration of the distinct historical periods in which traditionally accepted conceptions of manhood are widely perceived to be under threat can reveal the specificities of the paranoia directly related to the times. Although it is true that conceptions of "ideal" masculinity are always being contested, the topic of contemporary American men in crisis is particularly noteworthy because it has recently become so appealing to Hollywood producers and audiences. Susan Faludi's oft-referenced and controversial book, *Stiffed*, is particularly relevant in this regard because both the reasons it presents for the American male's purported fall from grace and the ways it offers to help him resurrect his authority are often vividly expressed by recent popular culture representations, including a number of misdirection films. According to Faludi, so many American men have become increasingly disillusioned because the institutions created by their predecessors to support their dominance have failed them. She theorizes that many of the changes precipitated by the U.S.'s emergence as a superpower after World War II, such as the shift from a production economy to a service economy as well as the gains made by the women's liberation, civil rights, and gay rights movements, have resulted in the depreciation of the roles that white, heterosexual men play in economic, political, and social spheres. Whereas their fathers were almost unequivocally considered the undisputed heads of their households, earned respectable livings in the production economy, and were revered as the authorities of culture, or so the story goes, contemporary American men do not have similar male-dominated institutional spaces to assert their traditional masculine control.

A cursory evaluation of the gendered makeup of corporate boardrooms, the military ranks, and the highest levels of government in the United States begins to raise doubts about the veracity of Faludi's claims. Regardless, Faludi's argument is relevant largely because of the ubiquity of contemporaneous mass media productions that echo her thesis that many men are now in an unenviable situation. She contends that American men are still expected to express their masculine control in the same manner as previous generations of men; however, they do not have the foundation necessary to display their manhood even though, paradoxically, their fathers came to power during a period of unprecedented abundance. Over the course of her research, Faludi eventually comes to the shocking conclusion that the younger men who were the subject of her quasi-ethnography had been forced to come "face-to-face with the collapse of some personal patrimony" because they almost inevitably suggested that behind all of their problems "lay their fathers' desertion" (596). The unfettered rise of consumerism and its corresponding mass media representations of "ideal" masculinity, she theorizes, also play crucial roles in the contemporary crisis in American manhood. Like the fifties housewife, who primarily acted as a domestic servant and the arbiter of consumption, Faludi claims that the "nineties man stripped of his connections to a wider world" has been "invited to fill the void with consumption and a gym-based display of his ultra-masculinity" (40). Unlike women, though, who have had men as the clear enemy oppressor, men have neither had a tangible nemesis nor a way to escape their predicament because there is no socially acceptable alternative to conceive of their gender.

For Faludi, the only way for men to rectify the situation is to find a way to regain their authority by "having authored something productive," which she admits has become increasingly difficult in a society where the kinds of contributions that most men now make in the service economy or on the high-tech warfront are much harder to quantify in the same terms as previous generations (86). Although Faludi ultimately argues that the task of men "is not, in the end, to figure out how to be masculine—rather their masculinity lies in figuring out how to become human," she never disputes that his "proper" role is as the active, and primary contributor to cultural, economic, and political arenas (607). I grant that she makes a valid point that men need to stop evaluating their worth based on how well they live up to gender standards that have long been codified as ideal in American culture. Her proposed solution, however, sustains, rather than redresses, the structural inequities that have kept white, heterosexual men on top and women and other minority groups on the bottom for centuries in the United States.

Irrespective of whether or not Faludi is ultimately right about either the culprits for or the appropriate responses to the contemporary crisis in American masculinity, *Stiffed* is particularly germane because, as Martin Fradley speculates, it has proven to be "symptomatic and representative of social perceptions and frustrations of many white, American men" (238). A number of Hollywood films that were released around the time of its publication indeed overlap with her fundamental claims about the status of American manhood, helping to produce cultural anxieties related to changing gender roles and relations in the United States. As J. Michael Clark observes, Tyler Durden (Brad Pitt) "virtually paraphrases Faludi" when he informs his fellow members of Fight Club that they have "no Great Depression, no Great War, no other dragon to battle heroically against, but that, instead, the 'great depression' is their own contemptuous lives lived so passively enslaved to consumerism" (67). These challenges prompted many men to respond in reactionary ways. In the 1990s, for example, there was a rise in men's groups, like the Mythopoetic Men's Movement, whose leader, Robert Bly, author of best-seller, *Iron John*, urged men to participate in wilderness retreats that enabled them to relocate their supposedly lost inner wild man.

Although the declarations that white, heterosexual, American men have recently been victimized by a series of unfavorable circumstances might be overblown, Faludi's claims are intriguing partly because many in this cohort have, in fact, fallen on harder times of late. The economic policies initiated by the Reagan and the George H. W. Bush administrations in the 1980s and early 1990s, strengthened by similar strategies enacted by subsequent U.S. presidents, had negative repercussions for many middle- and working-class Americans. A number of the developments associated with these neoliberal policies, as Kimmel documents, such as the "outsourcing of manufacturing jobs, plant closings, downsizing layoffs, cutbacks, and the gradual erosion of the safety net (health insurance, medical benefits, Social Security) instituted by the New Deal have ushered in a new era of 'social insecurity'" that is gendered because it "confounds men's sense of entitlement, their ability to be family providers and breadwinners" (218–19). The dramatic widening of the earning gap and the corresponding evisceration of the middle class since the early 1980s have made it increasingly challenging for many American males to continue fashioning themselves as self-made men. Moreover, the few mechanisms that were actually once deemed acceptable by many who subscribe to rugged individualism have been almost entirely eradicated. As Kimmel writes, the social programs that once "buttressed the self-made man's ability to be a successful breadwinner and provider—minimum wage, the GI bill, high wage employment, and unions—have eroded or disappeared" (220). Again, although these developments have diminished the economic standing of many white, heterosexual, American men, this group is still in a better position than minority groups to succeed. The real losses that many middle- and working-class white, American men have recently suffered, however, have caused confusion and anger for those who continue to struggle to demonstrate their cultural worth in a traditionally masculine fashion.

These paranoid responses convey worries about diminishing individual autonomy that jibe with Timothy Melley's aforementioned conception of agency panic. However, rather than address the culprits, such as the neoliberal policies that have consolidated wealth and bolstered corporate power, many disenchanted men instead blame familiar scapegoats, including big government, women, and other minority groups. Importantly, the perception that individual agency is dwindling has struck white, heterosexual men hardest because of their steadfast faith in rugged individualism and the American Dream, which, in spite of their meritorious myths, historically favor the privileged. In the 1990s, the destructive ramifications that could result from such reactionary fears were epitomized by the notorious cases of domestic terrorism committed by Timothy McVeigh and Ted Kaczynski, who, as Melley posits, believed that the supposedly "feminizing force" threatening their masculinity should be redressed by " 'regeneration through violence' " (14). Melley's reliance on Richard Slotkin's theory of regeneration through violence is significant because, as Slotkin argues, it was a crucial aspect of the frontier myth that "represented the redemption of American spirit or fortune as something to be achieved by playing through a scenario of separation, temporary regression to a more primitive or 'natural' state" (12). Centuries later, this logic endures for many American men hoping to find their mythical, primal manhood, as evidenced by groups like the Mythopoetic Men's Movement.

In contrast to the frontier era, there is now less unequivocal acceptance of men reverting to their supposed inner wild man. After the Reagan-era backlash against second wave feminism subsided, as David Greven documents, American masculinity "became aware of itself as both monolith *and* joke," resulting in growing Hollywood representations of a "post-Reagan New Man," that articulate a "*split masculinity*, which performed traditional roles of gendered identity while also acknowledging its ironic, meta-textual status" (16, emphasis in original). Brenton Malin, likewise, hypothesizes that this kind of dual portrayal characterized Bill Clinton's presidency and was embodied by a simultaneously dominant media representation of "conflicted masculinity that embraces and puts aside a variety of masculine stereotypes" (8). Until the Monica Lewinsky scandal calcified his budding reputation as a philanderer, for instance, Clinton was also consistently disparaged for being obsequious to his wife, Hillary Rodham Clinton. Such contradictions in masculinity, Malin argues, are palpable in many contemporaneous Hollywood films, featuring protagonists "salvaging the disturbing traditions from which the '90s man seemed to diverge" (10). Hollywood indeed released a number of Oscar Best Picture winners during the period under study, including *Braveheart* (1995), *Jerry Maguire* (1996), *American Beauty*, and *Gladiator* (2000), portraying broken protagonists who recapture their lost male spirit traditionally. In contrast to these depictions of explicit remasculinization, misdirection films often prey on the spectator's propensity to associate narrative agency with conventional protagonists by revealing that they are powerless at a time when other tactics are necessary to maintain male authority.

The substantial pressures on American men to prove their masculine prowess in a familiar manner without the same kind of supporting structures to do so has encouraged many men to seek alternative ways to counter their dwindling power. Throughout the 1990s, for example, some men turned their attention from displaying their competence at the workplace to showcasing their masculine proficiency in domestic affairs. As scholars like Jeffords argue, though, this turn to the home front did not represent a significant departure from the conservative agenda to maintain the patriarchal order. Although the home rapidly became a logical place for the dispossessed American man to reestablish his lost sense of worth, men did not necessarily change their approach to domestic affairs even though their role as the primary breadwinner was now often matched or exceeded by their female partners.

Many men stripped of power in the economic arena have thus sought to regain a foothold in the domestic sphere by reasserting their manhood as authoritative patriarchs. As a consequence, Kimmel argues that many men have focused on traditionally masculine activities, such as protecting their families and representing their family's interests in external affairs, which are "all valuable behaviors," but are "also behaviors that do not require that he ever set foot in his child's room" (237). This turn to the home front, then, is a classic case of hegemonic negotiation in action because it does not necessarily mean that men perform the child-rearing roles typically associated with women. Consequently, many men's movements in the 1990s attempted to determine the particular value that fathers, and not mothers, were thought to be well-positioned to provide to their families. Adrienne Burgess, author of *Fatherhood Reclaimed*, for example, cites the U.S. National Fatherhood Initiative as evidence that to help the family unit function most effectively, men must behave differently than women in the home because they should "contain emotion and be decisive" and should not be expressive or nurturing (27). For these kinds of activists, men need to assume a greater leadership role in the home because only they can provide the rational guidance that their purportedly over-emotional and irrational female partners are believed to be incapable of executing.

Not all proponents of the new family man, however, are opposed to men taking a more active role in parenting. For many throughout the 1990s, fatherhood was considered, as Stella Bruzzi claims, to be the primary "vehicle for teaching a man how to feel," making the "articulate, caring father the most valued male archetype" during the period (157). Unfortunately, though, the father often became highly prized in American culture not because of the actual contributions that he made around the house, but simply because he was actually there. In an era marked by the increasing presence of the single-parent household, the father who stayed and made time for his family, especially for his male offspring, became the prototype in some circles, such as the Mythopoetic Men's Movement. It became the job of dads to heal the "father wound" inflicted by a previous generation of men who had inexplicably deserted their families after promising so much to their sons. According to conservative thinkers, like Bly, this unfortunate trend began during the industrial revolution when men were encouraged to leave the home for extended periods to work in factory-style labor. The total disappearance of many men from the home in an era of post-1960s women's liberation only exacerbated this problem. As Kimmel documents, Bly and his followers expressed paranoia that this abandonment meant that many women "retained an incestuous dedication to their sons, excluding the father and keeping the boy dependent on her long after he needed to break away" (208).

Commercial U.S. films centering on young men who struggle to come to terms with the fathers who unexpectedly deserted them have been extremely popular for a number of decades, suggesting that Hollywood has played a key role in the ideological project to recapture masculine authority by turning to the home front. To wit, as Kimmel notes, some of the most commercially successful Hollywood films of the early blockbuster era—*E.T.: The Extra-Terrestrial* (1982), *Close Encounters of the Third Kind* (1977), and the films of the first *Star Wars* trilogy (1977, 1980, 1983)—use " 'healing the father wound' as both the motivation for and the ultimate result of the masculine quest" at the heart of their narratives (211). Indeed, both Steven Spielberg and George Lucas, arguably the most successful creative personnel working in Hollywood since the mid-1970s, have made veritable entertainment empires out of films that depict the efforts that young men make to establish relationships with the fathers who never taught them how to be a man. This paranoid drive to reassert patriarchal dominance by reclaiming fatherhood through often troubling means continues to be a central theme for some contemporary

Hollywood filmmakers, including many of the misdirection film genre's most prominent directors.

Unbreakable Masculinity: Reclaiming Men's "Rightful" Place

To coincide with the release of *Signs* (2002), M. Night Shyamalan's second film after his smash commercial hit *The Sixth Sense*, the August 5, 2002 edition of *Newsweek* featured a cover story on the director, touting him as "The Next Spielberg." The connection between the two filmmakers was logical for a number of reasons. To begin, just a few films into his Hollywood career, Shyamalan had already frequently professed his indebtedness to his filmmaking idol, such as numerous times in the cover story article by Jeff Giles in the aforementioned issue of *Newsweek*, and demonstrated a similar ability to create films that appealed to a family audience. Additionally, his films contain thematic preoccupations that align with Spielberg's favorite concerns. Most notably, Shyamalan's films are also obsessed with the influence of the meltdown of the American nuclear family on the lives of a generation of men and boys. *The Sixth Sense*, for example, centers on the plight of two male characters—one young (Cole Sear) and one middle-aged (Malcolm Crowe)—who both struggle to reconcile their small, splintering families. The two characters are only able to reconnect with their loved ones after developing a quasi-father-son relationship. Their bond finally enables Cole (Haley Joel Osment) to communicate openly with his mother (Toni Collette) about his problems and transforms him into a popular boy at school. Similarly, even though he is later revealed to be dead, the connection that Malcolm (Bruce Willis) forms with Cole allows him to reconcile with his wife (Olivia Williams) and provides him with the assurance that he is still an effective child psychologist.

Shyamalan already began to establish himself as a filmmaker in the auteurist mold before he made *Signs*, which also portrays a man's struggle to come to terms with death, albeit his wife's and not his own, to understand what it means to be a good father to his children in her absence, and to regain confidence in his chosen profession. *Unbreakable*, the film that Shyamalan made right before *Signs* also clearly showcases its direct connections to *The Sixth Sense*, its immediate predecessor. *Unbreakable*'s trailer, for instance, advertises the film as another collaborative effort by the writer/director of *The Sixth Sense* and Bruce Willis. Elijah Price subsequently rhetorically asks the audience if they are "ready for the truth?," alluding to the presence of another memorable changeover.

Unbreakable's trailer could not be accused of false advertising because the film contained many of the same narrative and formal attributes as *The Sixth Sense*. It also included a changeover, the use of a particular color to signal danger (purple, in *Unbreakable*'s case), and a fascination with the supernatural. Even more importantly, *Unbreakable*'s narrative similarly centers on the existential angst of a dispossessed white, heterosexual, middle-aged, male character—David Dunn—who aims to reclaim his positions of authority in the home and on the job. Moreover, as in his previous film with Shyamalan, Willis's character must seek the help of marginalized people to reassert his agency. As with *The Sixth Sense*, it is not until David is truly willing to listen to the advice of a young boy, in this case his biological son, that he is able to discover his calling. Interestingly, David's son Joseph was played by Spencer Treat Clark, who also had a significant role in *Arlington Road* just a year earlier, suggesting that Willis was not the only actor cast for his ability to perform in the misdirection film genre. Shyamalan's familiar narrative scenario, then, appears once again in *Unbreakable*, and is actually taken a step further, in this instance, because David also needs to heed the advice of Elijah, a physically disabled African-American man, to overcome the obstacles that stand in his way.

The remarkable commercial success of *The Sixth Sense* established Shyamalan's reputation as an up-and-coming Hollywood writer/director, significantly influencing the ways that audiences received a follow-up effort that was clearly packaged in auteurist terms. *Unbreakable* opened to a lukewarm reception from both critics and audiences upon its release in 2000. The film grossed a respectable $95 million during its run in U.S. theaters on its healthy $75 million budget; yet its small profit margin was nowhere near the box-office gold generated by *The Sixth Sense* (imdb.com). Like audiences, film reviewers were divided about *Unbreakable*'s merits. Many critics agreed with Eric Harrison of the *Houston Chronicle*, who claimed that "Shyamalan made the unfortunate, but predictable choice of trying to bottle *The Sixth Sense*'s lightning and reuse it" (Houston 1). By contrast, many other critics agreed with the *New York Post*'s Lou Lumenick, who wrote that "Shyamalan's dazzling reunion with Bruce Willis confirms that he's one of the most brilliant filmmakers working today" (47). Shyamalan himself also played a considerable part in encouraging these kinds of auteurist connections because he has made explicit efforts to establish his identity as the preeminent maker of misdirection films in many of his films since *The Sixth Sense*.

Another reason why Shyamalan has become widely referred to as an auteur is because of his penchant for working with a relatively consistent stable of actors. This anachronistic notion of authorship harks back to an era in which both actors and directors were forced to work under highly restrictive multi-picture contracts with a studio. Under the post-studio-era, package-unit system, in contrast, the teaming of celebrated directors with A-list actors on multiple films is instead often a marketing strategy because, as the industrial logic goes, there is a better chance to capture audiences if familiar names from successful collaborations are reunited on subsequent projects. Disney tried to repeat the success of *The Sixth Sense* by prominently featuring the pairing of Shyamalan and Bruce Willis in all forms of advertising in the hopes that *Unbreakable* would also attract both an arthouse and mainstream crowd. The re-teaming of Willis with Samuel L. Jackson was attractive to Disney for similar reasons: the success that the two actors had previously experienced together with both *Pulp Fiction*, another misdirection film with an indie sensibility, and *Die Hard With a Vengeance* (1995), the third installment in the highly successful action film franchise, could be leveraged to target these same audiences.

Although the Shyamalan/Willis and Willis/Jackson duos made sound economic sense, it was not merely a cynical marketing tactic. Shyamalan built his now fledgling brand in part by highlighting auteurist tendencies other than just the presence of an ending that forces spectators to reinterpret a majority of narrative information. In addition to the aforementioned thematic preoccupations, Shyamalan's films usually present faith in a divine plan, feature children or adolescents who see the world more clearly than adults do, are set in the Philadelphia vicinity, and so on. Among his stylistic tendencies are long takes, shots of reflected images, and the use of a mobile camera. The casting of Willis as the protagonist of *Unbreakable* can similarly be read in auteurist terms even though strong economic motives also undoubtedly drove the decision. In particular, Willis was an ideal candidate for the lead in *Unbreakable* because his secure position as a Hollywood action hero with limited acting ability could be used to the director's advantage, as it was in *The Sixth Sense*, to keep the audience from prematurely unearthing the changeover. Similarly, Jackson was a logical choice for Willis's ostensible sidekick because his familiar role as the prototypical "black buddy" in films, like *Die Hard With a Vengeance*, also effectively concealed his character's real motives.

Willis's performances in a number of profitable Hollywood action films released during the late 1980s and 1990s, including the first three films in the *Die Hard* series (1988, 1990, 1995), *The Last Boy Scout* (1991), and *Armageddon* (1998), helped to cement his reputation as a bad actor with great box-office appeal. Willis has subsequently become typecast as a wise-cracking, everyman hero in the mold of *Die Hard*'s John McClane, who relies on his traditionally masculine attributes, such as physical prowess, cool under pressure, and mental toughness, to overcome seemingly insurmountable odds. Although his particular acting style and hyper-masculine onscreen identity have proven extremely popular with audiences, critics have remained largely unimpressed by his performances. Reviews of *The Sixth Sense*, for example, almost universally claimed that Willis had little to do with its success because child actor, Haley Joel Osment, was believed to have delivered the film's most impressive performance. Critic Rod Dreher, for example, claims that "Willis is OK in this movie, but it's not his picture anyway. This film belongs entirely to an 11-year-old kid named Haley Joel Osment" (43). Fellow reviewer Mick LaSalle speculates that Willis "has more screen time, but his role is *reactive*. Osment carries the drama" (emphasis added, C1). As these comments suggest, even though Willis was the star of a film that ended up being a critical and box-office sensation, his unfavorable reputation overshadowed the part that his acting played in its success.

Willis's perceived limited range as an actor and his inextricable connection to the *Die Hard* films, though, are key reasons why he became the quintessential misdirection film star. His familiar performance style from the *Die Hard* films is inseparable from his onscreen persona in any genre and has been almost universally reviled by film reviewers. Critic Stephen Holden, for example, pejoratively remarks that Willis wears the same smirk to suggest his sensitivity for Cole in *The Sixth Sense* as he does when "he is about to shoot someone in the face" (14). In his review of *Unbreakable*, James Berardinelli similarly complains that Willis's recognizable acting style is "too laconic" and showcases little "more than a glimmer of emotion." His performances are thus typically deprecated because they lack the kind of psychological depth that is most prized by the critical establishment. Traditional evaluations of Hollywood film performance such as these, however, neglect to account for how choices that actors like Willis make with their faces, bodies, and voices can inspire audiences to draw conclusions that extend beyond just character psychology.

In contrast to these typical assessments of Hollywood film acting, in *Acting in the Cinema*, James Naremore discusses the performer's ideolect, a term which he adapts from linguistics, as another way to evaluate "the actor's set of performing traits systematically highlighted in films." (4). As Andrew Higson also speculates, by approaching film performance in this way, the physical and vocal utterances of the performer can be conceived of "as a field of discourse" composed of "visual and aural signs" because in that context acting becomes "not the enactment of a coherent, psychologically complex character, but a montage of gestures (or 'gests')" that is "refined for the requirements of the shot" (154). Extending Higson's and Naremore's arguments, Willis's wooden acting style can be interpreted as entirely appropriate for the constraints of the misdirection film genre. His recognizable, monotone voice and limited facial expressions are effective for the misdirection film because they evoke an existing set of acting conventions with which the audience is familiar. Such choices are master "fabrications," which, in *Frame Analysis*, Erving Goffman defines as the "intentional effort of one or more individuals to manage an activity so that one or more others will be induced to have a false belief about what is going on" (83). Actors in misdirection films, then, must perform in a way that does not raise audience suspicions. Even more importantly, as Goffman theorizes, fabrications depend on audience expectations because they "require the use of a model, the use of something meaningful in terms of primary frameworks" (84). Effective fabricators keep the equivalent of a straight face by making their actions appear to be customary even though they are ultimately revealed to be anything but reliable. It is no coincidence, therefore, that Willis has been cast in a lead role in six contemporary misdirection films, more than any other Hollywood actor. His decision to perform these roles, as he would John McClane, is not out of sync with the requirements of the genre. In short, Willis was so often selected to star in these films not because of his ability to create psychologically complex characters, but because his stock techniques never signal to the audience that their interpretations of his character traits will be violated.

In *Unbreakable*, Willis's character struggle stems from his decision to become a security guard after abandoning a promising football career by faking an injury in order to marry his wife, Audrey Dunn (Robin Wright), who detests the violent sport. After miraculously surviving a train wreck, David reluctantly discovers how to reclaim his masculine prowess without jeopardizing his marriage. At the encouragement of Joseph and the enigmatic Elijah, who, thanks to faith in comic book lore believes that David was the sole survivor because he is really a superhero who is impervious to most injuries, he covertly learns to harness his superhuman strength and psychic ability to see the past crimes of the perpetrators he touches. As the generically inspired alliterative name, David Dunn, suggests, a clandestine superhero persona becomes the perfect alter-ego for a seemingly ordinary man, like Clark Kent and Peter Parker, whose spectacularly brutal talents must be kept secret from his pacifist wife.

Without knowledge of the changeover, this familiar narrative trajectory looks like just another example of how Hollywood imagines that white, heterosexual male dominance still exists even though hegemonic masculinity is less universally approved. After all, it ostensibly focuses on how the protagonist's closeted revival of his authentic male identity helps him overcome feminizing forces and restore his family. Additionally, its apparent remasculinization project seems disconcerting because of its racist implications. Heather Hicks, for example, documents that numerous critics jumped to the erroneous conclusion that *Unbreakable* contains the same dangerous racial ramifications as other contemporaneous Hollywood films, such as *The Family Man* (2000), *The Green Mile* (1999), and *The Legend of Bagger Vance* (2000), which also feature stereotypically mystical African-American friends, who, like Elijah, leverage their powers "toward helping and enlightening a white character" (28). As she contends, such critiques neglect how the changeover can alter comprehensions of narrative information. In contrast to conventionally altruistic magical African-American sidekicks, Elijah's objectives are eventually revealed to be anything but noble, if the narrative epiphany is interpreted as exposing a different motive for the antagonist's actions.

Had *Unbreakable* been exclusively about how David's superhero identity frees his suppressed male spirit, then it would have ended in standard classical fashion, as it appears to do when David rescues helpless children by killing their captor, reconciles with his wife, realizes his job protecting people is actually meaningful, and solidifies his bond with Joseph by covertly divulging his secret identity. Although all narrative lines of action are resolved satisfactorily, the end credits do not roll. The film instead cuts to an apparent epilogue in which David visits Elijah's store to thank him. Before expressing his gratitude, David meets Elijah's mother (Charlayne Woodard), who agrees with him that her son is a "miracle" for surviving accidents that should have "broken him," suggesting that Elijah is really the film's titular character. Once Elijah and David reunite and shake hands, the revelation shows that Elijah is indeed the film's primary causal agent. As is customary in many misdirection films, the changeover contains flashbacks exposing what actually happened. When the two finally touch for the first time, a bright light flashes and a loud screeching noise plays, signifying, as it has throughout, David's psychic ability to see the past illicit actions of touched subjects. Both David and the spectator simultaneously learn that Elijah is actually an archvillain, and not a benevolent helper, who has committed many terrorist acts, including David's train derailment, to find his adversary. The final scene can thus be reinterpreted as more than just an epilogue, as Elijah's desire to understand his brittle bone disease is really why he mentors David. As the successive reverse zoom-outs on both characters after they release hands show, they are most linked by Elijah's insistence on discovering a nemesis, like David, whose superhuman physical resilience renders the antagonist's opposite disorder meaningful. The narrative is only resolved classically, then, because David's belated understanding that he is a superhero confirms Elijah is an archvillain.

This revised explanation of narrative causality inspired by the revelation alters the meaning of almost all narrative information. Just as the final scene can be reinterpreted to be more than an epilogue, the film's opening scene can now be read as no longer simply being a tangential prologue. Although it is not immediately apparent that it is a flashback, a superimposed title indicates that the scene takes place in a Philadelphia-area shopping mall in 1961, decades before David and Elijah meet and perhaps not coincidentally the same year that Marvel Comics became a household name with the publication of the first issue of the *Fantastic Four* (DeFalco 84). The pre-opening credit scene depicts a flashback of the birth of baby Elijah, who is swaddled in a purple trimmed blanket (purple is linked to Elijah throughout the film) after suffering fractures during his emergency delivery in a department store dressing room. Significantly, virtually the entire scene is shot in a mirror image reflection, one of Shyamalan's formal signatures, which functions as an important visual motif in this film. In classical fashion, the technique is not just an artistic flourish because it subtly references both the paralleling of the two primary male characters and Elijah's hidden, archvillain alter-ego: "Mr. Glass." To reiterate the unstated relationship between the two, after the prologue, the film surprisingly cuts to an image of David aboard the soon-to-derail train, and not to a grown-up Elijah. The film's misdirection has already begun, in other words, as the edit leads spectators to identify with David by misleadingly positioning him, rather than Elijah, as the primary causal agent.

David's character is subsequently introduced classically because important information about his psychological traits is communicated

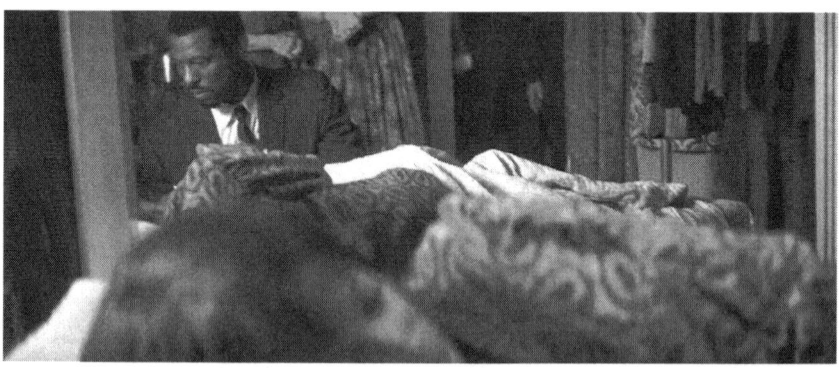

Figure 3.1. A mirror-image shot of Dr. Mathison examining baby Elijah Price after his mother's emergency department store delivery in *Unbreakable*.

rapidly. David first appears from an atypical angle that, on reverse shot, is revealed to be from a young girl's perspective. A purple-clad stranger, Kelly (Leslie Stefanson), then asks David if he is alone. David's affirmative response, which alludes to his isolation, prompts her to sit next to him. His sexual interest in Kelly is subsequently communicated nonverbally, as the camera gaze, mimicking the child's perspective, captures him removing his wedding ring. His attempted infidelity is inspired by his imminent separation from Audrey, which is later revealed to be driven by his admission that he keeps her and Joseph at an emotional distance. Rather than save the marriage, David has all but agreed to Audrey's wishes to take another security guard job in New York City and give up primary custody of his son. Although Joseph continues to admire David despite the impending separation, the film raises doubts about his parenting skills. For instance, when his injured son demands the school nurse call his father, David reports that Audrey "usually handles Joseph stuff" and asks if he has "to rub any smelly ointment" on him. David is on the verge of abandoning his family, then, because his conventional masculinity alienates him from his wife and kid. He thus begins to flirt with Kelly more aggressively in an awkward exchange always filmed from the child's point-of-view that never switches to the standard-shot/reverse-shot style of a classical conversation. In a matter of moments, David's introduction alerts viewers that the film contains non-classical and classical attributes as well as focuses on a man whose traditional masculinity is ruining his marriage and negatively influencing children.

David's impropriety is further established when he offers Kelly a copy of a women's-interest magazine left onboard. Her unexpected

Figure 3.2. David Dunn attempts to give Kelly a woman's-interest magazine in *Unbreakable*.

response exposes his gender bias because she informs him she would prefer a discarded sports-themed magazine. Kelly clarifies her preference by noting that she is a sports agent traveling to meet a football prospect, making her the kind of woman who many men believe has encroached on their cultural authority by entering once all-male bastions, like the professional sports industries. David responds to her unexpected request in sexist fashion by joking that he wants to become a synchronized swimmer. He quickly retracts the misogynistic joke about the female-dominated sport by admitting that he is afraid of water, information that turns out to be crucial because it is later revealed to be his kryptonite. As the train passes through a tunnel, ensconcing David's placid face in shadows, he lies to her by claiming he dislikes football. As if it was not already clear that David's behavior is inappropriate, Kelly's embarrassing rejection of his advances confirms it. Like McClane, who at *Die Hard*'s outset is revealed to be economically and socially inferior to his estranged wife, David's traditional masculine ways are outmoded and lead to embarrassing consequences when displayed explicitly. Such a reading of David's character was only amplified by offscreen events shortly before *Unbreakable*'s release, as Willis's then-wife, Demi Moore, shockingly filed for divorce.

If David's introduction is understood in relation to Willis's prototypical onscreen and changing offscreen personas, then it is clear why *Unbreakable* fools spectators into thinking that its classical ending will be David's discovery of a superhero identity that provides him with an acceptable way to reestablish his conventional masculinity, in secret. Such a reading is confirmed by Willis's performance because his relatively unexpressive acting style only seems to verify that he will again be playing a fallible action hero who uses his comedic wit, steady voice, and stoic facial expressions to combat and triumph over the now unfamiliar world that he inhabits. Like the viewer, though, it is David's proclivity to pigeonhole that most results in the surprise turn of events. In addition to misreading Elijah's and Kelly's true characters, David falsely accuses a man of South Asian descent, played by Shyamalan himself, of carrying drugs. As in *The Sixth Sense*, in which Shyamalan plays an archetypal Indian physician who misleads spectators by incorrectly diagnosing the situation, the director again uses his cameo not only to augment his burgeoning superstar image, but also to expose the audience's penchant for negative stereotyping. It is significant, then, that Elijah's disguise operates in relation to numerous markers of identity, extending beyond his race and the viewer's familiarity with Hollywood's interracial buddy film conventions, that are misconstrued as connoting weakness. His physical disability also helps him go undetected because it is misinterpreted

Figure 3.3. *Unbreakable* director, M. Night Shyamalan, appears in a cameo as a stadium attendee whom David Dunn searches for drugs.

as a flaw even though it is really the attribute that gives him the most strength by confirming he is David's foil. Indeed, the retroactive centrality of Elijah's disorder to his real identity counters cultural anxieties about disabled bodies being prisons for fully realized potential, as Vivian Sobchack theorizes in *Carnal Thoughts*, by transforming his supposedly debilitated body into one with "the transparent capacity for significant action and sensible meaning" (189).

The importance of Elijah's disorder to his authentic identity is reiterated by a final twist that again links the two primary characters. Elijah acknowledges that he should have long realized he is a criminal mastermind because, like David, who consistently ignores his son's insights, he should have listened more closely to children, who called him Mr. Glass, the alter-ego he now presumably adopts. Importantly, it is Elijah's belief in the veracity of comic books that fuels his quest to find his superhero opposite who confirms his true identity, which justifies his permanent retreat out of adulthood. According to the film's logic, men like David and Elijah only fulfill their true promise if they are unencumbered by emasculating demands supposedly placed on contemporary adult males. Such an understanding, of course, comes at a cost for both characters, as Elijah resorts to mass murder to find David and reignites the violent fire extinguished by the hero's wife. Although the generically motivated concluding superimposed titles indicate that Elijah is sentenced to a psychiatric facility, he ultimately triumphs. Undoubtedly, Elijah's institutionalization marks him as a deviant pariah and renders him temporarily impotent; however, such places typically do not contain archvillains for long in the superhero genre. In fact, Shyamalan has consistently expressed his desire to make a sequel, featuring an actual showdown between David and an escaped Elijah, a rumor that Willis reconfirmed in a 2010 interview (Marshall). In the end, despite Elijah's capture, the villain wins by showing David that overcoming their malaise requires them to resurrect a stifled male essence free from feminizing constraints that is veiled by impaired alter-egos.

Misreading *The Usual Suspects*: Feigning Fragility to Bolster Authority

Whereas *Unbreakable* depicts primary male characters as having to learn to deploy imperfect disguises to conceal their authentic identities, *The Usual Suspects* illustrates how masquerade is a powerful weapon for a man already certain of who he really is. *The Usual Suspects* was one of the first financially successful contemporary misdirection films, grossing over $23 million at the domestic box office on its $6 million budget (imdb.com). The film's complex narrative, which director Bryan Singer and screenwriter Christopher McQuarrie claim on their DVD commentary was partly inspired by John List's infamous 18-year disappearance after murdering his own family to shelter them from the shame of losing his job, was ultimately promoted as its primary draw; however, it initially scared off Hollywood. Singer and McQuarrie had to turn to Polygram Filmed Entertainment, a Dutch-owned company with ties to Universal Pictures, to finance and distribute the film theatrically (imdb.com). The gamble proved worthwhile because, in addition to its profitable theatrical run, Kevin Spacey won the Best Supporting Actor Oscar for his portrayal of Roger "Verbal" Kint and McQuarrie won the Best Original Screenplay Oscar. As with other contemporary misdirection films, a number of major players, including Columbia TriStar, MGM/UA, and Paramount subsequently distributed the film domestically and internationally in its various home video formats (imdb.com).

The film centers on U.S. Customs Agent David Kujan's (Chazz Palminteri) interrogation of Kint, who is about to post bail after being granted immunity by the District Attorney despite his role in the massacre associated with a purported $91 million cocaine deal at a San Pedro pier. Initially, the authorities and viewers suspect that Kint played a minor part in the crime because his riveting narration is revealed through a series of flashbacks from his perspective that accentuate his status as a crippled, small-time con artist. First, Kint's testimony to the D.A. reveals how a suspicious police lineup helped him team up with four seemingly more virile and accomplished crooks. Second, Kujan's interrogation of Kint in his friend's police station office depicts detailed flashbacks of the occurrences leading up to and during the events at the pier. In these flashbacks and the accompanying interrogation sequences, Kint presents himself as a weak lackey whose disabled body seems to inhibit his capacity to act authoritatively. Kujan and the viewer, therefore, are led to believe that Dean Keaton, the gang's most revered thug, is the film's primary causal agent. In standard heist film manner, Keaton is portrayed as the reluctant protagonist, who, despite his efforts to settle down by running a respectable business with his lawyer girlfriend, Edie Finnernan (Suzy Amis), possesses the traits to pull off the big job that will finally allow him to go legit. Classical standards are thus again deployed to trick viewers into thinking the alleged protagonist will inevitably prevail. Although Kint claims that Keaton is dead, Kujan refuses to believe it, leading audiences to presume that the con man is covering for his friend and co-conspirator. The interrogation, as a result, seems to be building to a climax in which Kujan finally gets Kint to admit that Keaton is really behind it all and escaped the law.

Kujan indeed hopes to use Kint's testimony to concoct his own furtive explanation to incriminate Keaton. As Kint effectively summarizes, Kujan's rigid theory demonstrates that "to a cop the explanation is always simple" because they just verify the suppositions they already believe. Kujan's construction of an alternative account, in other words, exemplifies how the authorities are depicted employing conspiratorial tactics to further their own agendas. To get Kint to participate in the interrogation, for instance, Kujan threatens to make up a story that, as part of his deal with the D.A., Kint ratted out Ruby Deemer, Kujan's most reliable, incarcerated informant. As Kujan also subsequently reports, during Keaton's stint with the NYPD, he was indicted seven times, including for multiple murder cases. In fact, Keaton was once involved in "New York's Finest Taxicab Service," a "ring of corrupt cops" handsomely compensated for chauffeuring smugglers. Keaton's insider-knowledge of this covert activity turns out to be valuable because he helps orchestrate a robbery of the Taxicab Service that also results in over 50 cops being busted. Ironically, the hit on the Taxicab Service only occurs because the police rely on unlawful means to rustle up the five criminals initially. As Kint claims, their "rights went right out the window" when the cops identified them as suspects. Kint's accusation that the authorities act unlawfully is verified by the police's interrogation of the five criminals when Keaton is punched in the face by a cop. Additionally, after Edie frees the five suspects, she reports that they were never officially charged.

Kujan similarly relies on underhanded tactics to pin the crime on his man. To get his information, Kujan challenges Kint to "convince" him that Keaton is dead by telling him "every last detail." In turn, Kint presents a byzantine account of events, eventually revealing that Keyser Söze, a legendary Turkish crime lord, is really the puppet master. Kint's recounting of the criminal scheme ultimately is believable, then, because it conspiratorially adheres to classical narrative conventions of causality and agency by attributing everything to the machinations of a powerful individual: Söze. Kujan, of course, is convinced that Keaton, and not the mythical Söze, is the mastermind. As a result of Kint's recollection, he concludes that Keaton is actually Söze. Consequently, when Kujan finally explains his theory to Kint about what really happened, the music on the soundtrack swells to a crescendo and the film frequently cuts to flashbacks that depict images from Kint's earlier testimony now taken out of their previous context. Kujan's acceptance of the totalizing plot of Keaton as the archcriminal seems logical, as events that ostensibly were initially unimportant to comprehending his "true" character now make Keaton look ruthless. In short, this scene appears to be the classical resolution in which the detective identifies the individual, whom he wanted to nail all along, as the real primary causal agent.

The film, though, does not actually uphold this conventional resolution by showing Keaton successfully fleeing with the money and Edie. Instead, its changeover provokes a new way to understand narrative causality. It stunningly shows that Kint is a master storyteller who *knits*—hence the anagrammed surname—the fictitious tale to escape the law and further his own legend as the mythic Söze. Upon Kint's release, Kujan and the audience simultaneously realize that the confession was fabricated because it is shockingly revealed that Kint both faked his cere-

Figure 3.4. Roger "Verbal" Kint reads the bulletin board that becomes the source for his narrative immediately before David Kujan's interrogation begins in *The Usual Suspects*.

bral palsy and used the contents of the interrogation room to create his contrived testimony. It is significant in this regard that Kint was briefly shown earlier scanning his surroundings when he first arrived in the police station office. The inclusion of such a seemingly narratively insignificant scene is crucial for two primary reasons. First, in classical fashion, it can be reinterpreted as anything but tangential because it becomes the most important scene for retrospectively reassessing the meaning of narrative information. Second, it helps to inoculate a film that is also packaged as a whodunit from complaints that it does not adhere to the tenet of "fair play," even though it is highly unlikely that viewers would be able to solve the mystery.

The changeover is depicted spectacularly, as the film cuts back and forth between Kujan's dumbfounded gaze, the objects that he observes in the office, and flashbacks of previous scenes from Kujan's explanation, which portrayed Keaton as the archcriminal, Söze, into whom Kint now transforms. Aural evidence also helps viewers make sense of what has really occurred, as earlier lines of dialogue are now associated with the objects captured by the camera's gaze. As Kujan stares at a bulletin board frame, for example, indicating its manufacture in Skokie, Illinois by the Quartet Corporation, Kint's offhanded remark that he once sang in a "barbershop quartet in Skokie, Illinois" replays. The new master thread of Kint as Söze reverses what both Kujan and spectators thought they knew about who really possessed narrative agency. Of course, once Kint's story is exposed as a fabrication, it becomes difficult to determine what, if anything, from his testimony is factual. However, although the revelation shows Kint's account is untrue, it leaves no question that he has been self-interestedly propelling narrative events all along.

Thus, it is Kint who is clearly revealed to be the film's master manipulator. Kint's brilliantly constructed narratives not only trick Kujan into confirming that Keaton is the perpetrator, they also bolster his own legend as a brazen criminal who is able to pull off seemingly impossible feats, perhaps suggesting he is even Söze himself. If he is also really Söze, then the methods he describes the crime lord deploying throughout also serve to amplify his reputation, as they are what enable him to convince the four other unsuspecting criminals to further his objectives. Specifically, Kobayashi (Pete Posthelwaite), Söze's purported attorney, gets the other felons to participate in the heist by presenting them with a mountain of surveillance evidence, revealing that Söze has the capability both to kill their loved ones and expose all of their previous wrongdoings. In fact, each of the criminals discovers that they once unknowingly stole from Söze, which is why they are being forced into his service at this time.

Kint/Söze also expertly creates a number of cover stories to conceal his agenda and prowess. First, his convincing performance as a cripple lowers everyone's suspicions that he could be an archcriminal. Second, to distract his partners in crime and the authorities from his actual mission, Söze leads everyone to believe that the large sum of money at the pier is intended for a cocaine deal. As the film ultimately shows, though, the real aim of the mission is to kill Arturro Marquez (Castulo Guerra), who recently informed the authorities that he could identify Söze. Consequently, he is able to dupe the four other criminals into massacring practically everyone on the pier and the boat, allowing him to assassinate Marquez and steal $91 million that a group of rival Hungarians had brought to purchase the informant from a gang of Argentineans.

The self-serving reasons for Kint's storytelling agenda become most apparent retrospectively in relation to his earlier retelling of Söze's rise to power. Before beginning the tale about Söze, Kint strategically authenticates it by informing Kujan that "One story the guys told me, the story I believe, was from his days in Turkey." Kint's disclaimer triggers the Söze flashback, which, in contrast to the other recollections that are clearly framed as such but not delineated stylistically, is shot in a dreamlike fashion, obscuring the image. These quintessentially classical techniques alert spectators that the scene should be differentiated from the film's other flashbacks, rendering it potentially more believable in retrospect. After Kint finishes the story, he verifies it further by noting that few believe that Söze really exists. Kujan then asks, "Do you believe in him Verbal?," indicating that the fable has made him and the specta-

Figure 3.5. The stylistically delineated flashback in *The Usual Suspects* that portrays Roger "Verbal" Kint's description of Keyser Söze's rise to power.

tor let down their interrogative guards. Kint seizes the opportunity to persuade him even further by exclaiming, "Keaton always said I don't believe in God, but I'm afraid of him. Well, I believe in God and the only thing that scares me is Keyser Söze." The kind of believable details that Kint provides, therefore, encourages viewers to rely on the fable to reconstruct the narrative according to the revised logic of Söze as the primary causal agent.

Kint's tale depicts Söze as a callous villain, who is especially fearsome because he commits horrific acts unfathomable to most other criminals. Specifically, during a raid on his home in which his wife is raped in front of his children, he mercilessly kills all but one member of a rival Hungarian gang as well as his own wife and kids. Söze's decisions to kill his family and spare one adversary are partly motivated by the hope that word about his exploits will spread. Accordingly, the spectator's revised understanding of Kint's true identity is inextricably linked to this legend. In a film virtually devoid of female characters and loaded with homoeroticism, doubts have been raised by Kint's feminized cover. In contrast to *Unbreakable*, by revealing that Kint's disorder was faked, *The Usual Suspects* does not depict disability as ultimately validating and enhancing masculine potential. Questions about Kint's real persona thus do not just evaporate along with his bogus cerebral palsy. To wit, after Kint is picked up outside the police station by his foreign and dandified associate, the man known as Kobayashi in his testimony, Kint smokes a cigarette effeminately. The film, then, does expose a few facts about Kint's authentic identity after revealing his lies, which could lead to a further interrogation of his manhood. The Söze legend, though, retrospectively secures his status as a former heterosexual family man who confects a pathetic façade to cover his ferocious male essence.

As Kint claims, it is Söze's ability to commit familicide that most defines his prowess and launches him to the top of the criminal underworld. Familicide, as Elizabeth Barnes argues, uses murder as "an expression of love as well as hatred" to enable "a man to (re)gain a sense of self-reliance (by eliminating his family) without abdicating his position as a devoted family man" (54). The horrific violence of familicide disturbingly allows offenders to free themselves from the perceived shackles of domestic obligations at the same time that it sustains their belief that they are fulfilling their familial duties by protecting their vulnerable kin from worse fates. This is exactly what happens for Söze, according to Kint, because his savagery saves his family from the consequences of his wife's rape and permits him to focus myopically on his criminal empire. Such tendencies, for Barnes, make familicide a distinctly male and characteristically American transgression. As her analysis of the prevalence of the crime and its literary representations in the immediate post-revolutionary United States demonstrates, during "a particular crisis in the history of U.S. masculinity, familicide perpetrators sought to exemplify manhood by asserting absolute sovereignty over their wives and children" (47). At a moment when American men were bent on distinguishing themselves from the British, the epidemic of patriarchs killing their own families to protect them from the embarrassment of having failed in a radically new economic context is especially telling. Söze's deeds are anything but foreign, then, as the actions of notorious American murderers, like List, reveal that familicide remains an ideal escape for men crushed by the pressure to provide for the families they so desperately want to protect.

The twisted fantasy of conflicted masculinity inherent in familicide relates to how manhood is represented in *Unbreakable* and *The Usual Suspects*. Both films demonstrate that men need to flee their emasculating predicaments by relying on elaborate disguises to hide a violent male core that enables them to assert control over their families. This veneer is necessary, the films imply, at a time when explicit displays of traditional masculinity are received with growing incredulity. In the end, these two films are troubling fantasies of male masquerade in which men secretly maintain their patriarchal supremacy by flaunting their purported fragilities. Although their duplicitous narrative structures are well-suited to reveal that gender is socially constructed, these films instead portray masculine performance as a way to conceal the "truth." They effectively counter pervasive paranoia about the loss of a male essence by showing how select men are capable of strategically protecting their power as well as reestablishing their authority in the family and beyond. In conspiratorial and classical fashion, the two films present narratives that privilege causality and agency to make order out of chaos. These films appeal to many spectators, therefore, by transforming everyday uncertainty into familiar causal narratives that support dominant ideologies, particularly the staunch belief that hegemonic masculinity endures and reigns supreme. Such a thematic preoccupation begins to suggest why they are attractive to viewers increasingly concerned about rediscovering who they "actually" are as well as reclaiming their "real" place in the home and in broader U.S. culture.

4

Start Making Sense

Narrative Complexity, DVD, and Online Fandom

Many young men have experienced hardships in recent years as they have struggled to overcome their perceived emasculation and maintain their dominance in the United States. A number of contemporary Hollywood misdirection films address these concerns by teaching young, white, heterosexual, American men how to adapt to a culture that has become increasingly intolerant of traditional ways that they have been encouraged to perform their gender. Rather than suggest that minority groups should be granted equality, however, the narrative solutions offered by these films typically give its target audience blueprints for maintaining authority in economic, political, and social spheres. Yet, because many misdirection films are difficult to interpret decisively, only those viewers who scrutinize the films most carefully are able to gain the privileged information that they believe their almost always male creators have hidden beneath the surface. In the end, although many misdirection films appear to revel in uncertainty, the work of devoted fans suggests that they can be made coherent by a high degree of interpretive labor, at least according to those who claim to have cracked the code definitively.

The presence of a way to make sense of seemingly ambiguous information renders most misdirection films hyper-classical because they can be reinterpreted according to a new narrative logic that is linked to the actions of a clearly defined causal agent who is almost inevitably male. The existence of this alternative explanation provides consolation to spectators who have grown accustomed to the narrative structure and relatively conservative ideological messages contained in an overwhelming majority of Hollywood films. Fans of these films thus often derive pleasure from a discovery of what they believe to be the filmmaker's "true" intentions.

The practice of turning films, which at first both seem to contain an unconventional narrative logic and depict a culture that has become increasingly unfamiliar, into ones that can be understood traditionally and coincide more closely with dominant ideologies, is one of the distinct joys that many viewers derive from watching misdirection films. Crucially, the spectator's ability to enjoy misdirection films in this manner has been greatly enhanced by the advent of new home-video and media communication technologies. In *Beyond the Multiplex*, her study of the impact that such developments have had on the production and reception of Hollywood films, Barbara Klinger contends that "familiarity" is one of the primary reasons why spectators revisit their favorite movies because it is "at once a central arena of satisfaction and the root of other functions and pleasures" of repeat viewing (152). Consequently, as Klinger argues, some recent Hollywood films seem to be designed specifically for consumption in the aftermarket since the familiarity offered by repetition "enables viewers to experience both comfort and mastery" not possible in one-time theatrical screenings (154). Many misdirection films, of course, are uniquely positioned to appeal to repeat viewers. It is only on subsequent viewings that spectators, who are initially dissatisfied with both their seemingly unconventional narratives and often confusing ideological messages, can potentially reread misdirection films coherently. In fact, once viewers have reinterpreted their narratives retrospectively, they are freer to focus on a number of different endeavors, such as gaining an even better understanding of narrative meaning, searching for evidence that was initially missed, ensuring that the trick was pulled fairly, more thoroughly comprehending the film's messages, and so on. Put simply, films that demand these kinds of viewing practices are tailor-made for audiences who use new media and communication technologies to gain a deeper appreciation of their complexities.

The misdirection film, then, encourages interpretation and viewing practices that differ from those typically enacted by the classical spectator. The ways that these films are usually comprehended challenge David Bordwell's conception of the classical film as a hermetically sealed entity that adheres to a recognizable narrative template and corresponding formal practices that make it easily understandable in one viewing. According to Bordwell, the classical narrative functions to retard the occurrence of the predictable conclusion because spectators derive pleasure from the way in which the protagonist overcomes a series of unknown variables, in the form of obstacles that stand in the way of his or her clear-cut objectives. Under this model, it is difficult to understand why spectators engage in multiple viewings of Hollywood films because once the narrative is consumed, it no longer effectively heightens the viewer's anticipation. Yet, misdirection films often cannot be interpreted classically in a single viewing and spectators generally do not enjoy them fully until they watch them repeatedly in post-theatrical settings.

I grant that it was difficult for Bordwell to contend with this development because in the years leading up to *Narration in the Fiction Film*'s publication in 1985, earnings from the box office still outpaced those garnered from home-video. In fact, although viewers typically would venture to the cinema to see their favorite Hollywood films on multiple occasions and would await their re-release in theaters or on television, repeat viewing was a less common cultural practice at the time and, especially, in the decades before then. However, now that Hollywood's profits from home-video far exceed the box-office take, it is no longer tenable to equate Hollywood film primarily with the theatrical experience. Instead, as Derek Kompare theorizes, under these radically new conditions of commercial film exhibition, it is misguided to think of playback devices, such as the VCR and the DVD player, as "mere enhancements of media" because these new technologies, which are "designed on the premise of mediated repetition," are "*reconceptions*, profoundly altering our relationship with dominant media institutions, and with media culture in general" (*Rerun* 199). For instance, the ability to own and replay Hollywood films as well as to manipulate the narrative trajectory and the image were virtually inconceivable prior to the home-video age. These changes, though, have not only had a significant impact on the ways that spectators interact with commercially produced films, as Hollywood has also had to adapt its production strategies to respond in kind.

In this chapter, I examine how the highly complex and seemingly ambiguous narratives of two contemporary misdirection films—*Mulholland Dr.* and *Memento*—epitomize strategies that Hollywood has devised in response to these changing industrial and technological contexts. These two films are especially germane because their convoluted narratives and seemingly eternal ambiguities make them among the most byzantine Hollywood films ever released. This complexity has inspired an inordinate amount of interpretive work devoted to figuring out their "true" meanings in online communities. Such developments raise a series of questions about how the industry has encouraged spectators to engage with new media technologies that have significantly altered the manner in which Hollywood films are now commonly viewed, interpreted, and discussed. How do these two films demonstrate the ways in which the industry packages products for a niche audience that enjoys games of discovery and decipherment made possible by technologies, like the DVD player and the Internet? What tactics have producers recently deployed to entice a particular group of spectators to interact with films that require a comparatively high degree of interpretive labor? Who makes up this audience and why is it so attractive to Hollywood? What do these spectators hope to gain by watching misdirection films repeatedly on DVD and discussing them fervently online? What might discursive evidence on websites associated with these films tell us about how fans respond to the industry's practices?

Hollywood in the Digital Era: Media Convergence and New Narrative Strategies

The recent proliferation of misdirection films exemplifies Hollywood's new economic logic amid changing industrial contexts because these films have been greenlit by media conglomerates even though their complex and often ambiguous narratives typically disappoint at the box office. Obviously, there have been enormously high-grossing misdirection films, like *Inception* (2010) and *The Sixth Sense* (1999), that are exceptions, as they both netted well over $200 million during their runs in domestic theaters; however, there are only a handful of other contemporary Hollywood misdirection films, such as *A Beautiful Mind* (1999), *Planet of the Apes* (2001), *Shutter Island* (2010), *The Village* (2004), and *Vanilla Sky* (2001), that have garnered as much as $100 million at the domestic box office. Yet, each of the misdirection films in the $100 million to $200 million club also had a substantial production budget that ranged from $60 million to $100 million, suggesting that their high revenues stemmed from expensive overhead costs that cut into profit margins (imdb.com). Although most contemporary Hollywood misdirection films have made at best only a modest splash at the box office, the theatrical performances of some smaller budgeted films, such as *The Usual Suspects* (1995) and *Memento*, are also of note because they greatly exceeded economic expectations. Importantly, the success of these films was attributable primarily to strong word of mouth and positive reviews because media conglomerates were initially hesitant to back them out of fear that their complex narratives would alienate audiences. *Memento*, for instance, earned $25 million at the domestic box office on a shoestring $5 million budget even though it was produced and distributed in the United States by Newmarket Films, an independent company that does not have the marketing resources to compete with the majors and their often astronomical advertising budgets (imdb.com).

In spite of their limited success at the box office, misdirection films typically perform well on DVD, which explains why Sony jumped at the chance to serve as *Memento*'s distributor when it was released on home-video. Hence a reason why I classify misdirection films, such as *Memento* and *Mulholland Dr.*, as Hollywood films even though they were produced independent of the U.S. commercial film industry. Although the ongoing nature of home-video sales as well as the studios' desire to conceal ancillary profits from parties seeking royalties and residuals make it difficult to locate exact figures on *Memento*'s DVD revenues, its standing as of August 2015 as the 44th greatest film of all-time on the *Internet Movie Database*'s Top 250 list suggests why Sony seized the opportunity to distribute the film on home-video. Its belated fan following is not out of the ordinary because a number of misdirection films that made little splash at the domestic box office are now consistently ranked among the greatest films ever made on lists created for popular cinema-related websites and entertainment-themed magazines. Drastic reassessments such as these indicate that many misdirection films do not find an audience, and do not become real moneymakers, until after they are released in post-theatrical markets.

Although earnings at the domestic box office continue to be the primary obsession of the U.S. entertainment-related news media, many scholars have demonstrated that theatrical receipts have long constituted only a fraction of a film's overall revenue. As Douglas Gomery asserts, in "little more than a decade after the 1976 introduction of the Betamax and the VHS alternative, rentals and sales of movies on tape surpassed the theatrical box-office take in the United States" (276). Even though the DVD player and the VCR were a boon for Hollywood, the industry actually struggled for years to reach a nontheatrical audience. As Peter Kramer summarizes, Hollywood has always striven to extend the life of its products beyond the silver screen: the "strong parallels between the integration of movies and domestic media technologies" that exist today were present at "the very beginnings of moving pictures in the late-nineteenth century" (13). In spite of these aspirations, industry executives have always been ambivalent about the development of moving-image exhibition technologies that supposedly threaten Hollywood's theatrical market. Fears relating to the loss of market share and the cannibalization of theatrical revenues have been present in the discourses surrounding every new platform for the nontheatrical exhibition of commercially produced films, including network television, cable television, satellite television, the Internet and, most significantly, home-video. The prevalence of such industry-induced hysteria is dubious, however, because it obscures the symbiotic relationships that have developed between the film industry and purportedly rival media industries since the start of broadcasting.

The well-publicized success of the DVD player, in particular, reveals that Hollywood is not primarily in the business of producing feature-length films for a theatrical audience. As Janet Wasko claims, DVD players became affordable to the middle class in the late 1990s, and by 2002 "the technology represented the fastest selling consumer electronic product ever" at that time, "having reached sales of 30 million units within five years" (133). Unlike VHS tapes, though, which initially flourished as a rental product and subsequently only experienced limited success in sell-through markets because Hollywood priced titles too high for most consumers to purchase thanks to concerns such as piracy, DVDs were immediately packaged for direct sale to consumers. The cheap cost to produce DVDs in large quantities, the difficulty to reproduce them illegally on DVD when the technology first appeared, their smaller packaging, and so on, instantly made them much more attractive to a sell-through than a rental market.

The advantages that DVDs provided to both consumers and producers all but eradicated the VCR and quickly made the DVD player the dominant home-video technology in the United States. Profits from DVDs rose steadily in the years after the technology first became widely available to the public in 1997. However, revenues from DVDs began their steady decline in 2007, slipping for the first time by "dropping three percent from 2006," yet still garnering a staggering "$23.4 billion" in "total sales and rentals," which "dwarfs Hollywood's $9.6 billion box-office total" for the same year (Snider, Life 1). Total sales of DVDs may have dipped slightly then, but the contemporaneous success of online DVD rental outlets, like Netflix.com, helped to stabilize the state of the DVD rental market, albeit precariously. The arrival of a number of new home viewing technologies such as Blu-ray (high definition DVD), video on-demand, DVR, and, particularly, streaming content online have now largely replaced the DVD, suggesting a major reason why the misdirection film genre went into a state of decline in the 2010s. Yet, the presence of all of these new technologies that purportedly threaten the theatrical feature-length film have only made the nontheatrical audience more important to Hollywood's bottomline.

Regardless of the continued importance of the domestic box-office for quickly paying off high interest loans and to a film's success in the aftermarket, the industry has adopted strategies to package the encounter with its films in each of its forms as distinct; the high sales revenue generated from DVDs in the late 1990s and early 2000s demonstrated that Hollywood also had success positioning post-theatrical interactions with its products as special. The marketing of home-video as a distinct form of entertainment is possible, as Gregory Waller hypothesizes, because "there is no 'film' apart from exhibition; we seek out, pay for, take pleasure or displeasure in the *experience* of a film—even if the film is shown in a 'home theater' rather than a public venue" (emphasis in original, 3). The industry has wisely understood that post-theatrical viewings, like the theatrical experience, are a unique recreational activity with a particular set of associated pleasures. Such tactics have become vital because Hollywood is working harder than ever to milk additional profits out of existing products to recover its investments. Klinger refers to this practice as "repurposing," which she defines as "the media industry's attempt to gain as much revenue as possible from a given property" by reselling it in ancillary markets (7).

The transfer of a litany of new, old, and otherwise unreleased Hollywood films to DVD was a temporary goldmine for an industry hoping to repurpose its products for nontheatrical audiences. Although clandestine accounting procedures made it difficult to obtain the precise amount that the media conglomerates pocketed from either the sale of a single ticket or post-theatrical products at the height of the DVD's popularity, Wasko reports that in 2002 a "studio head" claimed that they made an average of "$15 in profit on the sale of one DVD" (133). There was clearly great incentive for media conglomerates to encourage audiences to purchase films directly on DVD at the time because the money earned from those transactions greatly exceeded the take from individual theatrical admissions. Under these circumstances, only a niche audience had to be willing to buy a film on DVD to turn a profit from those that failed at the box office.

Games of Discovery and Decipherment: Interpretive Practices in the Digital Age

DVD helped the film industry to expand a customer base that derives pleasure from viewing and, even more importantly, re-viewing Hollywood films in the home. Prior to the VCR's widespread adoption in the 1980s, film collecting was the province of a select few, who had both the economic resources and technological expertise necessary to acquire, maintain, and operate a library of Hollywood films on celluloid. In recent years, however, the film-collecting customer base created by the VCR was greatly expanded by the immediate status of the DVD as a sell-through product with the technological capacity to replicate many of the pleasures of the theatrical experience. Although the large and diverse market for DVDs has democratized personal ownership of Hollywood films, the industry initially targeted audiences historically proven to be the most profitable with products customized to their tastes when the technology was first available. Klinger demonstrates, for instance, that when the DVD was released in the late 1990s, demographic research revealed that middle- and upper-class white men were the earliest adopters of the new technology. Unsurprisingly, Hollywood genres typically coded as masculine were consistently among the best-selling DVDs at the time. These sales trends influenced Hollywood's production strategies for years, as "younger, well-to-do white men" were the "most important purchasers of DVD players," meaning this group had "great sway over which films are approved for production" during the period (Klinger 64).

The success of the DVD sell-through market encouraged producers to create films that target niche audiences like never before. Prior to the home-video age, Hollywood primarily made movies that appealed to broad audiences partly because the theater was practically the only venue for the consumption of its products. Hollywood's best interests are still served by making family friendly and politically safe films; however, the emergence of the sell-through, post-theatrical market decreased the financial risks associated with producing films that have greater potential of alienating certain audiences. The economic importance of this market, especially at the height of the DVD-era, led critics like Aaron Barlow to speculate that "the change in income sources is having a tremendous impact on how films are made" even though "few filmmakers are willing to admit it" (9). DVD technology enabled producers to repurpose their theatrical products in obvious and cost-effective ways by adding attractive extras, such as director commentaries, multilanguage soundtracks, deleted scenes, and behind the scenes featurettes that differentiate it from the theatrical version with minimal additional necessary investment.

The misdirection film is also well-positioned to appeal to viewers who routinely use DVD players and the Internet to maximize their enjoyment by engaging in practices, such as aesthetic appreciation and close narrative decipherment. Like Klinger, Henry Jenkins argues that films, including those that comprise *The Matrix* trilogy (1999, 2003, 2003), are now attractive to Hollywood producers because their transmedia narratives are "encyclopedic, containing a rich array of information that can be drilled, practiced, and mastered by devoted consumers" (*Convergence* 97). Although *The Matrix* films do not necessarily contain a moment that inspires viewers to reinterpret narrative information retrospectively, some audiences have been drawn to them partly because they offer pleasures that are similar to misdirection films. In fact, many of the hidden clues buried within the *The Matrix* trilogy are neither possible to unearth nor understand without the use of new media and communication technologies. As Jenkins writes, although some of the trilogy's secrets, "pop off the screen on first viewing," others "become clear only after you talk about the film with friends," and "still others . . . may require you to move through the film frame by frame on your DVD player" (*Convergence* 99). For fans willing to play the game, *The Matrix* films contain an " 'encyclopedic capacity,' " a term Jenkins borrows from Janet Murray, to describe the "new narrative forms" enabled by technologies that allow audiences to "seek information beyond the limits of the individual story" (*Convergence* 115–16).

For some scholars, the participatory activity inspired by many recent Hollywood films, like misdirection films, is evidence that spectators have become liberated from the authority of producers. Graeme Harper, for instance, notes that the arrival of the videotape meant that "a film need not be viewed at one time," and that it was thus "no longer even a teleological, or goal-directed art-form" (93–94). Similarly, Barlow contends that the popularity of "hang-out movies," watched repeatedly by groups in the home, goes "hand-in-hand with the viewing habits developed in the decades after the advent of the VCR, with the most important being that complete control the viewer assumes over the movie" (18).

In contrast, Jenkins counters that these freedoms have not necessarily liberated audiences from the authority of producers. Jenkins claims, for instance, that Lana and Lilly Wachowski, the directors of *The Matrix* films, "have positioned themselves as oracles" who possess, but are intentionally hesitant to reveal, the answers to the many enigmas contained in the trilogy (*Convergence* 99). *The Matrix* films demonstrate, for Jenkins, how filmmakers have created transmedia products with such detail that spectators, particularly younger viewers with substantial discretionary time and income, who are granted little expert authority in other realms, are encouraged to "become informational hunters and gatherers, taking pleasure in tracking down character backgrounds and plot points and making connections between different texts within the same franchise" (*Convergence* 129). The fictional world of *The Matrix* is so vast, complex, and riddled with mystery that one person alone cannot possibly tackle it. Yet, a core group of devoted fans eager to pool their resources has a much greater chance of being able to solve the Wachowskis' dense puzzle. In sum, *The Matrix* films are tailor-made for the digital age because they capitalize on "collective intelligence," a term that Jenkins adopts from Pierre Levy to describe "the ability of virtual communities to leverage the knowledge and expertise of their members, often through large-scale collaboration and deliberation" (*Convergence* 281).

Klinger similarly contends that spectators are still expected to follow the filmmakers' orders, even in nontheatrical contexts, if they hope to receive maximum pleasure from films that require repeated viewings and encourage virtual communities to examine their complexities. The spectator who unearths the secrets of these films, she argues, seems to become their omnipotent makers, "something of an authority—an intrepid explorer who has discovered a terra incognita and mapped every path" (Klinger 161). Like fans of *The Matrix* trilogy, however, these viewers do not necessarily reclaim power from producers. As Klinger posits, these films require viewer mastery that, in the discourses surrounding home-video technologies, "has often been inscribed within traditional associations of men and machines, white masculinity and technology" (250). Fans of misdirection films decode their secrets partly because they believe that their skilled detective work gives them privileged knowledge of the authorial intentions of their almost always male filmmakers. Rather than try to encourage a multiplicity of readings, misdirection films often demonstrate that producers hope to control and profit from the consumption of films nontheatrically by directing how they are interpreted in that context. Consequently, it is not surprising that misdirection films have been most appealing to an audience largely comprised of men, who both fashion themselves as discerning consumers of Hollywood films and use new technologies to gain a better understanding of their favorite titles. The online reception of misdirection films ultimately reveals that they have successfully attracted a modest, yet lucrative, target market that derives pleasure from obtaining insider knowledge. Specifically, the discovery of the films' "true" meanings and the transformation of seemingly unfavorable messages into ones that often support dominant ideologies provide these fans with a sense of superiority from films that, as box-office results suggest, some other viewers may find unappealing.

Finding the Way on *Mulholland Dr.*: Willing Narrative Coherence and Closure

Although there is a strong correlation between the advent of new technologies and changing narrative strategies in Hollywood, these kinds of complex narratives are not solely a product of the digital age. There is perhaps no better example of this type of narrative experimentation in mainstream U.S. moving-image media prior to both the widespread adoption of the Internet and the advent of the DVD player than *Twin Peaks* (1990–1991), a television show co-created by Mark Frost and renowned Hollywood filmmaker, David Lynch. First broadcast by ABC in 1990, the show survived for only two seasons despite critical acclaim and a devoted fan following. *Twin Peaks* contained a remarkably complex narrative for network television, requiring multiple viewings and the shared expertise of a collective intelligence to try to decipher the show's core mystery of "Who Killed Laura Palmer?". As Jenkins observes in an essay about the discussions that the series generated on UseNet, a text-based computer networking platform that preceded the development of the contemporary World Wide Web, "Lynch's cryptic and idiosyncratic series seemed to invite the close scrutiny and intense speculation enabled by fans' access" to the VCR and the Internet ("Do" 54).

Twin Peaks indeed aired at a time in which both the VCR was the only playback device available to spectators who wanted to re-watch television programs repeatedly on their own schedules and in which the Internet was only in a rudimentary developmental stage. "It has been commonplace to remark upon the meteoric rise of the Web," Jeremy Butler writes, "but in 1991 it was essentially a text medium that seemed no more remarkable than other information distribution systems" (41). As he explains, the Internet did not really take off in the United States until the mid-1990s because before that time no browser was available that "could effectively handle images and position them on the screen" (42). It was not until the release of Netscape's Navigator in late 1994 and the subsequent development and dominance of Microsoft's Internet Explorer that the web became the medium that transformed the Internet into the enormously popular communication technology that it has since become. Although it is possible to speculate how the original *Twin Peaks* would fare with contemporary audiences, it is safe to assume that it failed, at least in part, because the technologies necessary to decode its narrative ambiguities were both relatively unsophisticated and available to only a select population.

The many viewers who did not or were unable to decipher the show's secrets thus likely echoed the primary complaints of critics, who, as Jenkins documents, grew impatient with *Twin Peaks* for dragging out the central enigma for too long. Even though a majority of middle- and upper-class Americans owned at least one VCR with time-shifting capabilities in the early 1990s, comparatively few U.S. households were connected to the Internet at the time. Fans attempting to crack the code, therefore, not only had to remember to record the show from week-to-week, but also did not have the ability to navigate or manipulate the show with the kind of precision that has been enabled by DVD technology. Additionally, although access to the Internet and the production of web content have been democratized greatly in recent years by the development of Web 2.0 as well as the sheer ubiquity and lower cost of personal computers with networking capability, it was initially available only to those technologically savvy few who possessed the substantial economic resources necessary to gain access. More specifically, the "digital divide," a term that entered the popular lexicon in the mid-1990s to describe the gap between those who had access to the Internet and those who did not, was tangibly raced, gendered, classed, and aged throughout the 1990s because young, white, middle- and upper-class men were most likely to possess the financial wealth and technological knowledge required to participate in the new communication technology. The show's deliberately convoluted narrative alienated many viewers and allowed only a select demographic to make the discoveries necessary to enjoy *Twin Peaks* in the manner that its creators seem to have intended.

These obstacles did not deter a core group, comprised of mostly men, from attempting to solve the dizzying puzzle at the center of the show. As Jenkins discusses, it is surprising that the show attracted a male audience because it was packaged as a nighttime soap opera. He also theorizes, however, that the show's unexpected success with men was attributable to the ways it encouraged interpretive practices that are typically gendered male. In comparison to groups of female fans of other cult television shows that Jenkins analyzes in *Textual Poachers*, who primarily "focus their interest on the elaboration of paradigmatic relationships, reading plot actions as shedding light on character psychology and motivations, the largely male fans in the *Twin Peaks* computer group focus on moments of character interaction as clues for resolving syntagmatic questions" (109). In particular, the male participants on the show's UseNet site rationalized their intense scrutiny of aspects of the show often considered the terrain of female fans, such as charting and imagining the details of romantic relationships, because the information was deemed essential for solving the puzzle. The show's dual generic status as both a soap opera and a mystery, as Jenkins claims, ultimately "provided the alt.tv.twinpeaks participants a space to examine the confusions of human interactions by translating them into technical problems requiring decoding" ("Do" 60).

The site's most active posters typically also relied extensively on their knowledge of Lynch's authorial tendencies both to support their devotion to the show and to validate their interpretations of its ambiguities. Although Frost shared the credit as creator, most fans attributed the show's complex narrative machinations solely to Lynch. The discourses of authorship effectively positioned Lynch as the show's primary creative force because of the authorial reputation that he already established, thanks to the critical success of films, such as *Eraserhead* (1977), *The Elephant Man* (1980), and *Blue Velvet* (1986). As Jenkins notes, fans on the Internet leveraged Lynch's auteur status to position him as a "master programmer" and "trickster author" who had engineered a sophisticated game of cat-and-mouse with loyal viewers ("Do" 61). Comments consistently made by the site's participants indeed revealed that one of the show's main sources of pleasure came from matching wits with the director. In particular, to display both their cultural capital and satisfaction with the show, a number of contributors routinely identified its many allusions to recognizable texts and Lynch's other works as well as offered their solutions to the complex narrative puzzle that they credited exclusively to him.

Although these core fans were not enough to sustain the show beyond a couple of seasons, in 1999, perhaps encouraged by substantial improvements in both Internet and home-video technologies, Lynch attempted to make another, similar foray into network television. He filmed a pilot for ABC for a show that was to be called *Mulholland Dr.*, which, like *Twin Peaks*, was supposed to be propelled from week-to-week by an ongoing central mystery that remained perpetually unsolved. As Lynch explained to film critic, David Sterritt, the show never aired because network executives were reportedly unhappy with early versions of the pilot (15). Moreover, as they eventually did with *Twin Peaks*, which, in a March 1997 interview with *Rolling Stone* Lynch claimed had failed because he was forced to present revelatory information prematurely, network executives balked at the idea that the show would be driven by a never-ending mystery (Gilmore 41). As a result, the director subsequently accepted international funding to turn the pilot into a feature-length film that was picked up by Universal for theatrical distribution. Even though *Mulholland Dr.* eventually was developed for release in U.S. theaters, then, it was intended to be watched in nontheatrical venues from its inception. Lynch finally executed such a distribution strategy with his follow-up to *Mulholland Dr.*, *Inland Empire* (2006), which contains many of the same narrative, formal, and thematic elements as its predecessor and was strategically shot using digital video so that it would be easy to disseminate widely on DVD after its extremely limited theatrical release.

In comparison to the success that it has experienced on DVD, the relatively poor performance of *Mulholland Dr.* during its run in theaters indicates that Lynch was correct to suspect that the film would fare better with a nontheatrical audience. However, its box-office disappointment is surprising because the discourses surrounding its domestic theatrical release were largely positive, suggesting that the film had a good chance to be commercially successful with some audiences. At the Cannes film festival in the summer of 2001, the film earned Lynch a share of the award for Best Director (the Coen brothers also won for *The Man Who Wasn't There*). Additionally, *Mulholland Dr.* was lauded by a number of America's most influential film critics in spite of its confusing narrative. Andrew Sarris, for instance, asserted that it is "one of the very few movies in which the pieces not only add up to much more than the whole, but supersede it with a series of (for the most part) fascinating fragments" (23). Similarly, Roger Ebert claimed to be "willing to forgive [Lynch] for *Wild at Heart* [1990] and even *Lost Highway* [1997]" because at last his "experiment doesn't shatter the test tubes . . . the less it makes sense, the more we can't stop watching it" (35). In particular, Ebert declared that *Mulholland Dr.* worked even though it contained virtually the same seemingly incoherent narrative structure as *Lost Highway*, which he bashed because he thought that he had been "jerked around" by a director who "knows how to put effective images on the screen, and how to use a soundtrack to create mood," but who does not seem to have "an idea, purpose, an overview, beyond the arbitrary manipulation of plot elements" (35).

Lynch's own comments prior to the film's theatrical release also advertised *Mulholland Dr.* as being more accessible than many of his other films. In fact, the director, who is notoriously unwilling to discuss the meaning of his films and maintains that some do not even contain coherent narratives, uncharacteristically claimed that there is a "correct" way to make sense of *Mulholland Dr.*'s narrative. In a 1997 interview for *Rolling Stone* that coincided with the release of *Lost Highway*, for example, Lynch complained that "every single element in a movie now has to be understood—and understood at the lowest common denominator," which, for him, is "a real shame, because there are so many places that people could go if they weren't corralled so tightly with those kinds of restraints" (qtd. in Gilmore 39). In contrast, after discussing *Mulholland Dr.* with Lynch at Cannes, Sterritt reported that the director informed him that the film "does tell a coherent and comprehensible story" and "though you may need multiple viewings to fit the pieces together, they'll form an elegant pattern if you ponder their perplexities long enough" (15). The positive reviews from critics and Lynch's own promotional efforts, however, were not enough to encourage Universal to release *Mulholland Dr.* widely in U.S. theaters. During its opening weekend in 2001, the film appeared on only 66 screens and, though that number grew to 247 screens the following weekend, it was never granted the kind of saturation booking that is typical of most Hollywood fare, contributing to its poor performance at the domestic box office. In the end, *Mulholland Dr.* recuperated less than half of its production costs during its short run in select U.S. theaters, bringing in approximately $7 million on a $15 million budget (imdb.com).

However, *Mulholland Dr.* has subsequently been elevated into the canon of contemporary Hollywood films even though it lost money at the box office. Critical praise and Lynch's Academy Award nomination for Best Director helped to fuel its delayed appreciation. Yet, its changing reputation has been bolstered most by how it was packaged for sale on DVD. The DVD version of *Mulholland Dr.* was designed with a number of features that encouraged viewers to watch it in a specific manner in post-theatrical settings. As with *The Straight Story* (1999), the original DVD of *Mulholland Dr.* contains no chapter stops, practically compelling spectators to watch it in a teleological fashion. The ploy forces repeat viewers to expend great energy to navigate the disc to unearth the meaning of its mysteries. Paradoxically, that version of the DVD also included an insert entitled "David Lynch's 10 Clues to Unlocking this Thriller," which read:

> 1) Pay particular attention in the beginning of the film; at least two clues are revealed before the credits. 2) Notice the appearances of the red lampshade. 3) Can you hear the title of the film that Adam Kesher is auditioning actresses for? Is it mentioned again? 4) An accident is a terrible event . . . notice the location of the accident. 5) Who gives a key, and why? 6) Notice the robe, the ashtray, the coffee cup. 7) What is felt, realized, and gathered at the club *Silencio*? 8) Did talent alone help Camilla? 9) Note the occurrences surrounding the man behind *Winkies*. 10) Where is Aunt Ruth?

Although no answers were offered to correspond to these hints, their presence strongly suggests that there is, in fact, a "correct" way to interpret the narrative coherently. It also signaled, however, that only those willing to engage in the interpretive work necessary to solve the puzzle would be rewarded with the privileged information that Lynch buried for their discovery.

The presence of an enigma to be solved eventually helped *Mulholland Dr.*, like *Twin Peaks* before it, appeal unexpectedly to Hollywood's most desired target market, even though the film's storyline and thematic preoccupations are not well-positioned for success with young, male spectators. The film centers on Diane Selwyn (Naomi Watts), an aspiring female actress, who both struggles to succeed in the male-dominated world of Hollywood and copes with being rejected by her dream girl, Camilla Rhodes (Laura Elena Harring). A film that exposes the misogynistic tendencies of the American film industry and focuses on a lesbian character who longs for an unrequited romantic partnership is not the kind of topical focus that generally resonates with men. Of course, although one of the film's taglines—"a love story in the city of dreams"—wryly encapsulates its narrative thrust, its primary causal lines of action are anything but readily apparent on first viewing. Instead, as is suggested by its alternative tagline—"A woman in search of stardom. A woman in search of herself—in the city of dreams. A key to a mystery—lies somewhere on Mulholland Drive"—the film's narrative can only potentially be made coherent retrospectively with significant interpretive labor, initially rendering it non-classical.

Mulholland Dr. is difficult to interpret in classical fashion because it appears to contain a series of loosely related vignettes featuring characters who, like the primary players in the purportedly narratively incoherent *Lost Highway*, switch names and identities without explanation. The female leads played by Watts and Harring, for instance, are called Betty Elms and Rita, respectively, for most of the narrative and are not referred to as Diane Selwyn and Camilla Rhodes until late in the film. The film is also populated by bizarre and threatening characters, such as a powerful dwarf (Michael J. Anderson), a menacing cowboy (Lafayette Montgomery), psychotic brothers—Vincenzo (Dan Hedeya) and Luigi (Angelo Badalamenti) Castigliani—who finance Hollywood films, as well as a frightening homeless person (Bonnie Aarons), who lives behind the dumpster of a Winkie's diner. Although these characters appear to be important, they each turn up briefly, never exchange dialogue with the protagonist, and thus seem tangential. Additionally, many of the film's most memorable scenes, including those featuring the strange events at club Silenco, filmmaker Adam Kesher's (Justin Theroux) discovery of his wife's infidelity, as well as Luigi's terrifying display of revulsion with his espresso, function as ostensible narrative digressions. The film's peculiar characters and occurrences appear to render *Mulholland Dr.* non-classical because they seem to obfuscate narrative meaning, suggesting that they exist for something other than compositional motives.

The presence of a mystery to be solved, though, alerted viewers that the film's strange scenes and characterizations could each have narrative significance. Consequently, before moving on to my presentation of the many plausible readings of the film's narrative that have been generated in a particular online fan community, I briefly present the most readily available way to reinterpret it retrospectively in coherent fashion. In particular, many fans believe that *Mulholland Dr.*'s incomprehensible narrative actually depicts a causally related series of events because once its master key is discovered, the film can be understood as being divided into three distinct, but narratively related, sections. In fact, the most commonly held interpretation maintains that the film begins with a brief prologue before Diane falls asleep, is followed by a portrayal of her extended dream sequence, and ends with a series of post-dream fantasies and flashbacks that explain the source material for her dream. According to this reading, Diane's dream is fueled by her failed attempt to become a successful Hollywood actress. Diane's frustration inspires her to hire a hit man (Mark Pellegrino) at a Winkie's diner to kill Camilla, the woman she blames for her demise. This alternative explanation is largely derived from the information presented during the film's extended changeover, which is instigated by the master keys—literally a stylized blue key and its corresponding blue box. However, as opposed to the standard changeover film, *Mulholland Dr.* never blatantly signals to the audience that it is imparting revelatory information. Specifically, although the chic blue key appears to be important, its significance is never explicitly stated during or after the opening of the blue box.

The stylized blue key that eventually opens the box initially shows up early in the dream sequence shortly after Betty discovers a naked Rita in her beloved Aunt Ruth's (Maya Bond) apartment. Importantly, Betty, who is new to L.A., is only staying at the place temporarily because her aunt will be away for a short period to work on a film shoot in Canada. The key immediately seems as though it will be significant because it is one of the few pieces of evidence available to help Betty discover Rita's true identity, which is the film's ostensible quest narrative. Rita, who is experiencing amnesia after a freak accident in which a serendipitous car crash saves her from two men who threaten her at gunpoint in a limousine, cannot remember basic information, like her name (the inspiration for her alias comes from a *Gilda* [1946] poster, featuring Rita Hayworth) or why her purse contains a large stash of cash and the blue key.

The one thing that Rita initially remembers is that she was going to Mulholland Dr. when the accident occurred. Her memory is further jogged when she sees a waitress (Missy Crider) at Winkie's with the nametag "Diane," who looks a lot like Betty, prompting her to recall that the name Diane Selwyn is somehow important. In turn, Betty calls the mystery woman to see if she can provide any information about Rita. As she dials the phone, Betty offhandedly tells Rita that "it's strange to be calling yourself." When the two recognize that the voice on the outgoing message is not Rita's, Betty innocently suggests that "maybe that's your roommate." According to this particular reinterpretation of narrative information, Betty's seemingly tangential remark is the kind of evidence that becomes vital, in retrospect, because it hints that Betty and Diane may actually be the same person. Upon their return from the mysterious club Silencio later in the film, Betty inexplicably disappears and the key becomes relevant again when it opens the strange blue box that magically appeared in Betty's purse at the club. As Rita opens the box, the camera zooms into its darkness, slyly signaling, but never announcing, that a change is occurring. Shortly thereafter, the frightening cowboy reappears and signals that the dream is over by literally telling Betty that "it's time to wake up." Unlike the always groomed and peppy Betty, the woman (also played by Naomi Watts) who wakes up in the bed looks unkempt and gravely depressed. In sum, the opening of the box becomes the changeover because it subtly depicts the end of Diane's dream in which she both imagined herself as Betty and Camilla as Rita.

However, *Lost on Mulholland Dr.* (*LOMD*), an unofficial website created and maintained by fans of *Mulholland Dr.*, demonstrates that some viewers are unconvinced that this particular rereading is the most persuasive. Consequently, they have leveraged their collective intelligence to resolve the seemingly eternal mysteries that it does not explain. On the site's "newcomer's guide," the contributors briefly summarize what they term the "classical interpretation" (the reading described above in which the opening of the blue box is deemed to be the changeover) because they consider it only "a useful starting point" for those interested in learning about *other* possible explanations. The site's participants, therefore, are devoted to discovering what they perceive to be alternative ways to reinterpret the film in a coherent fashion. Of course, there are a few posters to *LOMD*, like Dave H., who question the site's aims by wondering if the contributors are ultimately "reducing the beauty of this work of art by analysis." Yet, later in that same thread, he admits that he is "continually trying to figure it all out" even though he knows that this potentially ruins the film's pleasures. These contradictory statements exemplify participants' sentiments because although there is a desire to crack the code, *LOMD*'s contributors consider the film's ambiguity to be a great asset.

While the anonymity of online posting makes it difficult to determine information about the identities of the site's primary contributors, it is safe to assume that a majority are male because the most active participants use avatars such as HarryTuttle, Alan Shaw, and richdubya that suggest that they are men. Such skewed gender representation on the site indicates that Jenkins is right to speculate that the presence of a mystery compensates for men's anxieties with a film that is not ostensibly targeted at them. It is possible to deduce more information about *LOMD*'s creators from a link on the homepage that directs visitors to a list of the contributors' "recommended movies," which contains both their favorite films and films that they deem similar to *Mulholland Dr.* The lists are comprised primarily of narratively, formally, and thematically challenging films from a range of traditions, such as experimental, international art, and Hollywood cinemas. Unsurprisingly, Lynch's other films and a slew of contemporary misdirection films dominate both lists. This display of cultural capital is of note, then, because it signals that the site's creators consider themselves discerning cinephiles who possess exquisite taste in and an abundant knowledge about film.

LOMD's homepage also contains links to the site's primary sections, which each demonstrate that its contributors are highly devoted to solving *Mulholland Dr.*'s narrative puzzles. There is a link, for instance, to a page that features images associated with the film, such as photos and the corresponding addresses of primary shooting locations, snapshots from the making of the film and the television pilot, as well as still shots from the film deemed narratively significant. Additionally, there are pages that house sound clips from and related to the film, including songs from the soundtrack, key lines of dialogue, and interviews with creative personnel. Of most interest are the pages titled "theories" and "studies." The "theories" page provides detailed accounts of possible ways to interpret the meaning of the film. Similarly, the "studies" page offers explanations for the possible narrative relevance of just about every character, object, location, and event in the film.

On the "theories" page, visitors are invited to click on links to approximately 30 distinct ways to comprehend *Mulholland Dr.*'s narrative in a totalizing fashion. Although the content of the theories varies greatly, as is evidenced by their often outrageous titles, such as "The Abortion Theory," "Two Drug Trips," and "A Deal with the Devil," they each similarly aim to render the film classical by explaining how

Figure 4.1. Diane Selwyn at Winkie's, making arrangements with Joe, whom most fans identify as a hit man, to do something to Camilla Rhodes in *Mulholland Dr.*

something other than the opening of the blue box can make the film's ambiguities narratively relevant. For starters, many posters claim that the post-dream scene in which Diane meets with the seedy man at Winkie's holds the key to comprehending the film coherently. According to a number of these contributors, those who ascribe to the "classical interpretation" incorrectly assume that the man she meets at the diner is a hit man. In the "Bribery Theory" explanation, for example, a poster argues that Diane is paying the unidentified man "to influence the casting of Camilla Rhodes in a film—starting her off on the road to stardom." This alternative reading is persuasive because it can be supported by the events that transpire in the dream. Its proponents posit that the blonde Camilla (Melissa George) in the dream is selected as the lead in the film within the film—*The Sylvia North Story*—because an array of shady businessmen, including the Castigliani Brothers and the dwarf, influence personnel decisions in Hollywood. Such a string of events implies that someone, presumably Diane, has arranged for it. Consequently, it is just as likely that her dream is inspired by the guilt associated with her decision to give him the money to buy Camilla's fame as it is that she paid him to kill her.

In the "Dying Dream/Afterlife Theory," three *LOMD* contributors, who adopt the usernames smapty, cuttingedgenyc, and Alfred Romo, also marshal convincing evidence to counter the "classical" interpretation. They believe that "the bulk of the film takes place after Diane has committed suicide." For these contributors, the key to understanding the film in this manner is revealed in the pre-opening credit sequence in which, through a P.O.V. shot, a character, presumably Diane, falls to the bed to begin the dream. Significantly, in this scene, the sound is highly muffled, potentially concealing a suicidal gunshot. Following this logic, the dream thus actually begins after Diane pulls the trigger because she falls on the same bed that, in the dream, contains a rotting corpse that resembles her. The meanings of many of the film's ambiguities and the ten clues, then, change dramatically from the "classical interpretation." To begin, the two elderly people—Irene (Jeanne Bates) and her companion (Dan Birnbaum)—depicted in the opening jitterbug sequence and later accompanying Diane when she first arrives in L.A., can now be understood as representing "Diane's guardian angels" because they reappear in her apartment just before she shoots herself. Similarly, club Silencio is transformed into a depiction of hell, which explains why the film ultimately returns there after Diane sees her own suicide occur. In fact, its status as hell explains why virtually all of the club's performers, such as the magician (Richard Green) and emcee (Geno Silva), who also appears as the manager of the seedy Park Hotel, are either dressed in red or have a demonic appearance. It also reveals why the red-clad Rebekah Del Rio apparently dies onstage. For those skeptical about this interpretation, the authors present a freeze-frame of an image that only appears for a fleeting moment immediately before Betty and Rita get into the cab that takes them to club Silencio, containing a flyer attached to a telephone poll that reads in small letters "Hollywood is" and in big letters "HELL." This plausible alternative explanation is thus bolstered by DVD technology because it enables viewers to control the image in such a fashion. Moreover, evidence to support this theory is effectively and easily communicated on the web, which allows users who possess even a little technological knowledge the ability to distribute text juxtaposed with images to a wide audience.

Like many other contributors to *LOMD*, the proponents of the "Dying Dream/Afterlife" theory also rely heavily on their knowledge of Lynch's authorial tendencies and their ability to spot intertextual references to buttress their interpretation. To wit, as Camilla treks toward downtown L.A. after she survives the attempt on her life in the back of the limo, the camera tilts up to reveal that she has reached Sunset Boulevard. As the authors of this theory note, that street name is also the title of a famous 1950 Hollywood film that is "narrated by a person who is already dead" that "tells us how he came to be killed." This is

Figure 4.2. An almost imperceptible "Hollywood is HELL" flyer is affixed to a pole, as Diane Selwyn and Camilla Rhodes hail a cab to take them to club Silencio in *Mulholland Dr.*

relevant to their reading because they assert it is a film that "Lynch has referred to as his favorite," suggesting why *Mulholland Dr.* contains so many "homages to *Sunset Blvd.*" like "Lynch's use of the same car that Norma Desmond [Gloria Swanson] came to Paramount in." The authors cite similar evidence from Lynch's other works to validate their theory further. For instance, they contend that the cowboy has to be "a spirit" because when Adam meets him at his corral "the electricity in the lights overhead dimmer and flicker" and "in *Twin Peaks*, when a lodge spirit is nearby it alters the electrical charge of its surroundings." Most interestingly, to persuade readers that their interpretation is correct, they argue that "as an afterlife experience, *Mulholland Dr.* has NO unresolved issues." To discredit their opposition further, they also theorize that the "classical interpretation" is not plausible because "Lynch has never dealt directly with dreams. It's not his style." Put simply, the proponents of the "Dying Dream/Afterlife Theory" back their argument by claiming it explains everything and can be substantiated by the discourses of authorship.

Many of the ambiguities that are seemingly clarified by this theory can be even more sensationally and compellingly explained by other hypotheses on *LOMD*. Like conspiracy theorists, contributors to *LOMD* participate in a game of hermeneutic one-upmanship to obtain the kind of narrative closure that the text itself does not provide. According to the writers of the "Dying Dream/Afterlife Theory," for example, the meaning of Aunt Ruth's character is the key to understanding the film. They argue that Aunt Ruth's apartment represents a portal into the afterlife. Since their explanation assumes that Diane commits suicide after ordering the hit on Camilla, they speculate that it makes sense that viewers see "Aunt Ruth leaving with suitcases as Camilla arrives" because it is subsequently revealed that the two characters actually died in that order. Moreover, this logic explains why "Diane arrives in the apartment AFTER Camilla/Rita." Such an interpretation also convincingly highlights why the changeover occurs where it does and the significance of what happens during it. Indeed, as Rita opens the blue box in Aunt Ruth's apartment after they return from club Silencio, Betty inexplicably vanishes and Aunt Ruth magically reappears in the apartment.

In contrast, though, as Aleksandra H., one of the site's only contributors adopting a female avatar counters on the "studies" page devoted to Aunt Ruth, *Mulholland Dr.* can be interpreted as depicting Aunt Ruth's, and not Diane's, dreams and flashbacks. For this contributor, a reading of the film as being about "a young girl who came from Canada to make a career in Hollywood," in the 1950s, as opposed to an aspiring Hollywood actress from the present, renders many of the "anachronistic touches" and ambiguities insufficiently explained by many of the other theories as narratively relevant. A reading of Aunt Ruth as the primary character explains why the first of three different aged, red-headed women who look a lot like her briefly appears as a competitor in the 1950s-inspired jitterbug sequence in which Diane is never shown dancing. In fact, as another contributor to the Aunt Ruth "studies" page named blu-ray posits, each of Aunt Ruth's doppelgängers can be read as representations of different phases of her Hollywood career: the jitterbug contestant is the pre-Hollywood Ruth, the casting agent who appears in Diane's steamy audition scene is Ruth in middle-age after she has given up acting, and the comparatively older, red-headed woman waiting for a limo is a depiction of Ruth living in the Sierra Bonita apartments in retirement. Additionally, if the story is being told from Aunt Ruth's perspective, *The Sylvia North Story* no longer appears to be a period piece. Instead, it becomes a film that actually was shot when Ruth arrived in Hollywood in the 1950s. Thus, it is also easy to explain why many of the characters use terms like "horse pucky" and "smart aleck," which makes it sound as though they exist in a 1950s sitcom.

According to this theory, Aunt Ruth's reappearance in the apartment when Betty disappears can be understood as the end of Ruth's naïve reimagining of how her experience as a film actress could have gone differently because Betty and Diane are actually representations of the two sides of her Hollywood story. Betty is a talented, young woman, who has no idea how things really work in Hollywood. Eventually,

Figure 4.3. One of the red-headed Aunt Ruth doppelgängers appears in *Mulholland Dr.*'s opening jitterbug sequence.

though, she turns into Diane, who, like the film's other elderly women characters—Coco (Ann Miller) and Louise Bonner (Lee Grant)—becomes a hardened, presumably out-of-work actress. Finally, it also becomes evident why Camilla draws her inspiration for her alter-ego from Aunt Ruth's poster of Rita Hayworth in *Gilda*: the film is widely renowned for being a quintessential studio-era depiction of the objectification of women. Moreover, Hayworth was at the height of her popularity in the 1940s and 1950s and famously dyed her hair red to conceal her Latina heritage. In short, this astute reinterpretation effectively explains many of the film's most puzzling moments both by imagining the details of a seemingly tangential character's personal history and drawing on a vast knowledge of Hollywood history.

The remarkable explanation entitled "A Multi-Layered Analysis of *Mulholland Dr.*," posted by a contributor with the user name Alan Shaw reveals that the film has inspired the site's predominately male participants to engage in wild speculations about the personal histories of its characters to crack the code. Even though it is never explicitly stated in the film, Shaw posits, in a section of his analysis called "The Diane Selwyn Story," that Diane's parents died when she was a child. Consequently, she was forced her to live with her evil custodians—her grandmother Irene and her elderly male companion—in Deep River, Ontario. Diane's childhood was horrific, he theorizes, because the elderly man molested her. Worse still, her grandmother remained silent and demanded that Diane never speak of the abuse—hence, silencio. Fortunately, when Diane wins a jitterbug competition, she is able to try to fulfill her dream of becoming a Hollywood actress because it inspires her opportunistic custodians to give her the money she received from her recently deceased Aunt Ruth, who worked as a Hollywood casting agent.

Unfortunately, Diane's attempts to succeed in Hollywood are thwarted by consistent rejections. When her Aunt Ruth's money begins to run out, she is forced to become a waitress at Winkie's and moves into a room at the Park Hotel. To augment her meager income, Diane eventually becomes a prostitute, whose name gets placed in a pimp's black book, enabling her to move into the much nicer, yet still relatively humble, Sierra Bonita apartment complex. Such a reading is plausible, Shaw argues, "because her previous abuse as a child made her feel as though there was something inevitable about being treated like a commodity." Diane then tries out for the lead in *The Sylvia North Story*, a low-budget film produced by Wally Brown (James Karen), an old friend of Aunt Ruth's, which she believes is the perfect role for her because it depicts a woman in an illicit sexual relationship with an older man. However, as Shaw summarizes, "the role went to Camilla Rhodes" instead, who wowed everyone at the audition, including Diane, who told Camilla that she was impressed with her "ability to heat up what Diane thought was 'such a lame scene.'" Diane and Camilla subsequently develop a friendship after the fame-starved Camilla becomes enamored by Diane's flattery. The two eventually grow so close that they decide to move in together at Sierra Bonita and become lovers. Diane, who has been scarred by her male abusers, develops an unhealthy obsession for her female companion. Sadly, Camilla is not as committed to the relationship because she is only concerned with furthering her Hollywood career. After Camilla receives good reviews for her performance in *The Sylvia North Story*, she begins to be offered A-list parts, most notably in an Adam Kesher film. Camilla then agrees to get a desperate Diane some bit parts in her films, including Kesher's film, provided that she agrees to whore herself out to Hollywood executives like Luigi Castigliani, with whom Camilla routinely sleeps to secure her starring roles.

Camilla subsequently develops a romantic relationship with the director, which gives her financial stability and jeopardizes her relationship with Diane; however, even though Camilla moves out of the apartment, the two do not officially end their romance. To escape the trauma of once again being used, this time by a woman whom she loves deeply, Diane switches apartments with L. J. DeRosa (Johanna Stein), her neighbor at Sierra Bonita. Her attempt proves futile, though, because Camilla sadistically torments Diane by continually flaunting her promiscuity. Camilla's display of affection for another woman (the woman portrayed as the blonde Camilla in the dream) at a party celebrating her engagement to Adam becomes the final straw for the emotionally troubled Diane. As Shaw notes, "Diane had been able to hope that even if Camilla stayed with Adam" they "could still have an intimate relationship with each other;" however, "Camilla's kiss with another woman showed her that Camilla was not coming back to her." As a result, with the money she has earned from prostitution, Diane hires a hit man who promises to place a blue key behind a Winkie's dumpster after he kills Camilla. The sight of the blue key on her coffee table finally drives Diane over the edge. In turn, she falls into a drug-induced sleep and experiences the dream inspired by these traumatic events. Diane awakens from her dream more depressed than before and, presumably still under the influence of the drug, hallucinates the return of Irene and her companion. Horrified, she retreats to her bedroom, "the place," Shaw writes, "where her childhood abuse took place" and commits suicide.

"The Diane Selwyn Story" is only the start of his analysis because by hypothesizing that Diane was sexually abused by a number of perpetrators throughout her life, Shaw is able to close off a number of the film's most puzzling ambiguities and identify the narrative significance of the ten clues in a convincing fashion. Peppered throughout the "studies" pages, for instance, are his interpretations of how a variety of the film's mysterious characters, objects, and events can each be read as related to the master key of sexual abuse. He argues that the events at club Silencio portray Diane reliving her childhood sexual trauma. On the "studies" page devoted to the magician, he specifically theorizes that the magician's demonic performance, which culminates with both his almost imperceptible grunt and Diane's uncontrollable shaking in response, can be read as a coded representation of her childhood rape. Similarly, in his examination of Woody Katz (Chad Everett), Shaw speculates that his sexually charged audition with Diane can be understood as another time in which Diane's subconscious is contending with the horror of her abuse. He believes that Woody is closely related to Diane because of the scene's dialogue that suggests that he knows her parents well and because the actor, whose name has phallic connotations, prepares for the audition by saying "Dad's best friend goes to work." Moreover, evidence indicates that the liaison is both illegal and has occurred previously. During the scene, the two characters worry about going to jail if they are caught and Diane expresses remorse about the ongoing relationship. In sum, the sexual abuse theory provides an interpretive grid through which the narrative is made coherent by speculating about how unreferenced events from Diane's history shaped her Hollywood experience.

Figure 4.4. *Mulholland Dr.*'s Diane Selwyn and Woody Katz amplify the intimacy and sexual chemistry of their audition.

Shaw's highly imaginative reading of *Mulholland Dr.* also further showcases how *LOMD*'s contributors attempt to convince visitors that they have definitively solved the puzzle by relying on a knowledge of Lynch's oeuvre, their ability to catch intertextual references, and the capabilities of DVD technology. On the page devoted to a summary of Shaw's sexual abuse theory, a number of stills from the film are posted as evidence that characters, such as Irene's elderly companion, the magician, and Woody Katz, are each representations of Diane's abusers. Similarly, to support the idea that Diane's abusive past is what leads her to work as a hooker, the page also contains a freeze-frame of the hit man interacting with a battered prostitute from the dream, who looks a lot like Diane. Additionally, the cryptic narrative logic of *Twin Peaks*, which also contained thematic undercurrents about the horrors of incest, is consistently cited as being relevant to understanding *Mulholland Dr.* as a nightmare about the trauma of childhood sexual abuse. Those who support the sexual abuse theory also correctly point out that Diane claims to hail from a town called Deep River, which happens to be the name of the apartment complex in *Blue Velvet* where Frank Booth (Dennis Hopper) violently rapes Dorothy Valens (Isabella Rossellini). To validate their claims further, the unnamed authors of this summary note that many historians have claimed that Rita Hayworth was likely molested by her father. Finally, according to the "studies" page devoted to a painting, entitled "The Beatrice Cenci," which hangs in Aunt Ruth's apartment, the famous portrait depicts a "Roman noblewoman" from the sixteenth century who supposedly "hired two hit men to kill her incestuous father."

The sexual abuse theory illustrates the lengths to which this fan community will go to obtain narrative closure. The "studies" pages, in fact, feature many other examples of the kind of interpretive labor that the film's release on DVD has inspired on the site, such as diagrams that depict both the numbers likely dialed on a rotary phone to call the dwarf and the layouts of both apartments at the Sierra Bonita complex. Additionally, there are English translations of the Spanish and French dialogue as well as the Chinese writing that appears in the film. There are also "studies" pages devoted to revealing the ways in which a number of films, including *Sunset Blvd.*, *Contempt* (1963), and *The Wizard of Oz* are connected to *Mulholland Dr.* In fact, *The Wizard of Oz*, one of the most recognizable misdirection films in Hollywood history, has influenced Lynch throughout his career, especially in films like *Wild at Heart* and *Blue Velvet*. It clearly can be read as a narrative template for *Mulholland Dr.*, according to the "classical interpretation." Like Dorothy's (Judy Garland) experiences in Oz, after the blue box is opened, the people, events, and objects that appear in the nightmare can be understood as distortions of crucial moments from Diane's waking life. To help support this reading of the film, the authors of *The Wizard of Oz* "studies" page not only list the extensive narrative similarities between the two films, they also juxtapose freeze-frame images of *Mulholland Dr.* with the Hollywood classic to demonstrate that shots from the former have been constructed as explicit homages to the latter. This impressive display of cultural capital again reveals that making such elaborate connections in a convincing manner has become feasible in an age in which DVD and Internet technologies allow this kind of visual evidence to be presented with relative ease.

LOMD may be the most dazzling example of how *Mulholland Dr.* has successfully encouraged fans to use new technologies to decipher its ambiguous narrative, but it was not the first page of this kind to appear on the web. In October 2001, shortly after the film premiered in U.S. theaters, Bill Wyman, Max Garrone, and Andy Klein published an article on *Salon.com* entitled "Everything you were afraid to ask about *Mulholland Dr.*," which was an early attempt to forward what *LOMD* participants term the "classical interpretation." Although the authors do an admirable job of making narrative sense of many of the film's most notable ambiguities, they ultimately acknowledge that their reading cannot explain all of its enigmas. This admission, in turn, inspired fans to submit their interpretations of the film to the editors, a number of which *Salon.com* published just a few days later in an article entitled "Whaddaya mean, 'We don't know about the box?'." Interestingly, scattered through these alternative readings are the kind of statements that suggest that audiences conceive of misdirection films as constituents of a distinct genre. One responder, for instance, theorizes that "the first two-thirds of the movie are Betty/Diane's fantasy, either masturbatory or upon dying (a sort of *Jacob's Ladder* cum *Sixth Sense* thing)." Humorously, another similarly themed response simply reads "Rosebud." Finally, a pleased reader commends the site for publishing the interpretation, because "This—and the *Memento* article" that *Salon.com* "published last summer" are the "type of film discussion" there should be "more of," provided that there are "the right kind of movies to discuss."

Understanding *Memento*: Unreliable Memories and Untrustworthy Evidence

Salon.com readers were not the only ones to make these types of connections. The authors of the *Salon.com* article on *Mulholland Dr.* similarly note that "of recent American movies only *Memento* is remotely as challenging." Perhaps not surprisingly, then, in June 2001, just a few months before the *Mulholland Dr.* article appeared online, *Salon.com* published the aforementioned article on *Memento*. Written by Andy Klein, the article, entitled "Everything you wanted to know about *Memento*," aims to unravel the film's meaning. Klein justifies his decision to write the article about the film, which he initially compares to *The Usual Suspects* and *The Sixth Sense*, by eventually claiming that it is even more narratively complex than those predecessors. As he states, "*Memento*'s puzzle cannot be undone with a single declarative sentence." Instead, as he summarizes, it is difficult to make sense of *Memento*'s narrative because it is complicated by

> an elegant but brain-knotting structure; by an exceedingly unreliable narrator through part of the film; by a postmodern self-referentiality that, unlike most empty examples of the form, thoroughly underscores the film's sobering thematic meditations on memory, knowledge and grief; and by a number of red herrings and misleading clues that seem designed either to distract the audience or to hint at a deeper, second layer of puzzle at work—or that may, on the other hand, simply suggest that, in some respects, the director bit off more than he could chew. (Klein)

Like *Mulholland Dr.*, *Memento* is a film that contains such an uncharacteristically intricate narrative that spectators are encouraged to watch it on multiple occasions to sort out what "actually" happens. In the end, however, as Klein's comments also suggest, it may not be possible to determine *Memento*'s "truth." Although it is highly unconventional for a Hollywood film to contain such narrative characteristics, some viewers cite the existence of these seemingly eternal ambiguities as a positive artistic attribute. Yet, many of these ardent fans are most devoted to solving these mysteries in a way that renders the film classical, in retrospect.

Even though it presents information in a highly unconventional manner, *Memento* does contain a seemingly straightforward narrative, making it necessary to explain why its events may not have the same retroactive significance. The noir-inspired plot is ostensibly driven by Leonard Shelby's (Guy Pearce) attempt to avenge his wife's rape and murder. In particular, although he shoots and kills a culprit during the attack, he remains convinced that a second assailant, named John G. or James G., remains at large. When Leonard shares the details of the event with Natalie (Carrie-Anne Moss), however, he tells her the authorities consider the case closed because they believe that there was only one intruder. Leonard's quest for justice is further complicated by the anterograde amnesia (short-term memory loss) that he purportedly incurred as a result of a head injury that he suffered while attempting to save his wife. Leonard's condition makes him an unreliable narrator because he claims not to be able to store any new information in his long-term memory since the incident, meaning that it is difficult to trust any information he divulges about himself. The presence of his memory loss also casts doubt on the veracity of his motives. Indeed, the film consistently hints that his objectives and even the severity of his condition may not be as clear-cut as they seem. After murdering Jimmy Grants (Larry Holden), for example, Leonard steals both his designer clothes and Jaguar, which also happens to have $200,000 cash in the trunk for a proposed drug deal. He subsequently kills Teddy (Joe Pantoliano), a purported cop, whose real name is supposedly John Edward Gammell, and who admits to have been manipulating Leonard ever since being assigned to the Shelbys' case. The all-too-coincidental benefits of both murders suggest that Leonard may both be out for more than vigilante justice and able to remember more than he claims.

Other factors trouble Leonard's traits or motives as being legitimate. First, the film contains an unorthodox narrative structure that replicates Leonard's memory loss and consequently disorients the spectator in time and space, making it difficult to determine the film's causal relationship of events. Specifically, a majority of scenes—those that play in color—unfold in reverse chronological order. Complicating things further, these backwards scenes alternate with black-and-white segments that move forward in time. Eventually, however, the two distinct, yet related, plotlines seamlessly meld together into a forward-moving color sequence late in the film when Leonard develops a Polaroid photo that depicts Jimmy's murder. Second, Teddy discloses much of the "truth" about the attack on Leonard's wife and what has happened since the incident. As with the film's other secondary characters, most notably Natalie, who seems to manipulate Leonard to kill Teddy, Teddy takes advantage of Leonard's condition to further his own objectives. The information that he provides in the explanatory sequence thus cannot be trusted because it may simply be designed to trick Leonard. Finally, even though the film contains a changeover that appears to explain the meaning of events fully, its validity is troubled by both Leonard's status as a highly untrustworthy narrator and the fact that the film itself contains an unreliable *mise-en-scène*.

Although *Memento*'s meaning is complicated by its unconventional, nonchronological structure, theorists like Bordwell have demonstrated how the film's writer/director, Christopher Nolan, employs many techniques to help spectators comprehend it. The film contains a number of formal cues and narrative redundancies that indeed help spectators connect events in a classical fashion, such as the oscillation between color and black-and-white cinematography, Leonard's continuous reminders about the details of his condition, the parallel story about Sammy Jankis (Stephen Tobolowsky), who also suffers from anterograde amnesia and accidentally killed his diabetic wife by administering too many insulin shots, the use of dangling causes and dialogue hooks, as well as continuities and changes in makeup and costuming. Moreover, even though the film presents narrative information in an atypical fashion, its unconventional style and structure are tied directly to the subjectivity of the protagonist, rendering these decisions compositionally motivated. Although Bordwell grants that "closure operates retrospectively" in *Memento*, he ultimately claims that "the events still cohere through cause and effect," making its innovations contained by the classical paradigm (*The Way* 79).

Other critics argue, however, that even though many classical tactics are deployed to offset the film's complexities, it is still difficult to connect *Memento*'s narrative events according to a definitive causal logic. For example, Klein, who admits to seeing *Memento* five times before penning his analysis, speculates that the film is difficult even for repeat viewers to understand because "its puzzles are so intriguing and so impenetrable at first viewing that filmgoers are almost forced to go back for a second look if they want to figure just what the hell is going on." To assist viewers perplexed by the film's unconventional structure, he presents a method for systematically charting the chronology of narrative events. First, he assigns letters in reverse order to each of the color scenes in the sequence in which they appear in the film, starting with "V" and ending with "A." Second, he uses numbers, ranging from "1" to "22," to correspond to the distinct black-and-white scenes in the chronological order in which they appear. Accordingly, the scene in which Leonard develops the Polaroid of Jimmy and the film transitions from black-and-white to color, should be labeled "22/A." "If you want to look at the story as it would actually transpire chronologically, rather than in the disjointed way that Nolan presents it" Klein writes, viewers should "reorder the events by starting with scenes 1–22 and ending with scenes A–V," which he exclaims will "be fun to do on DVD!" As with *Mulholland Dr.*, Klein's provocative analysis of *Memento* inspired a slew of emails from readers, some of which *Salon.com* published on July 4, 2001. A number of these responses reveal that Klein was not the only one who believed that *Memento* was custom-made for DVD. One reader, for instance, tells Klein that "Like you, I am looking forward to *Memento*'s release on DVD." Similarly, another reader admits to "being a relative babe in the woods, having only seen the movie once" and is "anxiously awaiting its release on DVD for further viewing."

In 2002, as if they had read Klein's article and the responses to it, Sony subsidiary Columbia TriStar gave viewers the opportunity to watch the film chronologically by releasing a two-disc limited edition of *Memento* on DVD, which was packaged to look like Leonard's psychiatric case file and even included a few doctored excerpts from his dossier. In addition to these ancillary materials and the disc containing the theatrical version of the film, the limited edition DVD was accompanied by a supplemental disc with a number of extras that provided new evidence for solving the mystery. Among these are the text of Jonathan Nolan's (Christopher Nolan's brother) short story on which the film was based, excerpts from Leonard's journal, and a transcript of the shooting script, replete with Christopher Nolan's handwritten notes. Of most interest, however, is the supplemental disc's hidden feature that enables viewers to watch the film re-cut in the exact chronological order detailed in Klein's article. Of course, it is not easy to find the Easter egg that enables this special feature because users must navigate a maddeningly convoluted menu comprised of mock psychiatric tests to access any of the features on either disc. To do something as simple as view the theatrical version, for instance, viewers first have to wait for a couple of sample psychiatric questions to disappear and then have to locate and select the term "watch" from a long list of words on its quasi-main menu. Fortunately, instructions for doing this are included in one of the inserts that accompany the limited edition DVD. In contrast, to access the reedited, chronological version of *Memento*, spectators must execute a complex series of commands, resembling the kind of interactive participation that is typically required of videogame players to activate cheats. In sum, the existence of the film's alternative edit on DVD and the collective intelligence that it likely takes to discover its presence suggests that producers both understood how difficult it is to decipher *Memento* and hoped to entice viewers by rewarding only devoted fans with tools for decoding its narrative secrets.

The presence of this Easter egg, in addition to many of the other extra features, implies that the film's creators hoped that sales would be bolstered by suggesting that there is indeed a "right" way to crack the code. Christopher Nolan's own comments about the film support this further. In his article, Klein claims that when Scott Timberg of the *New Times of Los Angeles* spoke to Nolan "about the film's outcome" just prior to its domestic theatrical release, the director talked about his interest in "ambiguity and subjectivity," but also claimed to know "the movie's Truth—who's good, who's bad, who can be trusted and who can't" and ultimately maintained "that close viewing will reveal all." Despite his declaration that there is a "correct" way to interpret the film, evidence suggests that Nolan, like Lynch, may have purposely created an unsolvable mystery. Moreover, as Lynch did with his ten clues for *Mulholland Dr.*, the additional promotional materials that surrounded the film's various releases seem to have been designed with the intent of clouding narrative "truth." Such an apparently contradictory strategy makes perfect business sense because it helps to sustain a collective intelligence's attention for an extended period of time beyond the theatrical release by forcing fans to sort through both the film itself and the mountain of ancillary materials associated to it.

To market the theatrical release of *Memento*, for instance, cash-strapped Newmarket Films allowed Jonathan Nolan to create an innovative website that provides a critical backstory about Leonard and his wife that is never offered in the film. The official website, *otnemem.com* (cleverly, *Memento* spelled backwards), first greets visitors with the film's tagline "some memories are best forgotten." The tagline then disappears and is automatically replaced by a mock newspaper article, indicating that Leonard is the prime suspect in a murder investigation. Interestingly, the article also reports that Leonard escaped from a San Francisco Bay area mental institution in 1998. From the article, users are invited to click on a number of highlighted words that are hyperlinked to excerpts from Leonard's psychiatric dossier and his doctored copy of the police file, revealing information about his anterograde amnesia and what transpired since he was institutionalized. It notes that he was admitted to the mental hospital in late 1997, a number of months after the attack occurred. It also presents evidence that someone has been writing notes to Leonard in an attempt to warn him that another person may be manipulating him to kill the wrong individual to avenge his wife's death. These notes are what encourage Leonard both to tattoo important information to his body and to remember the tragic story of Sammy Jankis, whose all-too-coincidentally similar case Leonard had purportedly investigated when he worked in insurance prior to the attack. Additionally, evidence that helps Leonard eventually identify Teddy as the perpetrator, such as his driver's license and his license plate, is prominently featured on the site. It is ultimately difficult to determine what is factual on the site, however, because much of the information there is contradictory. For example, although a newspaper article reveals that Leonard's wife survived and that an accomplice is being sought by the authorities, hospital records suggest that she is dead and that Leonard fabricated the second perpetrator. Moreover, whereas some of his files indicate that he is incapable of making new memories, others suggest that his condition was improving before his escape.

Paradoxically, then, the insider information offered on the official website often makes it more challenging to determine the "truth" of many of the film's most troubling uncertainties, such as the actual severity of

Leonard's condition, what happened to his wife after the attack, the real relationship between Leonard and Sammy Jankis, and who is responsible for his wife's murder. In fact, answers to these questions may not be knowable. There is never enough evidence to determine if Leonard is manipulating all of the other characters through a Keyser Sözesque fakery of his condition, or if other characters are actually taking advantage of his very real short-term memory loss. The answer may seem to be evident in the scene that reveals that the motel clerk, Burt (Mark Boone Junior), is exploiting Leonard's purported disability by charging him for unknowingly renting two rooms simultaneously at the Discount Inn. However, after Leonard exposes the scam, Burt jokingly reminds him that "he's not going to remember" the ordeal anyway, to which Leonard retorts, "you don't have to be that honest, *Burt*." Leonard's use of Burt's name during an exchange in which it is never otherwise mentioned is suspicious because Leonard always seems to have to check his Polaroids to remember anyone else's name. Furthermore, in the other scenes in which Leonard and Burt interact both face-to-face and on the phone, Leonard explicitly asks the motel clerk his name because he claims not to be able to remember meeting him before. Although I grant that Leonard's inexplicable recollection of Burt's name might only indicate the presence of a continuity error, it may also more sinisterly reveal that Leonard is willing to appear to be taken advantage of to perpetuate his elaborate ruse.

The ambiguity about Leonard's condition lingers eternally because, like the promotional material associated with the film, the film itself is loaded with inconsistent information. For starters, although it seems Teddy's long explanation about Leonard's past is a revelatory sequence that provides key information about what "really" happened and what Leonard's "true" motives are, it actually further convolutes narrative meaning. During his explanation, Teddy suggests that Leonard committed the acts that he continually attributes to Sammy Jankis. In contrast to what Leonard claims, Teddy contends that Leonard's wife survived the attack, she did not believe that his anterograde amnesia was real, she had diabetes, and that Leonard's work as an insurance fraud investigator revealed that Sammy was a con man who did not have a wife. Interestingly, as Leonard refutes the diabetes allegation, the film replays an earlier flashback in which Leonard pinched his wife's leg; however, this time he administers an insulin shot to the same spot. A few seconds later, though, as Leonard vehemently denies Teddy's claim, the film cuts back to the earlier flashback of him pinching her leg. The incongruous visual evidence in this scene demonstrates that the veracity of everything that Teddy has just exposed as well as the information that viewers both see and hear Leonard recall about his past should be interrogated.

The events that follow this explanation sequence, which comprise the changeover, further muddy the film's meaning even though they seem to offer a coherent explanation for Leonard's motives and actions. In voiceover, Leonard confirms Teddy's allegation that he makes up his own truths by purposefully doctoring the evidence. Consequently, after Teddy reveals that he has been using him, Leonard leaves clues to trick himself into believing that Teddy is really John G., which finally explains why he kills Teddy in the film's opening moments. Yet the scene also subtly alludes to the fact that there may be a major problem with accepting Teddy's assertion that Leonard actually suffers from anterograde amnesia and manipulates himself to remember things how he would like them to be. To catch John G., Leonard has devised a system in which he tattoos his body with what he deems as the most crucial clues to solving the case. As a result, he writes himself a note on an index card to tattoo Teddy's license plate as fact number six. The scene's first indication that his memory loss may not be as severe as he claims, then, is that he remembers this clue to be the sixth fact without first checking his existing tattoos. Even more troubling is how he also erroneously copies the plate number as "SG13 71U" (the final three digits should read 7**I**U and not 7**1**U), which calls into question how he eventually determines that Teddy is the culprit. Importantly, though, the significance of his inaccurate transcription is only signaled visually because the film merely cuts back and forth twice between the index card and close-ups of the license plate. However, on a number of occasions earlier in the film, which are, of course, later in the sequence of narrative events, Leonard's incorrect notation of Teddy's license plate is further verified both aurally and visually. For instance, a tattoo artist

Figure 4.5. *Memento*'s Leonard Shelby writes himself a note, in which he fails to distinguish the number "1" from the letter "I," to tattoo Teddy's license plate number.

Figure 4.6. Shot of Teddy's actual license plate number that is juxtaposed with Leonard Shelby's notation of it to confirm his ambiguous transcription of the digits in *Memento*.

administers a tattoo with two ones instead of an I, as Leonard misreads the digits on his leg as "SG13 7IU" in voiceover. The question that thus arises is how did Natalie help Leonard track down Teddy if she gave her contact at the DMV the incorrect plate number? On one hand, it can be assumed that Natalie simply fabricated all of the documents that lead Leonard to Teddy. On the other hand, it could also be inferred that the error is irrelevant because Leonard is a faker, who is fully aware that he plans to kill Teddy. In sum, these revelatory scenes present considerable uncertainty, rather than closure, in relation to Leonard's traits, motives, and actions.

The unresolved issues that remain even after the explanation and changeover sequences transpire prompted fans to form knowledge communities on the web to solve *Memento*'s puzzle. Perhaps the most notable of these sites is the now defunct *Unofficial Christopher Nolan Web Site* (*UCNW*). The site, originally created and maintained by Johannes Duckner, contains links to each of Nolan's films; however, the amount of information posted in relation to *Memento* and the comparatively high degree of discussion that the film generated on the site's message board (as of 2008, there were over 400 posts related to *Memento*, which dwarfed its closest competitor) indicates that the film was *UCNW*'s main attraction when it was active. Additionally, the relatively few comments and pages related to *The Prestige* (2006) as well as the high number of postings that appeared in the years immediately following the release of *Memento*'s DVD reveals that the site was at the height of its popularity in the early 2000s. When *UCNW* was in full operation, Duckner was its main contributor and the most active posters on the *Memento* discussion board adopted usernames such as Michael, Chad, and Larry, suggesting that an overwhelming majority of its participants were men. Like *Mulholland Dr.*, therefore, the film successfully attracted a niche audience comprised primarily of male, tech-savvy cinephiles who largely derived pleasure from deciphering the film's mysteries. *Memento*'s discussion board was thus dominated by threads that focus on decoding the film's most baffling enigmas, including Leonard's inexplicable recollection of Burt's name, the mystery of the license plate, and the "true" identity of Sammy Jankis.

Unsurprisingly, the *UCNW* pages created by Duckner devoted to *Memento* also contain a number of tools for solving the mystery, such as links to both Klein's *Salon.com* analysis and the reader responses to his essay, an FAQ about highly disputed plot points, interviews with creative personnel, promotional materials associated with the film, and still images from the film deemed narratively relevant. The *Memento* section of *UCNW* also includes Duckner's own stabs at making sense of some of the film's most puzzling ambiguities. Significantly, Duckner's "*Memento* Trivia: Memory is Treachery" page again demonstrates how misdirection films encourage fans to use the distinct capabilities of Internet and DVD technologies to communicate and validate their particular readings of narrative causality. To provide evidence that Sammy Jankis and Leonard are likely the same person, for instance, Duckner posts a series of still images from the scene in which Leonard describes the circumstances surrounding Sammy's wife's death to an unidentified caller, presumably Teddy, whom he speaks to throughout most of the black-and-white sequences. As Duckner reveals, when the flashback nears its conclusion, Sammy can be seen seated in a mental hospital, where he has been sent for accidentally killing his wife. His juxtaposition of two freeze-frames from the DVD shows that Leonard replaces Sammy in the same hospital chair for a fleeting instant right after a doctor passes between him and

Figure 4.7. Leonard Shelby replaces Sammy Jankis in a mental hospital for a brief instant in *Memento* after a doctor passes between him and the camera.

the camera. This visual evidence strongly indicates that Sammy may not be real. Moreover, it suggests that it was likely Leonard who was institutionalized for killing his own wife with insulin injections. As a number of contributors to the site's *Memento* message board similarly maintain, it can be argued, therefore, that Leonard is a con man who committed insurance fraud by pretending to have anterograde amnesia and subsequently killed his wife to keep up the charade. According to this master key, he was institutionalized after her death and has maintained the façade since escaping the mental hospital to continue to attain his objectives.

Duckner presents other images likely captured from the DVD to encourage visitors to interrogate the validity of Leonard's condition even further. He questions the reliability of the information that leads Leonard to kill Teddy, for instance, by posting a freeze-frame of the photocopy of the driver's license that Natalie obtains from her contact at the DMV. As the site reveals, Teddy's driver's license expires on February 29, 2001, even though that was not a leap year, making it hard to believe that the document is authentic or that it actually helped Leonard identify Teddy as John G. As Duckner posits, "people could argue that this is a factual error," but "why would someone choose February 29th" and "not check if the year was really a leap year?"

It is Duckner's analysis of Teddy's license plate, however, that most persuasively demonstrates that it may ultimately be impossible to determine the "truth" about Leonard's condition. To explain the mystery of the plate, he initially posts a series of still images to show that Leonard erroneously transcribed and tattooed its digits. Taking things a step further, however, he also posts an image taken from much earlier in the film (later in the

Figure 4.8. A copy of Teddy's driver's license that contains an impossible leap day expiration date in *Memento*.

Figure 4.9. Teddy's license plate appears with changed digits to correspond to Leonard's tattoo in *Memento* when the two drive Dodd out of town.

chain of narrative events) in which there is a brief glimpse of Teddy's rear license plate when Leonard and Teddy drive Dodd (Callum Keith Rennie) out of town. Inexplicably, the plate's digits now read SG13 7**1**U (the I has now changed to a one to match Leonard's inaccurate tattoo!). To convince those who would argue that this is simply a continuity error, Duckner also posts scanned images of various iterations of the film's script, containing Nolan's handwritten notes, which confirm that the inconsistency was intentional. Consequently, Duckner's interpretation is predicated on the notion that the director purposely wanted spectators not to be able to trust the film's facts themselves because they have morphed to correspond to the whims of its unreliable protagonist. Following this logic, it once again becomes possible to believe that Leonard actually suffers from anterograde amnesia because even though he copied down the plate's digits inaccurately, the *mise-en-scène* has changed to render the transcription correct. Viewers are left with a conundrum because they too have to discern fact from fiction in a film in which there is no way to delineate between the two. Of course, by unearthing the purported intentions of the auteur, Duckner's reading suggests that the film's "truth" is ultimately knowable. His analysis of the license plate demonstrates that, like many of the contributors to *LOMD*, he believes that his particular interpretation should be accepted because it can be supported by both DVD technology and the discourses of authorship.

Even though some misdirection films contain narrative and formal attributes that appear to challenge classical conventions and are thus unappealing to many audiences, the economic motives for their increased production are clear. At a time in which DVD profits exceeded the box-office take, misdirection films, such as *Memento* and *Mulholland Dr.*, were well-positioned to be repurposed for post-theatrical markets. The viewing and interpretive practices that these films inspire depart from the standard activities of the classical spectator because they practically demand that viewers both watch them countless times in post-theatrical venues and examine them in communal settings to appreciate them to their fullest. However, producers are also careful to assure audiences that these films can ultimately be read classically, even if that may not actually be the case. Such a strategy enabled these films to be marketed as being both novel and familiar. The complex narratives contained in these films are created for a transmedia viewing experience because they effectively migrate viewers across media, which differentiates them from most Hollywood fare. An examination of the comments associated with these films in online fan communities suggests spectators find misdirection films attractive precisely because they believe that it is possible to find definitive answers to all of their mysteries. Interestingly, fans most often make recourse to the discourses of authorship to validate their totalizing accounts of what "actually" happened and why events "really" occurred. Although a number of misdirection films contain non-classical tendencies, interpretive activity in online fan communities reveals that the primary pleasure many viewers derive from them comes from striving to render them classical by discovering how each of their ambiguities can be retrospectively read as being narratively relevant.

5

The Masters of Misdirection

Branding M. Night Shyamalan and Christopher Nolan

As the ardent online analysis of *Memento* (2000) suggests, Christopher Nolan's authorial identity became associated with fervent fan activity in virtual communities at the same time that he began to become a marketable commodity. Despite the critical acclaim for *Memento*, there was no guarantee that Nolan would be able to parlay that film's success into a Hollywood career as a reliable auteur. This is partly because *Memento* was received as being dependent on the gambit of focalizing the narrative through an unreliable protagonist, who might be suffering from short-term memory loss. Roger Ebert, for example, claimed that the "device of telling his story backward, or sort of backward, is simply that—a device," leading him to report that, after re-watching the film, "greater understanding helped on the plot level, but didn't enrich the viewing experience." In addition to trying to avoid subsequently being associated with a narrative gimmick, Nolan had to contend with the fact that M. Night Shyamalan had already become recognized as being the misdirection film genre's preeminent director. By 2000, the remarkable performance of *The Sixth Sense* (1999) was leveraged to promote *Unbreakable* (2000) in auteurist terms as a similarly themed and narratively structured film from a Hollywood wunderkind. At the end of the decade, however, Nolan replaced Shyamalan atop of the genre with the release of *Inception* (2010), the most expensive and profitable Hollywood misdirection film made to date. How and why did such a rapid and unexpected turn of events occur?

By 2008, Shyamalan's once promising future in Hollywood had become a thing of the past. The critical and box-office disappointment of *Lady in the Water* (2006), the first Shyamalan film after *The Sixth Sense* to be a financial letdown, generating only $72 million worldwide theatrically on its $70 million budget, was a blow to the director's industrial standing (imdb.com). His next film, *The Happening* (2008), was almost universally panned by critics, cementing his declining reputation. Although it received terrible reviews, *The Happening* returned Shyamalan to box-office solvency, earning a respectable $63 million domestically and a healthy $163 million worldwide theatrically on its $48 million budget (Mendelson). Yet, studio executives could not bear continuing to advertise Shyamalan as an auteur in the same fashion after two consecutive films received such vitriol from critics. In fact, Shyamalan's two subsequent films—*The Last Airbender* (2010) and *After Earth* (2013)—were the first since the release of *The Sixth Sense*, when he was an unknown commodity, to be promoted with his name no longer featured as the primary draw in their marketing campaigns. In contrast, Christopher Nolan became a Hollywood superstar by 2008 largely because of the tremendous success of his first two installments in the most recent iteration of the *Batman* franchise, especially *The Dark Knight* (2008); however, Nolan did not achieve this lofty status merely by establishing a reputation as Hollywood's latest ruler of the blockbuster film. Instead, as *Time* critic Graeme McMillan summarizes, he has become renowned for making "smart, thought-provoking blockbusters" that do not simply adhere to the Hollywood formula. Nolan's reputation codified in this way, I argue, partly because he filled the void as the misdirection film genre's leading director in the wake of Shyamalan's critical misfires.

In this chapter, I chart the divergent career trajectories of Shyamalan and Nolan. Whereas Shyamalan's differentiation attempts have been disastrous, Nolan's continued linkage to the misdirection film has helped make him one of Hollywood's most powerful filmmakers. After *The Sixth Sense* and until *The Last Airbender*, marketing efforts attempted to distinguish Shyamalan's films and attract a fan following by promoting him as the master of the genre. His reputation began to decline precipitously, however, with *The Village* (2004), his third misdirection film, making it important to assess what transpired in relation to the film's release and in its aftermath. Nolan, however, has achieved great success, at least in part, by continuing to be tied to the genre. Shortly after the start of Shyamalan's demise, Nolan cemented his status as the heir apparent with *The Prestige* (2006), his second widely distributed misdirection film. The choices made on the film's production and promotion unabashedly announced his association with the genre, helping to transform him into its new dominant figure. A comparison of the discourses circulating around these two filmmakers, leading up to and since Nolan supplanted Shyamalan as the king of the misdirection film, reveals how closely genre and authorship are often intertwined in contemporary Hollywood. Consequently, I demonstrate the ways in which the misdirection film has been deployed, with varying effectiveness, to implement one of Hollywood's most reliable schemes for maximizing profit: manufacturing superstar auteurs to create brand-loyal enthusiasts. Such an analysis illustrates just how deeply authorial standing now depends on corresponding industrial strategies.

Nice Package: Product Differentiation and Authorship in Contemporary Hollywood

Authorship has long been a notoriously contentious issue in Film Studies. The story of how directors came to be known as auteurs is exceedingly familiar. The director was initially championed as the auteur by a group of French critics writing for the legendary journal, *Cahiers du Cinéma*, in the late 1940s and 1950s. Incidentally, many of these critics were aspiring filmmakers themselves, who would become members of the influential French New Wave movement. Most of these critics, therefore, had a vested interest in giving the director greater artistic credence than other creative personnel, especially screenwriters, who theretofore typically garnered more significant credit for their creative contributions. Obviously, this intervention ultimately had dramatic ramifications in Hollywood and beyond because many directors are now thought of as the primary artistic force in spite of the highly collaborative nature of commercial filmmaking. Indeed, once these theories about film authorship were relayed by influential English-language critics in the 1960s, most notably Andrew Sarris, the idea of the director as the major creative force on a film gained broader traction. Thanks to critics, like Sarris, directors, particularly those working in the most restrictive industrial conditions, began to become evaluated and ranked artistically based on how their thematic preoccupations and stylistic tendencies were expressed across their output. When the Hollywood Renaissance was at its peak in the early 1970s, it started to become standard practice, rather than the exception, as it was in the studio-era, to advertise a film's director as a main attraction.

On first blush, this recognizable account of film authorship being a product of a series of critical interventions is logical. Although not inaccurate *per se*, it contains omissions about why the notion gained a foothold in Hollywood and film culture. Chief among these exclusions is an acknowledgment of how shifting industrial contexts in Hollywood buttressed the strategic decision to promote directors as auteurs. In the midst of a serious economic crisis, stemming from a steep decline in movie attendance in the 1960s because of a confluence of circumstances, including the impact of the Paramount Decree, the rise of television, mass suburbanization, and so on, Hollywood scrambled to find a remedy. The weakened financial status of the studios leading up to this time made them ripe for takeovers. A wave of mergers and acquisitions thus began at the moment that laid the foundation for the formation of the media conglomerates that now dominate the industry, catalyzing a revised approach to handling creative talent.

This structural change ushered in new business strategies. Gone was a time when Hollywood could rely on vertical integration and its associated (now illegal) practices, like block booking, to ensure the profitability of its films. Accordingly, it no longer made financial sense for the industry to maintain the overhead that it did during the studio era when it relied on multi-picture contracts with creative personnel to control content and costs. To mitigate risk, Hollywood eventually turned to the package-unit mode of production that now characterizes the industry in which creative personnel on individual films are assembled on an ad-hoc basis. This strategy helped resuscitate Hollywood's bottomline in the late 1960s and early 1970s. The production of a series of films, directed primarily by young, film-school educated, directors and targeted at an enormous youth audience, which generated substantial revenues in relation to their small budgets became an ideal, albeit temporary, solution to the industry's financial woes. For the first time in Hollywood history, it was economically advantageous to amplify, rather than conceal, the contributions of the director. Whereas the studios once largely obfuscated directors' impact to curtail their bargaining power in long-term contract negotiations, it now served the industry to promote filmmakers as key players in the package. Directors became valuable commodities for Hollywood, provided that they generated revenues to justify the increasingly exorbitant salaries that they subsequently demanded.

As Timothy Corrigan documents, this industrial shift changed the roles of the director in significant ways. Clearly, it affords executives with a convenient scapegoat when high profile films fall short of financial expectations. Such an impetus was exemplified by what happened to notable Hollywood Renaissance auteurs, such as Francis Ford Coppola and Michael Cimino, held liable by the industry after the artistic freedom they were granted led to purported self-indulgences that resulted in their films going substantially over budget and schedule or disappointing at the box office. It also allows Hollywood to market directors like other presold properties, including stars and genre. Since the classical mode of narration calcified in the late 1910s, the industry has used presold properties, most routinely familiar source material, stars, and genre, to differentiate a largely uniform product line. Although few filmmakers were leveraged to distinguish films during the studio-era, directors are now typically constructed as auteurs by the industry to market difference. As Corrigan writes, "institutional and commercial agencies now work, whatever the filmmaker's intention, to define auteurism as publicity or advertisement or as the dispersal of the control of the auteur into the total flow of television monitors" (50). This "commerce of auteurism," as Corrigan terms it, is Hollywood's *modus operandi* at a time in which it is economically expedient to transform directors into celebrities often on par with the star performers traditionally featured in marketing campaigns.

Even though it may seem that romantic notions of the uncompromising, artistic auteur would contradict the industry's motives in light of the fall of the Hollywood Renaissance and the rise of the blockbuster, promoting directors in this way, whatever their actual roles, still benefits Hollywood. In *New Hollywood Cinema*, Geoff King persuasively argues that there are overlooked industrial continuities that closely link together the Hollywood Renaissance and blockbuster-era, which began in earnest in the mid-1970s and has been the dominant mode of production since the 1980s. Hence, one of the reasons why the ostensibly dissimilar periods are often both referred to as representing the same transition from "Old Hollywood" to "New Hollywood." For King, the fall of the studio system and its replacement with the package-unit is the defining feature connecting the two seemingly dissimilar production trends. In both situations, the industry's primary agenda has been to employ methods to replicate the guaranteed return on investment from the studio-era by devising strategies that ensure profitability. After the end of vertical integration, Hollywood wanted a way to rig economic outcomes, like it did when block booking was standard practice. The temporary solution of the Hollywood Renaissance, then, was doomed to be short-lived, as the baby boom was destined to age and the industry always had its eye on recapturing the mass market, anyway. As media consolidation and the dominance of television subsequently accelerated, blockbuster production, saturation releases, astronomically growing marketing budgets, and the requisite economic logic of synergy became the norm because these tactics are well-suited for the new conglomerate landscape and present significant barriers to entry. Under this model, advertising directors as superstar auteurs serves as another presold property to bolster the big opening weekends necessary to pay off the high-interest loans that underscore perpetually escalating negative costs of the blockbuster model quickly, propel films to generate additional revenue streams in increasingly lucrative ancillary markets, and keep independent players out of the competition.

Of course, Hollywood made spectacle-laden, event films with high production values confected to attract mass audiences to theaters before the dawning of the blockbuster-era. What distinguishes the blockbuster age, though, is that this mode of production is now the central focus of the industry and not the exception. For Warren Buckland, this shift has instigated important changes in how the industry conceives of and packages film authorship. As with King, Buckland, in his study of Steven Spielberg and the blockbuster film, theorizes that the move to the package-unit mode of production is the key to comprehending the new roles of the director. Whereas critics traditionally evaluated auteurs retroactively based on how their artistic signatures were discernable in the films themselves during the studio age and its corresponding producer-unit mode of production, many scholars have rightly determined that authorship is now more accurately linked to how a director's image is constructed, marketed, and managed. Specifically, Buckland posits that the contemporary director "needs to become a power broker, a talent worker (which involves mastery of management skills), and must also create a brand image in order to gain positional advantage over the competition" (24). This is neither to say that textual properties, like thematic preoccupations and stylistic tendencies, are irrelevant in the blockbuster age nor was brand management of directors nonexistent in the studio-era. As scholars, like Robert Kapsis, have shown, there were anomalous directors, such as Alfred Hitchcock, who became marketable commodities before the fall of the studio system because of novel self-promotional efforts across media. Likewise, contemporary auteurs' recognizable textual practices are frequently mobilized, in promotional materials and in the films themselves, to reify their authorial status. The industry's ability to create and maintain a director's distinct brand has become vital to deploying authorship as a presold property that reliably boosts the theatrical take, creates barriers to entry, and sustains strong performance in the aftermarket.

The phenomenon of brand identity management in the blockbuster age is crucial for examining the vastly different fates of Shyamalan and Nolan in relation to the misdirection film. Up until the industry orchestrated a drastic change in Shyamalan's image in 2010 with the *The Last Airbender*, the director's films, from *The Sixth Sense* to *The Happening*, strongly exhibit textual continuities that coincide with traditional notions for assessing studio age authorship. By all of these accounts, even Shyamalan's pre-*Airbender* disappointments bear the hallmarks of an auteur with artistic integrity, rooted in consistent thematic preoccupations and technical acumen that results in distinctly recurrent stylistic tendencies. Yet, as the eventual decision to reconstruct Shyamalan's image shows, this uniformity across his output was not enough to maintain a brand that remained profitable. I contend, then, that the drastic transformation of his reputation is mostly attributable to the misguided promotional tactics that preceded the shift. Perhaps even more interestingly along these lines, is the heretofore failed reconstruction model devised for and by Shyamalan, which is modeled on Nolan's subsequent success in the misdirection film genre. In particular, the strategic decisions to have Shyamalan helm the first installment of a proposed franchise (*The Last Airbender*) and a big budget, sci-fi vehicle for Will Smith (*After Earth*) were attempts to disassociate the director from the misdirection film by having him prove his mettle in other, even more economically viable, blockbuster-era production trends. Such a strategy aligns with Nolan's ascent to superstardom, which is tied to the effective promotion of his aptitude in both the misdirection film genre and blockbuster production. In particular, after experiencing moderate financial success with melding the two in *The Prestige*, Nolan's subsequent genre hybrid, *Inception*, became the most economically successful misdirection film ever made. The following analysis of the authorial discourses surrounding and running through the works of these two filmmakers thus illustrates how the industry markets auteurs in relation to genre to maximize profits in the blockbuster age.

A Surprising Authorial Twist: The Rise and Fall of M. Night Shyamalan

After his first two films, *Praying with Anger* (1992) and *Wide Awake* (1998), barely received theatrical distribution and netted next to nothing at the box office, the incredibly positive response to *The Sixth Sense* primed Shyamalan for authorial superstardom. The film received six Academy Award nominations (two of which, Best Director and Best Original Screenplay, were for Shyamalan himself), critical praise, became a cultural phenomenon, and, most importantly, was a box-office sensation. Although it might have been unreasonable to expect him to replicate those results, *Unbreakable* received generally good reviews, was widely interpreted as a continuation of the director's authorial vision, and turned a small profit at the domestic box office. *Signs* similarly garnered mostly favorable reviews and is Shyamalan's second highest grossing film to date, earning $228 in domestic theaters on its $72 million budget (imdb.com). *The Village* continued Shyamalan's profitable streak, bringing in $114 million domestically on a $60 million budget (imdb.com). Yet, it was his first film since before *The Sixth Sense* to be met with substantial critical scorn, precipitating a string of poor reviews on subsequent films and marking an important turning point in the director's career.

It is difficult to pinpoint why *The Village* had this impact on his reputation because it was profitable and not Shyamalan's first film to be branded in highly authorial terms. His name was previously sold as one of the primary attractions for both *Unbreakable* and *Signs*. As with *Unbreakable*, Shyamalan's name was featured in virtually all promotional materials for *Signs*. In contrast to *Unbreakable*, though, which evoked *The Sixth Sense* in conjunction with Shyamalan when it was uttered in the marketing campaign, the director had become familiar enough to advertise his second post-*Sixth Sense* film simply as "M. Night Shyamalan's *Signs*" in marketing materials, like the theatrical movie poster. The decision to rely on the exact same strategy with "M. Night Shyamalan's *The Village*," then, does not explain why that film experienced such a different critical fate than its immediate predecessors and initiated a sharp decline in the director's authorial standing. Whereas the favorable reception of *Signs* indicates that Disney's tactics to promote the director were well conceived, the critical backlash to *The Village* suggests that something elicited a very different reaction in response to his third misdirection film.

One change in the marketing of *The Village* is the amount of exposure the director himself received in comparison to his previous films. In addition to continuing to feature Shyamalan's name in promotional efforts, Disney capitalized on its television holdings to create a buzz for *The Village*. Just prior to the film's release in 2004, *The Sixth Sense* and *Unbreakable* were programmed on Disney subsidiary ABC in primetime specials. As Kim Owczarski summarizes, the network branded the event as "2 Days of Night," featuring "the presentation of *The Sixth Sense* on April 26 and the network television premiere of *Unbreakable* on May 3. Shyamalan hosted both airings by discussing his latest project and showing trailers and behind-the-scenes footage of *The Village*" (132). Clearly, Disney believed in the director's name and his now familiar persona to sell theatrical tickets as well as further enhance his authorial reputation.

These customary, synergistic marketing tactics were complemented by another, less routine promotional maneuver. Syfy television network (then Sci Fi), at the time a subsidiary of NBC Universal (now Comcast), aired a mockumentary entitled *The Buried Secret of M. Night Shyamalan* (2004) in the days leading up to the release of *The Village*. Importantly, the film was initially not packaged as a mockumentary. Although accounts of exactly what transpired during the making and marketing of the film differ, Shyamalan distanced himself from the mockumentary immediately before and after it appeared. Regardless of whether or not this was an elaborate publicity stunt, it had negative ramifications for Shyamalan's reputation. In the unlikely event that Shyamalan's trepidation was actually legitimate, there were justifiable reasons for his concern. The mockumentary portrays him in Orientalist fashion, as a mystical figure with strange powers, going as far as to suggest that his own biographical details inspired the supernatural elements of his three films released immediately before *The Village*. In particular, the film depicts Shyamalan's childhood as having parallels with primary characters in *The Sixth Sense* and *Unbreakable*. According to the film, the director, like *Unbreakable*'s David Dunn (Bruce Willis), miraculously survived a drowning accident as a child (revealing that, as with Dunn and the aliens in *Signs*, water is his kryptonite) and developed the supernatural ability to communicate with the dead (as in *The Sixth Sense*), as a result. All of this would perhaps not be so bizarre if the mockumentary and the story surrounding its production had been handled differently. As part of its attempt to position the film as nonfiction, rather than as a mockumentary, Syfy "leaked" reports to the Associated Press of Shyamalan's purported desire to disassociate himself from it. Ultimately, Syfy's public relations moves crumbled right before the airing, as network representatives acknowledged that the film and its marketing campaign were a hoax, foreshadowing the kind of trouble that was to come for Shyamalan's branded identity after a subsequent series of similarly miscalculated promotional ploys (Taylor).

Of course, a little-seen mockumentary run on a niche cable channel is not primarily responsible for Shyamalan's rapidly declining marketability. It is indicative, however, of the kinds of ill-advised tactics that contributed to the radical transformation of his reputation. The strong box-office returns from *The Village* suggest that Disney's decision to present it explicitly as an "M. Night Shyamalan" film in virtually all promotional materials did little to hamper its initial box-office returns. If anything, its $50 million opening weekend box-office take suggests that the marketing campaign was initially effective, providing Disney with the quick revenues necessary to reimburse creditors and ensure post-theatrical success (imdb.com). Like many films in the blockbuster-era, in other words, its strong opening weekend performance was mostly attributable to successful advertising. *The Village* struggled subsequently, however, earning only an additional $16 million through its second weekend and just another $7 million at the end of its third weekend in theaters (imdb.com). Such an abrupt drop off at the box office often indicates that the expectations generated by the marketing campaign were not met by the film itself.

The theatrical trailer for *The Village* explicitly positions it as a product of Shyamalan's distinct imagination and implicitly connects the film to his earlier works. Although the primary actors are featured in the trailer's clips from the film itself, their names are never identified in the preview. Instead, the only name mentioned is the director's, as the trailer includes title cards that read "from writer and director M. Night Shyamalan" and "M. Night Shyamalan's *The Village*." Shyamalan's previous successes are also never explicitly uttered in the preview. However, the trailer evokes his association with both *The Sixth Sense* and *Signs* by affiliating it with the horror genre and alerting audiences that suspense will be generated by a mysterious, invading force that threatens primary characters. In contrast to most misdirection film marketing and *Unbreakable*'s promotion, though, it never alludes to the changeover's presence. The decision to package it blatantly as a horror film aligns with the typical advertising strategies for the misdirection film by ostensibly packaging it in familiar genres that do not necessarily encourage retrospective reinterpretations of narrative information. Yet, the choice not to reference its status as a misdirection film even obliquely contradicts the genre's standard promotional tactics. This atypical strategy suggests that Shyamalan had become so closely linked to the genre by the time that *The Village* was released that marketing executives believed his name alone would be more than enough to signal to audiences that it is a misdirection film.

Rapidly declining box-office performance is not only a product of unmet expectations in relation to presold properties like genre. In addition to poor word of mouth that may have stemmed from the film failing to satisfy horror fans because of its PG-13 inspired lack of lurid material or it not being marketed as a misdirection film, negative reviews also strongly contributed to its steeply falling financial trajectory. Overall, reviews of *The Village* were mixed, but many who attacked the film were particularly venomous. Roger Ebert, for example, begins his review by describing the film as "a colossal miscalculation, a movie based on a premise that cannot support it, a premise so transparent it would be laughable were the movie not so deadly solemn." *The Washington Post*'s Stephen Hunter notes that Shyamalan is "riding a one-trick pony and that poor pony is nearly dead" (C1). The one-trick pony that Hunter cites, of course, is Shyamalan's penchant for the changeover. This critique is not entirely accurate because *Signs*, Shyamalan's first film since before *The Sixth Sense* not to contain a changeover, had already interrupted the director's successive misdirection releases. Its unanticipated ending, in which the primary characters thwart an alien invasion, is affiliated with the misdirection film because it reveals how a divine plan imbues seemingly inconsequential events those characters previously experienced with great narrative meaning; however, although *Signs*' ending does inspire audiences to reconsider the narrative functionality of some information, it does not encourage viewers to reinterpret the significance of almost everything that precedes it in the way that the changeovers do in *The Sixth Sense* and *Unbreakable*. Although *Signs* represented a slight departure for Shyamalan, his decision to return to using a pure changeover in *The Village* was not well-received by critics who interpreted it as an ineffective gimmick from a director in need of fresh material. Reviews of *The Village* consistently show that critics were tiring of the changeover formula. Hunter epitomizes this by claiming that "Shyamalan really has to do some reconsidering. His surprises don't work anymore because we expect them. It was his obscurity, his lack of reputation that made the ending of *The Sixth Sense* so unforgettably jolting" (C1).

Yet, the consistent presence of significant narrative surprise is one aspect that should have *helped* rather than hindered Shyamalan's reputation as an auteur, according to traditional approaches. Indeed, it was employed as a quintessential and successful authorial calling card for Shyamalan on *Unbreakable* because the director's connection to the changeover had already became recognizable enough to sell his films almost on its own. I say almost because, as with *Unbreakable*, Shyamalan's name shared billing with *Signs*' star, Mel Gibson, in the marketing campaign. For *The Village*, however, virtually all promotional materials followed the logic of the trailer by featuring Shyamalan's name as the sole draw. This was not because the film was devoid of marketable actors, as it starred Sigourney Weaver, William Hurt, Joaquin Phoenix, and Adrien Brody, fresh off his Best Actor Oscar win for *The Pianist* (2002). None of these actors were cast as the film's lead, though. Instead, relative newcomer, Bryce Dallas Howard, Ron Howard's daughter, played the protagonist, Ivy Walker. Although Howard's first leading Hollywood role received heavy media coverage, her name and image were absent in most of the film's promotions. This decision was connected to fears about her bankability as an unknown actress in spite of her marketable genealogy. Rather than gamble on Howard or promote the ensemble, Disney exclusively foreground Shyamalan's name in *The Village*'s marketing campaign, contributing to the direct backlash against the filmmaker after its negative reception.

Compounding matters was Shyamalan's choice to cast himself as the character who exposed the changeover to audiences in *The Village*. Shyamalan previously used the cameo in Hitchcockian fashion partly as a self-promotional maneuver to familiarize audiences with his image. He also deployed the device in cleverly self-reflexive ways to comment on his outsider status as a South Asian living in white, American culture and working in Hollywood, exemplified by his brief turns as an incompetent physician in *The Sixth Sense* and an alleged drug dealer in *Unbreakable*. These unlikable characters helped endear Shyamalan to audiences by making it seem as though he did not take himself too seriously and was unafraid to comment on the prejudice that South Asian Americans face, albeit tangentially. Shyamalan continued to develop his onscreen persona with *Signs* by casting himself as Ray Reddy, the man revealed to be responsible for the tragic and accidental death of the protagonist, Graham Hess's (Mel Gibson) wife, which leads to the existential crisis that provokes the film's classical quest narrative for the widower to regain his faith in his profession as a reverend. Although Shyamalan again plays an unlikable individual in *Signs*, his character is different than its immediate predecessors. Most significantly, his part in *Signs* is more than just a peripheral cameo because of Reddy's key narrative role. In particular, Reddy's apology to Hess for his part in his wife's accidental death and his hypothesis that the aliens are afraid of water help to tie all of the ostensibly random occurrences together at the end. This narratively significant role in a hit film helped make Shyamalan more recognizable than ever before, giving Disney the confidence to cultivate his growing authorial persona further to promote his next film. Such success not only resulted in more prominent use of his name in advertisements. It also encouraged Shyamalan to cast himself in similarly narratively significant roles in *The Village* and *Lady in the Water*.

In *The Village*, Shyamalan reverts to a smaller cameo because his brief appearance does not occur until near the end of the film, during its changeover sequence. Moreover, the director strategically chose not to feature his image prominently in front of the camera. Specifically, he plays an unfriendly park ranger who obliquely explains to a security guard surreptitiously helping Ivy, and, by extension to the viewer, what has really been happening. Their discussion reveals that Ivy and the members of her community actually exist in contemporary American society, but have just been living in secret in her family's Walker Wildlife Preserve, shielding them from outsiders. This changeover forces the spectator to realize that her ostensible pre-modern reality is actually a fabrication. It shows that the alternative community that her father, Edward Walker (William Hurt), and the other "elders" seeking a utopic refuge from violent American society created was deliberately constructed to shelter their offspring, explaining why the founders engage in farcical rituals to scare their children about fictional bogeymen in the surrounding woods.

The changeover, then, can be read as more than just a narrative gimmick because of its possible links to similar scare tactics enacted by the George W. Bush administration in the aftermath of 9/11. For some critics and fans, the changeover inspired a retrospective reinterpretation that connected it to contemporary U.S. culture in precisely this way, a thematic concern that Shyamalan began exploring in *Signs*, his first post-9/11 film, which also presents paranoid reactions to the threat of shadowy, invading others. *Chicago Reader* critic, Ben Sachs, for instance, posits that *The Village*'s twist ending "recasts it as allegory" because the director described it as "his 'post-9/11 film,' " making the changeover "more provocative if read as an indirect critique of the Bush administration's war on terror." The changeover is thus significant not only for being precipitated by Shyamalan's character, but also because it moves the film into possible master key territory by potentially imbuing what precedes it with symbolic meaning related to the cultural context in which it was produced and received.

Shyamalan's formal choices during the changeover also have implications for his authorial brand because they suggest that he wanted to return to a more traditional cameo in *The Village*. To wit, he is shot from behind the head, reading *The Philadelphia Inquirer*, making him identifiable only through his voice, a fleeting reflection in a glass door, and his authorial links to his hometown. Although Shyamalan does not occupy as much screen time as he does in *Signs*, his role is even more narratively important than it is in that film, and especially than it is in *The Sixth Sense* and *Unbreakable*, in which his appearances serve a primary narrative function of comic relief for those in the know. This overlap between Shyamalan the filmmaker and Shyamalan the onscreen persona strongly underscored his connection to the changeover, which marketers for *The Village* hoped would be evoked exclusively by his name. In this instance, he was actually the one delivering the device to which he had become inextricably linked. Such a conflation between Shyamalan the character and Shyamalan the directorial master of the changeover provoked a shift in his reputation when the device was poorly received.

Mixed reviews for *The Village* were not enough, though, to prevent Buena Vista (a Disney subsidiary) from continuing to promote Shyamalan's association with the misdirection film in the aftermarket. The blurb on the back cover of the DVD version, for instance, links the director to other masters of the misdirection film by claiming that the film "ranks with the best of Hitchcock." It also advertises its array of special features, which includes clips starring "M. Night Shyamalan—That Reveal Clues To The Movie's Twists and Turns." Obviously, good overall box-office returns convinced executives that Shyamalan's authorial standing had been preserved despite some poor reviews since audiences seemed to respond favorably to the theatrical marketing campaign. In the end, *The Village* performed well globally, garnering an additional $144 million internationally in theaters, exceeding its respectable domestic take (boxofficemojo.com). The fact that Shyamalan's name was again used as a main attraction for his next film, *Lady in the Water*, is a testament to the confidence that remained in his authorial brand despite the often unfavorable critical reception of *The Village*.

If *The Village* signaled potential trouble for the Shyamalan brand, *Lady in the Water* unequivocally inflicted serious damage from which the director has yet to recover. As with *The Village*, *Lady in the Water* was marketed by positioning Shyamalan as the film's biggest star, though it represented a return to having the director share billing with other creative personnel. Although the theatrical trailer copies the tactics from *The Village* by explicitly mentioning Shayamalan's name only, print ads for *Lady in the Water* generally positioned the director as being part of a package with the film's lead performers. The theatrical movie poster, for instance, prominently depicts Bryce Dallas Howard's face, yet her and her costar Paul Giamatti's names are situated below the director's, as his name is featured atop of the poster in a larger font than the actors, advertising it as "A Film by M. Night Shyamalan." Howard's and Giamatti's names then appear below the image of Howard and above the film's title and tagline, which reads "Time is running out for a happy ending." This prototypical promotional artifact illustrates that there were minor changes in the marketing strategy after *The Village* because the director's penchant for unexpected endings and the stars were again more explicitly packaged as major selling points.

The return to the previously successful marketing campaign strategy for Shyamalan's films on *Lady in the Water* concealed a sordid production history that has become contemporary Hollywood legend. Shyamalan claims he initially got the idea for *Lady in the Water* based on a bedtime fairytale that he created for his daughters about what happens in their backyard pool, which he also turned into a children's book of the same name that was published in conjunction with the film's theatrical release (Sampson). Such a project seems ideal for Disney's family-oriented and synergistic logic. Yet, *Lady in the Water* was the director's first film since before *The Sixth Sense* not to be distributed by the media conglomerate. Disney had initially agreed to back the project; however, it was ultimately distributed by Warner Bros. after Shyamalan had a disagreement with executive, Nina Jacobson, his longtime advocate at the media conglomerate.

The details of the Shyamalan and Jacobson kerfuffle were chronicled in another unwise publicity ploy leading up to *Lady in the Water*'s release that resembles Syfy's mockumentary for *The Village*. *Sports Illustrated* columnist Michael Bamberger penned an obsequious biography entitled, *The Man Who Heard Voices: Or, How M. Night Shyamalan Risked His Career on a Fairy Tale*, published just days before the film hit domestic theaters. In the book, Bamberger presents the circumstances that led to the film eventually being released by Warner Bros. instead of Disney. Purportedly out of concern for the script's confidentiality and because he insists on working out of Philadelphia instead of Los Angeles, Shyamalan had a personal assistant hand-deliver it to Jacobson in Hollywood. Shyamalan reportedly got angry when he learned that she was unable to read it immediately because of family obligations and then disputed her revision suggestions after she did review it. Even though Disney subsequently agreed to let him proceed with the production without making all of the edits, the director was upset enough to shop around the script. In light of his outstanding track record at the box office and eager to house the then-valuable Shyamalan brand, Warner Bros. agreed to back the film. Stunningly, Disney was so concerned about the situation that they subsequently fired Jacobson, even though her reservations would be confirmed by the film's box-office disappointment (Whipp U6).

One of Jacobson's biggest problems with the script was Shyamalan's ego-driven decision to cast himself in a more prominent role than he had in any of his films since before *The Sixth Sense* (Whipp U6). In *Lady in the Water*, Shyamalan plays Vick Ran, one of the apartment tenants of The Cove, a Philadelphia-area apartment complex, where a mystical creature named Story (Bryce Dallas Howard) magically appears. In turn, she relies on Vick and the other apartment denizens, most notably the complex's superintendent, Cleveland Heep (Paul Giamatti), to help her return to her native land. Like most of the apartment dwellers, Vick is initially reluctant to help. In *Signs* fashion, however, the unexpected ending reveals that he and the other Cove residents all live there for a fateful reason because they actually have unrealized special talents that they each need to deploy for her safe return. *Lady in the Water*, therefore, was Shyamalan's second film since *The Sixth Sense* not to contain a changeover because its big twists instead function like the ones in *Signs*, rendering allusions to the film's status as a misdirection film in promotional materials misleading. As it relates to Vick's hidden talent, specifically, he is portrayed as an aspiring author suffering from writer's block, whose book, Story reveals, needs to be written for her to return because it will eventually save the world, though, she claims he will be assassinated because of its ideas. Also disconcerting to Jacobson was Shyamalan's decision to depict a film critic, Harry Farber (Bob Balaban), as an idiot incapable of drawing correct interpretations about the world around him, which puts the film's other primary characters in grave danger (Whipp U6). As a consequence of his ineptitude, Farber is horrifically killed. Clearly, Shyamalan was not short on confidence after some critics dinged him for *The Village*. The decisions to portray Faber as he did and cast himself as a heroic martyr, who prevents the apocalypse with his unappreciated brilliance, indicate that the director hoped to highlight the inability of critics to understand his previous films fully.

Unsurprisingly, *Lady in the Water* was slammed by critics upon its release. The sometimes brutal disdain Shyamalan received for *The Village* pales in comparison to the almost universal disgust from reviewers about *Lady in the Water*. More than anything else, it was the director's decision to cast himself as the savior that made critics attack Shyamalan. Michael Booth of *The Denver Post* typifies this tendency by writing that "Shyamalan has sucked way too hard on the tailpipe of his fearsome publicity machine" and is "Blinded by his own aura." *Slate*'s Dana Stevens is even more vicious, as she claims that "*Lady in the Water* marks Shyamalan's official leap off the deep end" and that the director "appears to have completely lost his marbles." Michael Atkinson of *The Village Voice* similarly wonders if Shyamalan "has lost his mind" and then rails against the director's narrative signature by noting that "It's beginning to chafe as a formula . . . Authorial vision is a non-issue, in the face of so much rootless, repetitive mumbo jumbo." For Mick LaSalle of the *San Francisco Chronicle*, the film was indisputably Shyamalan's alone, as he asserts that it "has the strengths and weaknesses of a one-man show," but ultimately notes that Shyamalan is misguided for making artistic originality a central theme "in a movie that's a dead ringer for [his] last two efforts." Finally, James Berardinelli of *Reelviews* declares that *Lady in the Water* is "the biggest misfire of M. Night Shyamalan's career, including his pre-*Sixth Sense* movies" and warns "For those who thought Shyamalan was stretching it in *The Village*, you ain't seen nothing yet." Although Berardinelli apparently ignores the big twists that unite all the characters by claiming that the film only contains "several minor misdirections," he does not believe that such a change will prevent "whatever luster still remains to Shyamalan's reputation" from being completely removed by *Lady in the Water*.

The overwhelmingly negative reaction from critics and box-office disappointment did not stop Fox from subsequently backing Shyamalan and packaging his next film, *The Happening*, in auteurist terms. Like his other post-*Sixth Sense* releases up until then, *The Happening* was marketed as a product of the director's distinct artistic vision. The theatrical trailer, for instance, contains a title card that explicitly marks it as "An M. Night Shyamalan Film." It subsequently presents title cards, though, that suggest marketers were growing weary of Shyamalan's bankability because it directly references his highest revenue generating films by identifying him as "Writer and Director of *The Sixth Sense*" and "*Signs*." Additionally, at the end of the trailer, star Mark Wahlberg's name is featured in a title card even though he had already been the centerpiece of the assorted film clips comprising the preview. Such decisions reveal that industry executives' faith in Shyamalan's ability to sell the film on his brand alone had waned because the preview for *The Happening* explicitly mentioned the name of the film's primary star for the first time since the trailer for *Signs* as well as linked Shyamalan directly to his biggest box-office hits, *The Sixth Sense* and *Signs*, instead of assuming his identity alone sufficed.

There was an even larger shift in the way *The Happening* was promoted differently than Shyamalan's preceding films. Likely in response to perceived issues with mismatched generic expectations, it was blatantly advertised as Shyamalan's first R-rated film in some promotional materials. Although the trailer does not accentuate this aspect explicitly, it is peppered with horrific images of death, such as people jumping off buildings, that are not only frightening because of their visceral impact, but also because they evoke footage of the World Trade Center suicides recorded during the 9/11 attacks. The film, therefore, was still packaged in auteurist terms despite the growing reservations about Shyamalan's fading brand. For starters, even though the film is ostensibly about nature taking revenge on humanity for destroying the planet, it marks a thematic return to *The Village*'s allegorical representation of post-9/11 U.S. culture by consistently referencing the events of that day in its imagery and narrative. It centers on unearthing the reasons for the mystifying and terrifying mass deaths that begin on an otherwise mundane Tuesday (the same day of the week as the actual 9/11 events) morning in New York City, which are initially believed to be the result of a terrorist attack, and eventually lead the film's primary, Philadelphia-based characters to

Figure 5.1. Superimposed title from opening scenes of *The Happening* that detail the time and place of the horrific mass suicides that stem from a yet-to-be-determined cause.

flee to rural Pennsylvania, the site of the final 9/11 plane crash. It also explicitly linked Shyamalan back to the horror film, the genre to which his previous box-office smashes had been most clearly connected. As with those films, *The Happening* was similarly marketed as a horror film that would generate suspense from an unknown force threatening its primary characters, with the additional promise that it would meet those expectations this time because its R-rating would enable Shyamalan to produce terror in a more gruesome manner than he did in *The Village*.

Reviewers did not respond in ways that suggest the marketing plan was effective. For many critics, *The Happening* represented a nadir in Shyamalan's career from which he might not recover. In his review, *Time*'s Richard Corliss opines that "M. Night Shyamalan has lost the touch that made *The Sixth Sense* a suspense classic and his standing as a young master of creepiness in the grand Hitchcock tradition. He's just 37, but his best films are so far behind him, it's as if he's forgotten how he made them work." Kyle Smith of the *New York Post* is just as harsh, as he bashes the film and then situates it in auteurist terms by characterizing "the oeuvre of M. Night Shyamalan since *The Sixth Sense*" as "stupid ending, stupid ending, stupid ending and, in a change of pace with his last film *Lady in the Water*, stupid all the way through." Similarly, the *Newark Star-Ledger*'s Stephen Whitty believes that *The Happening* denotes the end of Shyamalan's career as a bankable director. Echoing the sentiments of others about the film's ineffective marketing, Whitty claims that "*The Happening* was supposed to mark a fresh start" by "being almost defiantly rated R, as if to signal Shyamalan's decision to move away from subtler PG-13 films" and because "Shyamalan had been complaining he was tired of being known as the writer with the 'twist'—indicating that this story would try something riskier." Whitty ultimately notes that had "Shyamalan been serious about getting an R-rating, then he should have pushed the material in disturbing ways; if he wanted to eschew easy 'twists' then he should have embraced chaotic, even existential turns of the plot."

As these reviews demonstrate, *The Happening* was received by critics as anything but a departure from form for Shyamalan. His decision to pander to his detractors by incorporating more disturbing material to get an R-rating did little to change opinions about his continued inability to produce genuine fear in his audience. Although the film depicts numerous gruesome and imaginative suicides, especially in its opening sequences, reviewers still largely agreed with critics, like Whitty, who believed that it failed to generate sufficient terror. Additionally, his strategic choice not to incorporate a twist at the end that completely resolves all causal lines of action unexpectedly, regardless of if it is a changeover or not, did nothing to lessen his now detrimental connection to the misdirection film. Yet, it is inaccurate to claim that *The Happening* contains an ending that aligns it with the director's previous, post-*The Sixth Sense* films. In particular, just after it appears all causal lines of action have been satisfactorily resolved because the threats posed to characters have been thwarted, the film cuts to an eerily prescient concluding scene in relation to the actual spread of al-Qaeda and ISIS sponsored terrorism since 9/11, as the mass suicides that mysteriously ended in the United States have suddenly started to impact people in Paris. Rather than show what occurs next in Europe or around the globe, the film abruptly cuts to the end credits, making *The Happening* Shyamalan's most pessimistic and ambiguous film to date. Unlike the similarly gloomy *Unbreakable*, which also has a threat to humanity triumph in the end, there is no epilogue in *The Happening* to suggest that order is ultimately restored. In contrast to most reviewer accounts, then, *The Happening* actually represents a significant shift for Shyamalan because it was his first film to contain a concluding twist that amplified lingering narrative uncertainty instead of retrospectively resolving all causal lines of action classically.

The Happening thus seems to signal Shyamalan's effort to begin orchestrating a transformation of his image to salvage his brand. Undoubtedly, many of his auteurist signatures remain, such as his insistence on

Figure 5.2. *The Happening*'s conclusion, depicting the spread of the mass suicides, which have mysteriously ended in the U.S., to Paris, where they inexplicably restart.

setting the film in the Philadelphia region, featuring an unknown menace that threatens the primary characters, casting himself in an unlikable cameo role (this time Shyamalan plays a man trying to court the protagonist's wife, but viewers only hear his voice), and so on. In spite of these similarities, his decisions to present more graphic images to elicit horror and abandon his signature twist ending that inspires a classical reinterpretation are notable divergences from the director's *Sixth Sense*-inspired filmmaking formula. The continuities outweighed the differences, however, as critics received it as anything but an actual tangible change of direction for Shyamalan.

The remarkable shift engineered for the making and marketing of Shyamalan's next film, *The Last Airbender*, reveals that consistent critical derision mixed with poor authorial marketing strategies and the financial disaster of *Lady in the Water* had tarnished Shyamalan's reputation beyond repair in the minds of executives. Shyamalan was hired by Viacom's Paramount film division to make *The Last Airbender* because of the media conglomerate's synergistic desire to transform its subsidiary, Nickelodeon's, successful animated children's show, *Avatar: The Last Airbender* (2005–2008), into a film franchise. Although the project appeared to be largely unrelated to Shyamalan's previous films on the surface, there was potential to evoke his authorial brand in the marketing campaign because of previous efforts to promote *Lady in the Water* as a fairytale for family audiences. Of course, that film's failure made executives reticent to associate the director with it in advertisements for *The Last Airbender*. His name was still deemed marketable enough, however, to feature it in promotional materials, such as the theatrical movie poster, which positions *The Last Airbender* as an "M. Night Shyamalan Film," albeit in small font, much less prominently than for any of his other previous films after *The Sixth Sense*. The film's teaser trailer similarly highlights the director's involvement, as it packaged it as being "From M. Night Shyamalan" from that preview's opening shot.

The attachment of Shyamalan's name to the film in spite of his recent failures was a calculated gamble. *The Last Airbender* was initially conceived of as the first installment in a trilogy that was to be helmed by Shyamalan. Executives had so much faith in the proposed franchise that Shyamalan was given an $150 million production budget for *The Last Airbender*, his largest to date, and an additional $130 million was reportedly spent on the film's marketing (imdb.com). Although such a risk seems misguided in hindsight in light of the film's extremely poor critical reception, it made sense in relation to recent Hollywood trends. Despite being lambasted by critics and failing to recover its production costs at the domestic box office, the film ended up grossing over $300 million internationally, revealing why executives were willing to invest so much in the project and in Shyamalan (imdb.com). In particular, the industry is especially keen on developing big-budget, franchise films with international legs, adapted from presold properties with recognizable directors attached, such as Peter Jackson's critically acclaimed, box-office smash, *The Lord of the Rings* trilogy. Even more notable in this regard was the incredible performance of *The Dark Knight*, the second film in Nolan's *Batman* trilogy, which garnered over $1 billion worldwide at the box office (imdb.com). Considering the exploding popularity of Nolan's brand at the time, it is logical that executives attempted to capitalize on a similar marketing approach for Shyamalan by positioning him as a director also capable of making both cerebral, challenging fare, like misdirection films, and blockbuster franchises.

Ever conscious of his authorial reputation, Shyamalan contributed to these rebranding efforts in ways that made it seem as though he was not compromising his artistic integrity by transitioning to franchise production and the blockbuster formula. In numerous promotional statements, Shyamalan reiterated that he became aware of the Nickelodeon series on which the *The Last Airbender* is based because his daughters were fans of the show and the fairytale aspects were attractive to him. Additionally, in an interview with *The Telegraph*'s Philip Horne, Shyamalan expands on the source material's appeal by noting that "There are Asian themes" and that it allowed him to depict aspects of his "life that [he] hasn't talked about," such as the "need for family," the ecological disasters that humanity is precipitating, and discovering "the reasons each of us are born." Of course, this self-promotional discourse is unreliable, as the thematic concerns that he claims are unique to *The Last Airbender* are featured in his preceding films. Such contradictory assertions indicate a central tension that helped damage Shyamalan's brand. On one hand, the director wants to sustain his reputation as a traditional auteur. Expressing frustration with the reception of his authorial intentions, Shyamalan told Aseem Chhabra of the *Mumbai Mirror* that he "just doesn't get it" and must be "speaking a different language" because he makes films "with great respect, integrity, and effort." Yet, on the other hand, he also tells Chhabra that if his "name is on top" of the movies "that means they are doomed."

Shyamalan's contradictory self-awareness suggests that he is fully cognizant of how the construction of his authorial reputation contributed to his demise. In other interviews surrounding *The Last Airbender*, he even identifies the culprit explicitly. Shyamalan told *The Philadelphia Inquirer*'s Stephen Rea, for example, that "It's the presentation of the movies as author-driven . . . Here in the United States that comes with a stigma of hubris."

Repeating these opinions, the director explained to Mark Naglazas of *The Western Australian* that he "has been cut down to size because American audiences are still not comfortable with the idea of the auteur" (TOD 6). These assertions suggest that the rebranding efforts orchestrated by and for Shyamalan in an attempt to repackage him as a franchise filmmaker did not go far enough to disassociate the director from his earlier releases and the authorial legend that calcified in response. As a consequence of keeping his name on the promotional materials and positioning the film as affiliated thematically with the rest of his oeuvre, audiences and critics received *The Last Airbender* as another disappointment from a director who had lost his touch and was only able to make misdirection films. Undoubtedly, *The Last Airbender* was constructed to represent a substantial shift for Shyamalan, as it is his first post-*Sixth Sense* film not to have significant plot twists, to be adapted from a presold property, set somewhere other than the Philadelphia region, and so on. These changes, however, were not enough to counter Shyamalan's status as a director incapable of anything other than the same tired, changeover formula.

Shyamalan's belated transition to blockbuster-style production collapsed after the originally proposed *The Last Airbender* sequels were shelved in favor of Sony's *After Earth*. *After Earth* continued the trend of the director getting bashed by critics even though his name went unmentioned in the marketing campaign, and it represented another departure from his post-*Sixth Sense* filmmaking template by embracing the blockbuster. *After Earth* also returned him to box-office disaster for the first time since *Lady in the Water*, as the film only garnered $60 million domestically on its $135 million production and estimated $100 million marketing budgets (imdb.com). Shyamalan shouldered most of the blame for *After Earth*'s failure despite production history evidence that suggests the director had less creative clout than in the past. The film's treatment was written by its star, Will Smith, and Shyamalan claims that he agreed to make the movie when the actor "called him for his birthday," they "talked about his son Jaden's acting career," and he presented the director "a 45 second version of a story that just clicked" (Hiscock). Such circumstances are a testament to just how drastic the attempts to revise Shyamalan's reputation were at the time, as his comparatively limited artistic input on the production is a far cry from the kind of original screenplay project that established his industrial cachet as a coveted writer/director. After two successive disasters, the blockbuster rebranding strategy was abandoned. Shyamalan himself noted that "while there was a lot more action" in *After Earth* than any of his other films, he now wants "to try to make smaller movies based on [his] experiences with this one" (Hiscock). Consequently, Shyamalan's next projects were his first foray into television, the current Fox series, *Wayward Pines* (2015–), and *The Visit* (2015), a micro-budgeted $5 million film (imdb.com). In the end, Shyamalan has been unable to undo the marketing tactics that inextricably connected him solely to the misdirection film, and executives are still trying to find a way to untangle him from that negative association.

Authorial Hybridity: Christopher Nolan as Indie Auteur for the Blockbuster Age

In contrast with Shyamalan, Nolan has not become exclusively associated to the misdirection film. Although this is partially attributable to his desires to stay behind the camera instead of also appearing in front of it and eschew ill-conceived publicity stunts designed to augment his authorial legend, it is mostly a consequence of production and marketing strategies better suited for contemporary industrial contexts than those linked to Shyamalan. Rather than immediately capitalize on his connection to the misdirection film after *Memento*, Nolan delayed his return to the genre by directing two films more aligned with New Hollywood's focus on remakes and franchises: *Insomnia* (2002), an adaptation of a 1997 Norwegian film of the same name and *Batman Begins*, the inaugural film in his superhero trilogy as well as his first film co-financed by Syncopy, the production company started by the director and his wife, Emma Thomas. These decisions have helped both inoculate Nolan from the sorts of critiques that have plagued Shyamalan and made him the most renowned director of the misdirection film genre.

Whereas Shyamalan met expectations by immediately following-up *The Sixth Sense* with another project that directly mobilized that film's most distinctive qualities, many reviewers were surprised by Nolan's choice to direct more mainstream-style fare after he established a reputation as a narrative innovator with *Following* (1998) and *Memento*. *Time*'s Richard Schickel exemplifies such reception by noting that *Insomnia* "does not tell its story backward" because directors are "allowed one gimmick that sensational per career" and that the film's narrative unexpectedly unfolds "rather conventionally, almost ploddingly." John Powers of *LA Weekly* agrees and also identifies a potential motive for the shift by claiming that fans of Nolan's first two features will likely be disappointed by this "conventional thriller without any of the time-jump shenanigans that gave *Memento* its special kick," but sees value in "his honorable, old-Hollywood knack for making entertainments geared to an intelligent audience." These typical responses to *Insomnia* appear to do anything but set up Nolan for the kind of authorial brand recognition constructed by and for Shyamalan in the wake of *The Sixth Sense*. Instead, *Insomnia* positioned Nolan as a budding studio-style director, willing to shed his arthouse reputation in favor of more customary fare. Industrially, the film established him as more than an indie director by earning generally positive reviews and netting a respectable $114 million global theatrical return on its modest $46 million budget (imdb.com). More importantly, it demonstrated that Nolan was capable of helming a more traditional Hollywood product, replete with A-level talent, including Al Pacino, Robin Williams, and Hilary Swank.

Nolan's post-*Memento* industrial savvy is best exhibited by his shrewd decision to use Syncopy to co-produce all of his films after *Insomnia*. As King documents in *New Hollywood Cinema*, the lots of auteurs during the late 1970s and 1980s is instructive for understanding how authorship actually functions in the blockbuster age. Building on the work of scholars like Jon Lewis and Corrigan, who both detail the reasons for Coppola's spectacular decline after his tremendous success in the early 1970s, King argues that the director's demise was most attributable to poorly conceived industrial strategies in relation to New Hollywood's changing economic logic. Specifically, he juxtaposes Coppola's short-lived Zoetrope Studio, as a haven for both filmmakers bent on preserving their artistic integrity and developing alternative distribution strategies, with directors, like George Lucas and Steven Spielberg, who founded production companies more congruent with Hollywood's financial motives and standard business practices. While Coppola's studio dovetailed with traditional notions of authorship being linked to consistent thematic preoccupations, stylistic tendencies, and artistic freedom, Lucas's Industrial Light and Magic concentrated on producing technical expertise, particularly special effects, for any Hollywood film, and Spielberg's Amblin Entertainment gave him the flexibility to serve as an executive producer on projects directed by other filmmakers as well as synergistically leverage his branded identity across a conglomerate's media holdings, especially television. Such tales of artistic success and failure relate directly to the fates of Nolan and Shyamalan decades later in an industry still governed by the same blockbuster economic logic. While Shyamalan has struggled to discard his seemingly unshakable, conventionally constructed authorial reputation and has used his own production company, Blinding Edge Pictures, only to co-finance films he directed, Nolan has thrived as an auteur and as a businessman adept at producing his own films and the works of others.

Although Syncopy was founded by Nolan and his wife in 2001, the company did not serve as a producer on *Insomnia*. It was not until the 2005 release of *Batman Begins* that the company co-produced its first film. After proving himself capable of helming studio-style production, Nolan further delayed his return to the misdirection film by instead next agreeing to direct an updated installment of the once-lucrative *Batman* franchise that had been temporarily abandoned after the box-office and critical disaster of *Batman & Robin* (1997), which failed to recuperate even its $125 million production budget at the domestic box office (imdb.com). The tenuous state of the *Batman* films and of superhero franchises in general at the time is important to stress now that they have become the centerpiece of contemporary blockbuster filmmaking. Although the success of misdirection veteran Bryan Singer's *X-Men* (2000) and *X2* (2003) as well as the first two installments of Sam Raimi's *Spiderman* franchise in 2002 and 2004 signaled the potential for recently established auteurs to transition into the highly commercialized genre, the disappointment of Ang Lee's *Hulk* (2003) was cause for concern in relation to attempts to revive the severely damaged *Batman* brand. Perhaps this partially explains why Nolan received no guarantee from Time Warner subsidiary, Legendary Pictures, which co-produced the film, to make the requisite sequels that would revive the franchise after his first attempt. In fact, when asked by *New York Times* reporter Dave Itzkoff if he always had planned to follow up his *Batman* installments with films outside of the franchise, Nolan replied that "he's only ever done one film at a time" and initially "had no thoughts of doing a sequel at all" ("A Man"). Regardless of the veracity of these claims, the spacing between the *Batman* films indicates that there was no agreement for him to make additional films for the franchise immediately after *Batman Begins*.

In spite of any reservations that may have existed about Nolan's potential fit for reviving the *Batman* brand, the success of *Insomnia* and the creation of his own production company to co-finance the project gave Legendary Pictures enough confidence that he was ready to manage a blockbuster film that might ignite a resurrection of the franchise. They agreed to help back the $150 million budget for *Batman Begins*. The wager worked, as the film grossed $374 million globally in theaters (imdb.com). Although this revenue generation was impressive, it is nowhere near the enormous profit margins garnered by Nolan's two subsequent sequels in the franchise. The success of the sequels is partially attributable to savvy production strategies. Rather than copy the successful *The Lord of the Rings* trilogy's model, in which Jackson's three installments were unprecedentedly produced all at once and released in uninterrupted succession, the two misdirection films, *The Prestige* and *Inception*, that solidified Nolan as the genre's new master were interspersed between the *Batman* sequels. Moreover, as opposed to the standard production tactic set by other Indiewood directors, such as Steven Soderbergh and Richard Linklater, who oscillate between higher-budgeted classical fare and cheaper films with arthouse sensibilities, Nolan has leveraged his

Hollywood standing since *The Prestige* to finance original projects with increasing negative costs, culminating most recently in *Interstellar*'s huge $165 million production budget (imdb.com). This is notable because it highlights Nolan's unique status as a director renowned for his ability to blend narrative complexity with mass appeal, making him not exclusively linked to the misdirection film. Indeed, the most frequent criticism of his films—their extensive expository dialogue that caters to the masses—exemplifies Nolan's efforts to capture both arthouse viewers with narrative innovation and blockbuster fans alienated by radical experimentation or a filmmaking formula that is deemed too narrow for a wide audience.

Whereas virtually all promotional materials for *Insomnia*, such as the trailer and movie posters, explicitly emphasized that the film was "From the Director of *Memento*," references to Nolan were left off of a majority of the advertisements for *Batman Begins*. This runs counter to New Hollywood's tendency to highlight any element of the package that can bolster the theatrical take, which is especially salient considering that Nolan's two previous films were successful at the box office and generally liked by critics. Consequently, the conspicuous absence of his name is an indication that executives aimed to preserve the director's still tenuous reputation as an arthouse innovator and were unsure that he would be able to make the transition to blockbuster filmmaking without jeopardizing his status as a marketable, indie commodity. Despite these concerns, the trailer does feature some of the thematic preoccupations and stylistic tendencies that were already evident in Nolan's films, like his penchant for setting parts of his films in snowy mountainous regions, focusing on the links between obsession and revenge, as well as his protagonists' battles with past traumas that haunt them and their pining for lost women. Most importantly, however, the preview centers on the film's convoluted narrative structure. Perhaps the most novel aspect of Nolan's first installment in the franchise was his decision to use a complex, flashback-laden narrative structure that is atypical of blockbuster production. In classical fashion, this risky choice was made compositionally motivated because *Batman Begins* presents the origin story of Bruce Wayne's (Christian Bale) development of his superhero alter-ego, making its constant temporal shifts, such as those referencing his childhood, subservient to narrative demands. As it relates to his authorial standing, however, it was a cunning move by Nolan to maintain the burgeoning reputation he had cultivated as a narrative experimenter capable of satisfying a mass audience that can be easily alienated by departures from classical standards.

Reviews of *Batman Begins* reveal that the critical establishment largely received the film as an effective mix of blockbuster and arthouse qualities, which had great potential to spawn sequels. Lisa Schwarzbaum of *Entertainment Weekly*, for instance, writes that the film, "directed by indie-oriented storyteller Christopher Nolan (*Memento*) is a triumph—a confidently, original, engrossing interpretation . . . that announces, from the get-go, someone who knows what he is doing is running the show, and he's modestly unafraid to do something new." Schwarzbaum then ends the review by proclaiming that the world the director created "is a vertiginous time warp where only a risk-taking artist can navigate. Nolan ought to get back there soon and tell us what happens next." LaSalle concurs, noting that "the film adopts an elegant narrative strategy," which gives him confidence that even though "now that Batman has begun, the Batman movies will never end, at least for another 10 years. But maybe this time around they won't get so awful." As these reviews highlight, the film was discussed by most critics in authorial terms despite the fact that Nolan's name was left out of the marketing campaign. Although the promotional tactics might have been designed to protect Nolan's brand in case of failure, such a response helped to augment his budding reputation as much more than an indie experimenter and began to fuel anticipation for the director to make sequels in the franchise.

Rather than immediately work on the next *Batman* film after pleasing critics and audiences of *Batman Begins* with its complex narrative atypical of the blockbuster formula, Nolan returned to the misdirection film next with *The Prestige*. The director leveraged his consecutive post-*Memento* successes to convince Warner Bros. and Disney subsidiary, Touchstone Pictures, to co-finance *The Prestige* with Syncopy. Just a few years after the release of *Memento*, then, which had to be produced and distributed theatrically independent of Hollywood, the majors were now willing to back a project that directly evoked Nolan's breakthrough hit. Although the film's $40 million price tag is modest in relation to other contemporaneous Hollywood films, it dwarfed *Memento*'s meager $5 million budget (imdb.com). Industry executives now had enough faith in the director to co-support a film with high potential to turn off audiences. Indeed, as *The Prestige*'s sole theatrical tagline—"Are you watching closely?"—suggests, marketers were even willing to package the film's misdirection narrative explicitly as its defining and most spectacular element (imdb.com).

In contrast to the tagline, a majority of promotional materials for *The Prestige* accentuates its narrative structure as a primary, but not the exclusive, attraction. Instead of advertising Nolan as only connected to the misdirection film, the preview identifies him as "The Director of *Memento* and *Batman Begins*," firmly situating him in both the narratively complex, indie and blockbuster traditions. In addition, the trailer does not present Nolan as the film's only, or most prominent, star, as the names of its headlining performers—Christian Bale, Hugh Jackman, Michael Caine, and Scarlett Johansson—are all explicitly highlighted with individual title cards. The preview also markets generic hybridity by advertising it as a period drama, science fiction film, misdirection film, thriller, mystery, and so on. The clips from the film itself in the trailer additionally stress its link to the blockbuster model, as its most special-effects-laden facet—the CGI-enhanced, electricity generating, cloning machine—is heavily featured. Yet, it balances that spectacular element with arthouse attributes by emphasizing its narrative complexity because it contains key lines of dialogue that strongly reference the presence of the story's twists, secrets, and surprises. As scholars like Rick Altman and Steve Neale show, Hollywood's penchant for promoting films as constituents of multiple genres has always been the industry standard because it amplifies opportunities to capture a mass audience. King agrees that the industry's emphasis on genre hybridity is not new, but he grants that promoting genre mixing has become more pronounced for New Hollywood films. Like all other elements of the package, genre is an important component of what Richard Maltby calls "the commercial aesthetic," a kitchen-sink approach that Hollywood deploys to mitigate financial risk, which has only escalated since the fall of the studio system (14). Accordingly, genre hybridity, like authorship and stardom, is a significant and reliable presold property used to allay economic uncertainty in New Hollywood. Consequently, it is logical that the industry would try to position authorship similarly by constructing Nolan as a hybrid auteur, equally adept at blockbuster and indie-style filmmaking.

The foregrounding of *The Prestige*'s particular narrative structure and its corresponding authorial mastermind did not stop at its theatrical marketing campaign. Nolan incorporated a number of overt diegetic references to its impending changeover to signal its status as a misdirection film and announce an intellectual competition with the audience from the film's opening frames. Like Shyamalan, who augmented his authorial reputation by alluding to his relationship with the misdirection film in *Unbreakable*'s dialogue, Nolan used *The Prestige*'s script as a means to cement his status as a preeminent maker of misdirection films. Immediately after the opening credits roll, magician, Alfred Borden (Christian Bale), reiterates in voiceover the tagline by asking viewers if they are "watching closely?" The film then cuts to a scene that depicts John Cutter (Michael Caine) performing a magic trick, as the stage engineer describes, in voiceover, how illusions work. His narration, parts of which are also featured in the trailer, first informs viewers that magicians commence their acts by requesting that the audience inspect props that appear to be mundane. He goes on to explain that the illusionist then "takes the ordinary something and makes it do something extraordinary." Subsequently, he claims that although audiences try to guess the secrets, they do not see through the ruse because they are "not really looking, don't want to know," and "want to be fooled." The film's opening blatantly warns viewers that they will be encouraged to draw incorrect conclusions by being lulled into relying on habitual forms of comprehension. However, it also alerts spectators that something remarkable will happen to violate preliminary interpretations. In sum, the film's first few minutes set expectations that the fun will derive from a spectacular narrative and the eventual exposure of an unforeseen revelation that drastically alters initial readings of narrative meaning.

The Prestige's metanarrative commentary, then, cleverly references how it will deceive and thrill viewers by both depending on and departing from Hollywood conventions. On one hand, the film is highly reliant on classical narrative and formal techniques to trick spectators into arriving at false causal suppositions about the significance of narrative information. On the other hand, its changeover reveals that an alternative explanation for narrative meaning has existed beneath the surface all along. At first, it appears that the film's narrative centers on how illusionist Robert Angier (Hugh Jackman) exacts revenge on Borden, whom he holds responsible for his wife's tragic on-stage death during their days as magicians' assistants. It focuses on Angier's efforts to develop his own version of "the transported man," his rival's most famous magic trick, in order to use it to frame Borden for his murder. After the opening voiceovers conclude, the narrative begins *in media res*, presenting scenes that appear to depict Angier's drowning and Borden's subsequent death sentencing for killing his rival. As a result, viewers expect that the ensuing flashbacks will showcase how Angier bested his nemesis. Up until the changeover, this is exactly what happens. The film presents the struggle between the two men, as they plot to ruin each other. Initially, it seems that Angier wins because he develops a version of the trick that is more popular than his adversary's is and destroys Borden's life in the process.

The changeover, though, unexpectedly reveals that Borden may actually get the better of Angier. Viewers shockingly discover that Borden's stunt only worked because the magician successfully kept its secret from everyone, including his nemesis. The sequence exposes the fact that Fallon, the magician's purported trusty stage engineer, is really a double, in disguise, who performed the trick in tandem with his doppelgänger. That is, although Borden convinced even his own family that he was just one person, he actually had a double, which he claims is a twin brother, with whom he took turns playing different roles on- and off-stage to give the appearance that the stunt was done by a single man. This is the reason that he was unable to maintain a healthy relationship with his closest confidants, including his wife, who commits suicide as a result of their troubled marriage. Even though the film hammers viewers over the head about the presence of the revelation from the beginning, then, it is hard to predict its exact contents. This is largely because critical information related to a primary character is either withheld or made to appear as though it has little narrative importance. For instance, characters consistently allude to the changeover by making what seem to be innocuous remarks about Borden's persona. In retrospect, though, ostensibly off-handed observations, such as the fact that a great magician always stays in character, "the transported man" could only be executed with a double, and that Borden often seems to have a split personality, take on great narrative significance. The epiphany is primarily effective, therefore, because viewers have been conditioned by the classical film to expect that main characters will possess a set of clear-cut traits that remain stable. As with many other changeover films, *The Prestige* demonstrates that a revelation that the protagonist is a much different person than viewers initially thought is particularly well-suited for an audience accustomed to classically constructed narratives.

Despite its presentation of a seemingly neat alternative explanation of narrative meaning, *The Prestige*'s epiphany does not provide viewers with the kind of narrative closure that is customary in most changeover films. In fact, as with *Memento*, the more carefully the film is scrutinized in light of the changeover, the harder it is to determine what "really" happened. It is difficult to believe that Borden has a biological twin, for example, because Angier went to great lengths to clone himself in order to perform his own version of "the transported man." Moreover, Angier learns about the existence of the device that enables him to replicate himself after meeting with Nikola Tesla (David Bowie), the famous inventor with whom Borden previously collaborated and whose name is the cipher to his encrypted journal. It is thus possible that Borden used a similar apparatus to create facsimiles of himself before Angier. Additionally, it is hard to say definitively that Borden actually kills Angier in the end. After Borden fatally wounds Angier, the film's final shot reveals that his rival has produced multiple clones of himself, raising the possibility that other doubles may still exist. Put simply, the film's ending does not tie up all causal lines of action despite appearing to be an explanatory changeover.

At a time in which fans now routinely use digital media technologies to dissect and discuss their favorite films, misdirection films that inspire these interpretive activities have become more common in Hollywood than ever before. In the same year *The Prestige* was released, Hollywood distributed two more highly self-reflexive misdirection films: *The Illusionist*, another magician-themed film, and *Lucky Number Slevin*, in which there

Figure 5.3. The final shot of *The Prestige* that suggests Robert Angier might still be alive by showing one of the many facsimiles killed during his act.

are similarly many diegetic references to the presence of its changeover. In addition, three Hollywood misdirection films—*Perfect Stranger*, *Shattered*, and *Atonement*—hit U.S. theaters in 2007. Interestingly, each of these films portrayed a female character as ultimately being the unexpected primary causal agent, indicating that producers had a growing awareness that contemporary misdirection films tend to center almost exclusively on the exploits of male characters and that a shift to focusing on women in the genre might represent an innovation to attract audiences tired of sameness. Executives thus believed that a potentially profitable audience recognized that films containing these particular narrative structures constituted a distinct genre with its own set of conventions. The decisions to begin *The Prestige* with a direct challenge to the viewer's interpretive acumen and to end it in an ambiguous manner, therefore, were calculated choices designed to appeal to viewers who enjoy participating in games of discovery and decipherment.

The Prestige was indeed targeted at spectators who derive pleasure from matching wits with a director already renowned for being a master of misdirection. This strategy worked. Critics were mixed, but many of them praised the film and applauded Nolan for his progress as a director. Booth epitomizes this critical discourse by noting that Nolan "first twisted *Memento* into a feverish dream," followed that with the "dark puzzle of *Insomnia*," and then his "most commercial success *Batman Begins* was disarmingly smart," which leads him to exclaim that "All those directing talents are in evidence with *The Prestige*." Although the film made little splash at the domestic box-office, netting a relatively modest $53 million, as of August 2015, it is ranked as the 51st best film of all time on the

Internet Movie Database's Top 250 list. Such belated fan appreciation suggests that the film's reputation has been elevated by its run in post-theatrical markets. For Henry Jenkins, the increased production of films that require a comparatively high degree of interpretive labor indicates that they are "part of a corporate strategy to ensure viewer engagement with brands and franchises" across multiple media platforms (*Convergence* 56). Extending this logic into the realm of authorship, I contend that filmmakers like Nolan and Shyamalan are similarly branded commodities largely because of how they have become associated with the misdirection film. The presence of the director's name alone, then, is enough to differentiate these films from other Hollywood fare; it informs audiences that they should be prepared to perform interpretive activities that depart from habitual forms of comprehension simply because the directors are attached.

For Nolan, a key to his enduring appeal in relation to Shyamalan is how he has been consistently and effectively marketed as capable of combining tent-pole production with narratively complex fare that is more challenging than run-of-the-mill blockbusters. His success is linked to how he has never been exclusively associated to the misdirection film. Despite his string of indie and blockbuster hits, his name was still absent from the trailer for the *The Dark Knight*, which became the film that propelled him to the authorial stratosphere thanks to its gargantuan theatrical revenues and almost universal critical acclaim. By the time he completed the trilogy with the similarly lucrative *The Dark Knight Rises* (2012), marketers had enough confidence to package it in the preview as being "From Christopher Nolan" without referencing any of his other films. Nolan's *Batman* fame has even enabled the director to leverage his production company to back superhero franchises for other directors. Specifically, he served as executive producer for *Man of Steel* (2013), a second recent attempt to revive the moribund *Superman* franchise after Singer's *Superman Returns* (2006) failed to meet expectations at the box office and was largely panned by critics. Although *Man of Steel* received mixed reviews, it performed well at the box office, netting $115 million in its opening weekend and nearly $300 million during its run in U.S. theaters (imdb.com). Its big opening weekend take was partly attributable to how prominently Nolan was featured in the marketing campaign. Even though the film was directed by Zack Snyder, promotional materials, like the film's trailers, explicitly positioned the film as being from Snyder and Nolan, who was packaged as the "Director of *The Dark Knight* trilogy." Just a few years after *The Prestige* made him the leading director of the misdirection film, effective promotional strategies in relation to his blockbuster films transformed him into an authorial commodity that could also be mobilized on franchise films that he did not even direct.

The trailers for *Inception* are the most telling, though, about how the strategies used to promote Nolan as an auteur effectively respond to contemporary industrial contexts. Instead of positioning Nolan as the director of misdirection films and the *Batman* franchise, like was done for *The Prestige*, *Inception*'s assorted previews advertise him only as the director of *The Dark Knight*. They also highlight the film's action-packed, spectacle-laden elements over its mind-bending narrative structure. Such a choice seems odd, considering that the film's complex narrative was one of its most defining attributes and a primary reason for *Inception*'s massive profitability. Clearly, executives deemed it safer to activate Nolan's blockbuster persona than his misdirection identity because of the *The Dark Knight*'s phenomenal performance. Yet, the final image of the trailers does allude to its status as misdirection because the film's title appears embedded in an intricate maze that mirrors Syncopy's logo.

As these emblems suggest, Nolan's link to the misdirection film may often be downplayed, but it has not yet had to be categorically denied like it recently has for Shyamalan. This is because Nolan has strategically avoided being pigeon-holed as only tied to the misdirection film genre. The same cannot be said for Shyamalan, whose career has suffered a significant setback from imprudent marketing tactics that ineffectively positioned him as the genre's top filmmaker. In contrast to Shyamalan's myopic use of Blinding Edge Pictures to back only his own authorial efforts, Nolan's decision to found his own production company early in his career has helped keep his image largely under his control and has made him just as associated with franchise filmmaking as he is with the misdirection film, enabling him to combine the two together in his films effectively as well as to produce blockbusters by other filmmakers. This crucial move has allowed Nolan to maintain a branded identity that aligns with New Hollywood's emphasis on authorship as a marketable commodity connected to other representative aspects of the package-unit logic, such as genre hybridity and a diverse production portfolio characterized by both blockbuster films as well as artistically innovative films with an indie sensibility, albeit within relatively familiar parameters.

6

Genre Prestige

The Misdirection Film as Blockbuster and Middlebrow Art

The decision to market *Inception* (2010) primarily as a blockbuster, action film paid dividends at the box office. The film essentially matched *The Sixth Sense*'s (1999) almost $300 million domestic, theatrical take and exceeded its predecessor's worldwide run in theaters by over $100 million, making it the highest grossing misdirection film ever released (imdb.com). Of course, this kind of data needs to be put fully into context to have significance because its comparative value is contingent on other factors, such as adjustments for inflation and who defines the genre's parameters. A review of the current evidence on *Box Office Mojo* (boxofficemojo.com), for instance, reveals some of the challenges associated with relying on these statistics to measure the economic merits of a genre's constituents. Among the many options for sorting all-time box-office figures, the website allows users to cull it according to genre. The site's genre label with the clearest connection to the misdirection film is the "mindbender" category. According to this classification logic, *Inception* indeed generated far more theatrical revenue than its closest competitor, almost tripling the category's second-place finisher: *Shutter Island* (2010). Its strong financial performance appears more remarkable than it might otherwise be because of the arbitrary choice not to include in the mindbender genre misdirection films that exceeded *Shutter Island*'s theatrical take, including *A Beautiful Mind* (2001), *Planet of the Apes* (2001), and *The Sixth Sense*. These results reveal a potential ramification of random genre classifications. Such data suggests that 2010 was when the misdirection film was at its peak, as it marks the release of the two highest grossing films in the site's most closely affiliated genre.

A more careful review of the circumstances complicates the claim that 2010 was the misdirection film's definitive moment culturally and industrially. The genre's breakout year was 1999, when the modestly budgeted *The Sixth Sense* became a popular sensation as well as *Fight Club* and *Magnolia* received significant critical acclaim in some circles in spite of their box-office disappointment. To capitalize on this momentum, the industry rapidly backed more prestigious misdirection films than ever before, three of which landed in the top 20 grossing films of 2001: *A Beautiful Mind*, *Planet of the Apes*, and *Vanilla Sky* (boxofficemojo.com). Each of these films had a healthy production budget of at least $60 million and was directed, respectively, by an established Hollywood auteur—Ron Howard, Tim Burton, and Cameron Crowe—indicating the industry's growing willingness to allocate more resources to the genre than just a few years earlier when the misdirection film was primarily relegated to lower budgets and helmed by young directors striving to become branded commodities, like M. Night Shyamalan, Paul Thomas Anderson, and David Fincher.

The 2001 crop of films also represents a milestone for the genre because *A Beautiful Mind* captured the Best Picture Oscar, the only contemporary misdirection film to win it. Yet, as *Box Office Mojo*'s failure to include any of these films in the mindbender category suggests, the 2001 slate of high profile misdirection films was not necessarily conceived of as primarily in connection with the genre. Instead, *A Beautiful Mind* was most prominently received as an esteemed biopic with some narrative surprises and *Planet of the Apes* and *Vanilla Sky* were largely considered part of a spate of recent Hollywood remakes. That is not to say that evidence of these films being constituents of the misdirection film genre is unavailable. It does suggest, however, that although the industry's faith in the genre had increased, it remained limited. This is why it mitigated risk by combining the misdirection film with Oscar bait content and source material that already proved successful elsewhere. In contrast, by 2010, the releases of *Inception* and *Shutter Island* illustrate that Hollywood briefly had enough faith in the genre to make artistically daring and expensive misdirection films designed to garner windfall profits and industrial cachet.

In this chapter, I examine how the production, marketing, and reception of *Inception* and *Shutter Island* reveal that the misdirection film had become an ideal genre for some of the broader conditions that most impacted Hollywood in the years leading up to the end of the first decade of the millennium. Specifically, my discussion of these two films shows that they exemplify the ways in which the genre was particularly well-suited for a number of the most significant cultural, industrial, and technological circumstances shaping the production and reception of Hollywood films at that historical moment. Rather than consider the misdirection film to be an anomalous genre in the industry's production agenda, my exploration of these two films highlights how it had developed into one of Hollywood's most reliable options for maximizing profits and amplifying its cultural capital for a short period of time before it quickly fell out of favor thereafter.

Middlebrow Tastes: The Blockbuster Film and Award Show Accolades

Although the blockbuster film has been Hollywood's central focus since discovering it is ideal for the post-studio landscape and its associated package-unit system, media conglomerates have not been solely in the business of making expensive, spectacle-laden films constructed to lure audiences to theaters and synergistically optimize ancillary market revenues. Numerous scholars explain how and why Hollywood maintains a diverse production portfolio even though blockbusters are most likely to garner the biggest revenues in the domestic theatrical market and beyond. One of the issues that such critics must contend with first is the difficulty of identifying exactly what characterizes a blockbuster. Building on the work of discursive genre theorists like Rick Altman and James Naremore, Julian Stringer argues that the blockbuster is most appropriately conceived of as a cultural category, created and sustained by utterances that compare and contrast it to standard Hollywood fare, which is itself also always a constructed classification. As with any genre, the blockbuster is an unstable grouping subject to change based on variables, like when people acknowledge constituents and who labels them accordingly. Some films never designed to be, or packaged as, blockbusters get retroactively categorized as such by groups, like critics, because of their enormous box-office takes. A few of the top grossing titles of their respective years since 1990, including *Forrest Gump* (1994), *Saving Private Ryan* (1998), and *American Sniper* (2014), showcase how films not initially positioned as blockbusters can become ones based largely on how they unexpectedly dwarf modest box-office expectations. This phenomenon leads Stringer to claim that the blockbuster is a relative term, linked to "the money/spectacle nexus" as well as to a film's "size factor and bigness and exceptionality" (8). The blockbuster, therefore, is a genre that is entirely comparative. A film's status as one is predicated on how it is discursively differentiated from what is conceived of as run-of-the-mill Hollywood output by various groups in relation to an array of possible factors, such as budget, box-office take, spectacle, run-time, promotional ballyhoo, casting decisions, release date, synergistic tie-ins, and so on.

The haphazard and volatile classification logic of the blockbuster genre's constituents begins to demonstrate why the industry has never simply produced films confected with this sensibility since it became the most attractive option for New Hollywood's business model. If some films are only recognized as blockbusters retroactively and if it is a comparative term, then other kinds of films have to be backed by the industry for the blockbuster even to exist and for the genre's constituents to be so varied. Genre theory aside, there are other, more pragmatic reasons why the blockbuster did not turn into the only Hollywood product. In *New Hollywood Cinema*, Geoff King argues that, regardless of the central importance of the blockbuster to the media conglomerates' fiscal health, these companies maintain strategically diverse production portfolios for important reasons, including trying "to leave no opportunity for profit unexploited" and sustaining a positive "image of the studios, a matter of some significance given their potential vulnerability to federal regulation" (83). The industry's desires to generate better than anticipated revenues from lower-budgeted fare and to keep the patina of art to protect its remarkable history of self-censorship by avoiding the kind of government intervention that could result from the appearance of crass commercialism are strong incentives for Hollywood to continue varying its products. Blockbusters are often referred to as tent-pole films for precisely this reason: their synergistic revenue streams can prop up the fortunes of an entire media conglomerate, giving them the potential to offset losses that result from the other films it continues to back. Even though lucrative ancillary markets usually make blockbusters profitable in the long run, their huge negative costs also mean they are risky investments because of the initial hits they may take at the box office when high-interest loans need to be repaid rapidly. To allay the blockbuster's economic uncertainty, it behooves Hollywood to continue to churn out cheaper films that often turn modest profits and even can become box-office smashes.

For Thomas Schatz, New Hollywood's assorted production docket can be separated into "three classes of movie: the calculated blockbuster designed with the multimedia marketplace and franchise status in mind, the mainstream A-class star vehicle with sleeper hit potential, and the low cost independent feature targeted for a specific market and with little chance of anything more than 'cult film' status" ("The New" 35). Schatz prudently acknowledges that such divisions do not mean that Hollywood is akin to a caste system in which these three production categories are mutually exclusive or absolute. Yet, I argue even more strongly than he does that the blockbuster category should not be limited to films specifically constructed with synergistic revenue generation and the potential for franchising in mind. As his use of the ambiguous term "sleeper hit" to characterize a primary motive for the production of the second class of films indicates, there are films from his other categories that can go beyond just being unexpected hits and become blockbusters because of how groups, like audiences and critics, receive them as a consequence of the huge profits that they surprisingly garner at the box office.

What is most notable about the misdirection film in relation to New Hollywood's production logic is that its constituents have steadily migrated from the bottom- to the top-tier during the period under study. In the early 1990s, misdirection films were lower-budgeted and produced by independents, as evidenced by *Jacob's Ladder* (1990, Carolco), *Total Recall* (1990, Carolco), *The Crying Game* (1992, UK co-production), *Pulp Fiction* (1994, Miramax), and *The Usual Suspects* (1995, Polygram) (imdb.com). Always eager to capitalize on missed chances for profit, Hollywood first benefited from these films by distributing them more widely in their various formats. In the late 1990s, the industry moved to backing higher budgeted misdirection films, which mostly fall into Schatz's second class. Unsurprisingly, this began in a largely risk averse way, as Hollywood's initial attempts to support higher budgeted films in the genre were characterized by remakes: *Diabolique* (1996) and *Psycho* (1998). After *The Sixth Sense* shockingly became more than just a sleeper hit, the industry took the final step by making a misdirection film that was constructed with clear blockbuster aspirations from the outset: Fox's remake of *Planet of the Apes*, the first misdirection film with a nine-figure production budget, which was also both released in the midst of the summer blockbuster season and accompanied by video game tie-ins for a variety of popular console and handheld systems. Although the film performed well at the box office, garnering over $360 million in theatrical receipts globally, it received generally poor reviews and initial plans for a sequel were shelved (imdb.com). Yet, Fox's decision to resurrect the property a decade later with *Rise of the Planet of the Apes* (2011), *Dawn of the Planet of Apes* (2014), and additional forthcoming sequels indicates that executives were right to conceive of it as having franchise potential. As this belated revival suggests, the lackluster critical reception of the *Planet of the Apes* remake gave the industry pause about the genre's blockbuster possibilities, preventing it from returning to Schatz's top-tier for years.

In addition to the relative disappointment of *Planet of the Apes*, the incredible critical success of *A Beautiful Mind* helped cement the misdirection film in the A-list star vehicle category for most of the decade. The film's four prestigious Academy Award wins not only gave it enormous cultural capital. They also made the film into a moneymaker, as it ultimately took home $313 million at the worldwide box office on its $60 million budget (imdb.com). The importance of the Academy Awards for Hollywood's production calculus epitomizes why the blockbuster is most appropriately conceived of as a synecdoche for the industry's total output that conceals its actually more varied product mix. The industry indeed packages some of its films as designed primarily for something other than just pure entertainment. The Academy Awards provide a key way to recognize products that are heralded for other virtues, such as artistic expression and social commentary. Awards ceremonies, particularly the Oscars, serve the important function of publicly identifying the cultural value of these products, especially because the entertainment news media is otherwise fixated on box-office results. The industry is not opposed to this journalistic obsession, as it creates barriers to entry by making Hollywood films practically the exclusive focus in the public sphere as well as helps to propel these products to achieve greater success theatrically and in the aftermarket. To milk the most out of films that are not part of the blockbuster class, the industry relies heavily on award show accolades to create a buzz around selected constituents of mostly Schatz's second class of films. This crucial facet of the business further maximizes revenues on existing products, transforms creative personnel who win awards into more valuable presold properties in the future, and inoculates the industry from accusations that it is myopically focused on the bottomline.

Although films packaged as blockbusters generally fare poorly in the most prestigious Academy Award categories and are instead typically consigned to the technical awards, Gillian Roberts posits that Best Picture Oscar winners are often constructed in ways that actually have much in common with their seemingly distant big-budget, franchise relatives. This is because they are both primarily designed to appeal to a mass audience. As with the commercial aesthetic that drives blockbuster production, Roberts argues that Oscar winners usually possess qualities that exhibit Pierre "Bourdieu's characterization of middlebrow culture, namely as one that offers a negotiation between the accessibility of low culture and the prestige of high culture" (157). Bourdieu seminally theorized that culture industry production is characterized by an opposition to "intellectual art" because it is constructed to garner "investment profitability," which often results in appropriations of revered art forms to legitimize its status (126). Roberts's argument may seem to run counter to conventional wisdom because Oscar voters are typically chastised for being out of sync with mass taste; however, this is often not the case despite the box-office discrepancies that usually exist between Oscar winners and blockbusters. In addition to ignoring instances when indisputable blockbusters, like *Titanic* (1997) and *The Lord of the Rings: The Return of the King* (2003), dominated the ceremony, this false dichotomy fails to account for how frequently Best Picture winners are created for wide audiences. As Roberts contends, the Oscars provide "the impression of bringing legitimate culture within the reach of all by bestowing legitimacy on accessible cultural products" (157). As Best Picture winners from the period under study, like *The Silence of the Lambs* (1991), *The Departed* (2006), and *No Country for Old Men* (2007), illustrate, the Academy can bolster the cultural capital of films from familiar genres, such as the serial killer, gangster, and crime film, which are extremely popular, but are generally debased by the intelligentsia.

Most misdirection films coincide closely with a middlebrow cultural appeal that blends artistic legitimacy with mass audience accessibility, as they contain a combination of a reliance on classical conventions with narrative and formal innovations that challenge those very standards. This combination of low- and high-art tendencies is often cited by scholars as evidence of a postmodern turn in Hollywood cinema. Such contentions relate to Fredric Jameson's influential notion, articulated in *Postmodernism*, of the epoch being partly characterized by artistic production that increasingly exhibits the qualities of "pastiche," which indiscriminately samples disparate forms of expression, often resulting in "the effacement in them of the older (essentially high-modernist) frontier between high culture and so-called mass or commercial culture" (2). As I argued in chapter 2, although the mixing of high- and low-culture has recently intensified across various media and art forms, I conceive of the misdirection film as embodying a late phase of modernity, rather than of postmodernity, largely because its dependence on classical principles and general support of dominant ideologies exemplifies how it is most reliant on conventional aesthetic practices and entrenched epistemologies that have not yet been replaced by different ways of thinking or new modes of expression. Moreover, it is a stretch to claim that taste formations separating the elitist from the popular have collapsed to a point in which the two categories have become culturally indecipherable. If anything, allusions to high-art are most often deployed by Hollywood filmmakers to imbue their mass cultural productions with greater legitimacy precisely because such distinctions persist and film canons continue to be defined by traditional conceptions of artistic value.

The misdirection film's production trajectory illustrates Hollywood's enduring reticence to take radical artistic chances and instead highlights how it relies on familiar conventions. It is unsurprising, in an industry characterized by risk aversion and artistic conservatism, that it was only after a few lower-budgeted, independently produced misdirection films—*The Crying Game*, *Pulp Fiction*, and *The Usual Suspects*—won prestigious Academy Awards and subsequent representatives from the second class—*Magnolia* and *The Sixth Sense*—garnered numerous, non-technical Oscar nominations, that it finally won big in the genre in the most coveted categories with *A Beautiful Mind*. In addition to being well-suited for post-theatrical markets, the misdirection film thus served the industrial purpose of earning prestigious Oscar wins and nominations for ensuing films from Schatz's second-tier. The Oscar wins and nominations in non-technical categories from films, like *Adaptation* (2002) and *Atonement* (2007), which, thanks to its seven nominations became the second most decorated misdirection film by the Academy, are a testament to the industry's use of the genre to bolster its cultural capital during the 2000s.

The misdirection film's high critical acclaim and strong post-theatrical performance positioned the genre well for even more in the years leading up to 2010. Hollywood's backing of *Inception* and *Shutter Island* demonstrates that the misdirection film had become more than just a reliable genre for Schatz's second-tier at that moment. There was perhaps no better choice, therefore, of a director to appeal to middle-brow tastes than Martin Scorsese, who, by the 2000s, as Marc Raymond summarizes, "had come to represent the industry's best possible version of itself and the artistic quality it is capable of delivering" (201). At the time of *Shutter Island*'s release, Scorsese had become Hollywood's crown jewel director, renowned for his image as the industry's foremost public intellectual, recent Oscar success, artistic integrity, and reliable, if often unspectacular, box-office returns. Scorsese's reputation for consistently directing aesthetically innovative films that do not alienate the masses made him ideal for helming an esteemed misdirection film because of its similar blend of those qualities.

As is the case under the package-unit model, the hiring of a director who has become a marketable commodity can serve as a valuable presold property. Scorsese's eventual participation in the project was critical to getting the film into production. The rights to *Shutter Island*'s 2001 source novel of the same name, which was written by Dennis Lehane, who also penned the book that was adapted into Academy Award winner, *Mystic River* (2003), were optioned to Columbia Pictures in 2003; however, the project did not actually come into fruition until Scorsese and Leonardo DiCaprio subsequently signed on to direct and to star in it in 2007 (Fleming). Importantly, Scorsese and DiCaprio had established a track-record of working together on films with similar sensibilities that performed admirably at both the box office and the Academy Awards, including *Gangs of New York* (2002), *The Aviator* (2005), and *The Departed*, which finally earned one of the director's films the Best Picture and Best Director Oscars that many critics claimed he had been unfairly denied until then. As with *Shutter Island*, *Inception* was a gestating project that had been put on hold for a number of years. Nolan reportedly began toying with the idea before becoming a Hollywood filmmaker and originally pitched the project to Warner Bros. after directing *Insomnia* (2002), his first studio-style film. In contrast to Scorsese, however, who had already established a reputation as a filmmaker adept at making both critically acclaimed, arthouse films, like *Mean Streets* (1973), *Taxi Driver* (1976), and *Raging Bull* (1980), as well as commercially driven fare, like *The Color of Money* (1986) and the remake of *Cape Fear* (1991), Nolan had to prove his acumen in mainstream filmmaking before getting the greenlight to make *Inception*.

Although a name brand auteur might be enough to get the industry to back a film in Schatz's second-tier, the greater risks associated with blockbuster negative costs almost always require multiple presold properties to get them into production. Such a gamble is amplified for misdirection films because of their potential to turn off the mass audience. Both directors, then, relied heavily on stardom as an additional guarantee by casting DiCaprio, arguably Hollywood's most coveted leading man at the time, as their lead actor. After breaking into the industry as a teenager in the early 1990s, DiCaprio's star soared in popularity with *Titanic*, a blockbuster *par excellence* that shattered box-office highs and won a record-tying 11 Oscars. His performance, though, was not among the also record-tying 14 nominations that the Academy bestowed on *Titanic*, precipitating similar results on subsequent films that turned good profits and received Academy recognition, but long failed to net DiCaprio an acting Oscar (imdb.com). Despite being denied by the Academy for years, DiCaprio has become known for being the rare actor able to capture both arthouse and mainstream audiences. As Scott Bowles documents in his *USA Today* article on the actor's casting in *Django Unchained* (2013), DiCaprio has "a reputation for being one of the most selective actors in the industry," choosing to work with directors who, like Scorsese and Nolan, have proven capable of making films that are popular with wide audiences and have Oscar appeal, including Danny Boyle, James Cameron, Clint Eastwood, Baz Luhrman, Steven Spielberg, and Quentin Tarantino. This has not negatively impacted the actor at the box office, as DiCaprio's films have earned over $2 billion in domestic theaters, for an average of $97 million per film to date (boxofficemojo.com). Before finally winning his Oscar in 2016, DiCaprio was nominated for four Academy Awards as a performer, won three Best Actor Golden Globes, and helped the films in which he has been cast as the lead accumulate many coveted prizes (imdb.com). Clearly, DiCaprio has a reputation for starring in films that capture mass and arthouse audiences, situating him among the industry's top middlebrow performers.

The reasons for DiCaprio's appeal, however, extend beyond just savvy career choices. As with the success of the misdirection film more broadly, DiCaprio's stardom is also a product of the ways in which his persona is linked to salient cultural conditions. The protagonist that the actor typically portrays is a paragon contemporary of broken manhood. Such roles are epitomized by *Inception* and *Shutter Island*, in which he plays men who ostensibly struggle to regain their traditional masculinity after losing patriarchal control of their families because of the underhanded actions of their wives. These onscreen representations, which build on the doomed, romantic partner persona that DiCaprio developed in his star-making, melodramatic lead roles in *Romeo + Juliet* (1996) and *Titanic*, are emblematic of a culture in which there is a perceived crisis in hegemonic masculinity.

The connections between DiCaprio's image and anxieties about the persistence of traditional masculine dominance extend beyond his seminal film performances. As Richard Dyer argues in *Heavenly Bodies*, the star's persona is "made up of screen roles and obviously stage-managed public appearances, and also of images of the manufacture of that 'image' and of the real person who is the site or occasion of it" (7). This blend of textual and extratextual discourses means that the star is not associated with a single performance, as the image that calcifies supersedes a one-off role. Even more interestingly, Dyer contends that stars are attractive to audiences for the same reason that ritual genre theorists often cite for its appeal: the star's image often dovetails with dominant ideology by representing a satisfactory mollifying combination of cultural oppositions that are actually incompatible off screen. DiCaprio's popularity is linked to how his persona reconciles competing notions about appropriate forms of masculinity. According to his recent biographical legend, DiCaprio has become arguably Hollywood's most eligible bachelor, famous for his womanizing exploits. Perhaps most notoriously, the tabloids were headlined with news of the actor leaving a Miami club with 20 models after he and his then-girlfriend, Toni Garnn, reportedly split just weeks before the release of his most recent collaboration with Scorsese, *The Wolf of Wall Street* (2013), in which he is cast as real-life philanderer, Jordan Belfort (Saad). Those overlapping discourses, which position DiCaprio as an irresistible catch, express cultural desires for supporters of conventional masculinity about its endurance at a time when such notions of ideal manhood are less universally accepted.

Inception and *Shutter Island* resonate culturally not only because of how DiCaprio expresses their shared wishes about antiquated modes of masculinity remaining appropriate amid pervasive paranoia about changing gender roles and relations. They also depict the kind of agency panic about anxieties related to the loss of individual sovereignty that permeates many misdirection films. Both films contain changeovers that can be interpreted as depicting how their protagonists' free will is severely restricted by powerful forces beyond their control. As a consequence of how much these two films typify the misdirection film's connections to some of the most significant cultural, industrial, and technological conditions shaping Hollywood production and reception from 1990 to 2010, they are the ideal final case studies of this book. The following examinations of the ways in which they were interpreted by audiences as well as constructed and promoted by the industry, therefore, tie the book's arguments together by demonstrating how the misdirection film was specifically fashioned in response to its contexts.

You Mustn't Be Afraid to Dream a Little Bigger: *Inception* and the Misdirection Film's Blockbuster Leap of Faith

A key aspect of Christopher Nolan's authorial lore that the director himself often repeats is that the decision not to make *Inception* as early in his career as he hoped turned out to be fortuitous. As Nolan explained in a 2010 interview with Dave Itzkoff of the *New York Times*, he "first pitched the film to the studio probably nine years ago, and [he] wasn't ready to finish it. [He] needed more experience in making a big movie" ("A Man"). This is a primary reason why he directed the initial film of the *Batman* franchise first. Whether or not this is revisionist history that conceals lasting concerns Warner Bros. had about the project's economic potential, Nolan is right to position the film's timing as auspicious. *Inception* was a risky film to back because its complex narrative threatened to turn away some audiences. In contrast to the typically modestly budgeted films in the genre, though, it was a bigger gamble than any misdirection film before it, as its estimated $260 million negative costs put it in indisputable blockbuster territory in terms of budgetary size (imdb.com). Moreover, whereas most films with that kind of gargantuan initial investment are greenlit because of their capacity to be franchised, tied to reliable presold source material, and capitalize on ancillary market revenues, *Inception* had few such opportunities, aside from likely exorbitant home-video sales and possible sequels, which have yet to be made. To alleviate risk, Warner Bros. chose to promote *Inception*'s action-packed and spectacle-laden qualities most heavily, assemble a star-studded cast led by DiCaprio, as well as adhere to the template from *The Prestige* by highlighting generic hybridity, packaging it as a constituent of the action, blockbuster, heist, science fiction, and misdirection film genres. Most crucial to the production logic, however, was Nolan's development into a marketable auteur. Putting the production rationale in crude terms, President of Worldwide Marketing for Warner Bros., Sue Kroll, told the *LA Times* that "We don't have the brand equity that usually drives a big summer opening," but "Christopher Nolan as a brand is very powerful" (Fritz and Eller).

Nolan's status as the mastermind behind the *Batman* franchise was mobilized more prominently than any other aspect of his branded identity in *Inception*'s promotional materials. This makes sense in light of the director's immediate predecessor to *Inception*, *The Dark Knight*, and its incredible performance at the box office, with critics, and at the Oscars, where it bucked the trend of blockbusters only netting technical Academy Awards by earning Heath Ledger a posthumous statue for Best Supporting Actor. Such a marketing strategy is logical because the film needed a wide audience to offset its high negative costs, which explains why *Inception*'s affiliation with the blockbuster and its prototypical action-packed, spectacle-laden sequences was more central to its marketing than any other element in the package. Virtually all promotional materials, however, reference its links to the misdirection film, albeit often obliquely and fleetingly. For starters, the film's two taglines—"Your mind is the scene of the crime" and "The dream is real"—only allude to its convoluted narrative structure by foregrounding other generic links, including the heist and science fiction genres, as explicitly (imdb.com). *Inception*'s trailers, which are dominated by clips of the film's most spectacular moments and images of its cast, also raise the specter of the misdirection film, but only briefly and implicitly. The teaser trailer, for example, bookends its featuring of *Inception*'s blockbuster qualities with insinuations to the misdirection film by opening with extended shots of the spinning top, ostensibly the most important clue for deciphering its narrative mysteries, and ending with an image of the film's title in the middle of a gigantic maze that appears to be unsolvable. In short, although executives did not ignore the film's connection to the misdirection film in the marketing campaign, its blockbuster elements were the primary emphasis.

The strategic decision to position *Inception* as a blockbuster paid off at the domestic box office, where the film grossed approximately $63 million in its crucial opening weekend in mid-July during the blockbuster release season, allaying fears that its unfamiliar source material would turn off mass audiences (imdb.com). The film's initial success was buttressed by favorable reviews that highlighted its blockbuster status, but also lauded its misdirection film attributes. Elizabeth Weitzman of the *New York Daily News* typifies these responses by noting "*Inception* blends the blockbuster enormity of *The Dark Knight* with the indie insights of *Memento* to create an all-encompassing experience that makes other summer films seem mediocre." *The Seattle Times* reviewer Moira Macdonald makes practically the same assertion by claiming that the film merges "the twisty appeal of *Memento* with the cool chic of *The Dark Knight*," resulting in "the rare would-be blockbuster that demands close attention and surely would reward rewatching." Clearly, Nolan's reputation as a filmmaker with an uncommon history of pleasing both arthouse and wide audiences was enthusiastically activated by many reviewers despite the ploy to market *Inception* as a blockbuster film most conspicuously. In his review, Bill Goodykoontz of *The Arizona Republic* identifies why Nolan is able to blend indie and blockbuster filmmaking effectively. Evoking David Bordwell's theory that compositional motivation drives classical film form, Goodykoontz writes "The visuals are stunning, perhaps the most fully realized of any film . . . in this context it is not simply showing off for the sake of doing so, but a believable part of the story." Such hyperbole pervades Goodykoontz's astute review, in which he also acclaims DiCaprio's "trademark wounded man" performance and extols Nolan's construction of an "interlocking puzzle for the audience to figure out. (Don't worry, it's more fun than that sounds)." Similarly, praising the film's appeal to fans, Roger Ebert speculates that it "is sure to inspire truly endless analysis on the web."

These critics' predictions about the film's likelihood to generate fervent fandom online proved accurate, as *Inception* immediately became an Internet sensation and remains one of the most frequently discussed films on the web to this day. A Google search in August 2015, using the terms "*Inception* analysis," for example, yields over 46 million results, while the terms "*The Dark Knight* analysis," returns a still impressive, but comparatively measly, two million hits even though that film is Nolan's biggest box-office moneymaker. As with other misdirection films that initially spawned this sort of rabid fan activity online, such as *Magnolia* and *Mulholland Dr.* (2001), much of *Inception*'s appeal to virtual communities can be linked to Nolan's decision to construct a narrative puzzle that resembles the ones he created in *Memento* and *The Prestige* because it similarly appears to be irresolvable. In contrast to the reception of those earlier misdirection films, particularly *Memento*, however, the advances of Web 2.0 technologies have made fan responses to *Inception* more common and diffuse than its generic predecessors. As a result, there is not a single online location housing the preponderance of *Inception*'s virtual community activity, as there was for a film, like *Mulholland Dr.*, because it was released when users needed coding skills to publish to the web, making the *Lost on Mullholland Dr.* (*LOMD*) website an unparalleled aggregator of that film's fan interpretations at the time.

Another key distinction between fan reception of *Inception* and earlier misdirection films is the specific kinds of interpretive activities it has inspired. In comparison to Nolan's previous misdirection films, most notably *Memento*, which provoked considerable online discussion dedicated to figuring out its "true" meaning, many fans of *Inception* begin from the premise that there is no conclusive solution to the film's central mystery of delineating dream from reality. For example, in an article on the *Ropes of Silicon* website, a once popular amateur movie blog, Brad Brevert challenges Michael Caine's earlier publicly stated assertion that he knows that the film's ending reveals it was not all just a dream by noting that it is unlikely that "we'll be hearing Chris Nolan explaining the ins and outs of *Inception* or confirming Caine's statement any time soon" because he would "expect to hear him talk about *Inception*'s ending just as much" as he would envisage the director to provide "a final explanation for the existence of a certain tattoo in *Memento*." As this emblematic viewer response indicates, the discourse of authorship has strongly contributed to this shift in the reception of Nolan's films. Indeed, Nolan and DiCaprio alike both balked at opportunities to explain definitively what "really" happened in the immediate wake of *Inception*'s release in their assorted interview and promotional appearances. Some of the director's fans thus continually make reference to his penchant for eternally lingering ambiguity and his tendency to avoid giving concrete answers about meanings of his previous misdirection films as evidence of why *Inception*'s many enigmas cannot be explained definitively. Despite this admission, most fans still cannot resist attempting to offset the uncertainty associated with the film's truth being unknowable by deriving interpretations that resolve all of its mysteries.

Paradoxically, Nolan's own comments about the film's "true" meaning also have helped to fuel speculation that refutes claims that *Inception* is intentionally constructed to be eternally ambiguous. As he did with *Memento*, the director coyly leveraged publicity opportunities to encourage fans to search for an absolute answer even though he simultaneously claimed one might not actually exist. In an interview for *Wired* magazine published shortly after the film's theatrical release, Nolan responds to a question about the presence of an absolute explanation for what "actually" happened by claiming he does have a conclusive answer to the inquiry. Expanding on that response, he tells the interviewer that "I've always believed that if you make a film with ambiguity, it needs to be based on a true interpretation. If it's not, then it will somehow contradict itself and end up making the audience feel cheated. Ambiguity has to come from the inability of a character to know—and the alignment of the audience with that character" (Capps). In addition to suggesting to viewers that there might be a correct way to interpret *Inception* without giving it away, this assertion is significant for identifying a key characteristic of the misdirection film. It reiterates why these films should be differentiated from those in affiliated categories, such as Thomas Elsaesser's "mind-game film" genre, that also includes films in which only diegetic characters are fooled into jumping to erroneous conclusions about narrative information. In contrast, misdirection films center on tricking the spectator, irrespective of the fate of onscreen characters, even though both are often duped simultaneously. Additionally, Nolan's response is relevant for referencing how central focalization is to the misdirection film's particular brand of deceptive magic, as the viewer's strong identification with the classical film's prototypically goal-oriented protagonist, who surprisingly turns out to have less narrative agency than other characters, is the most common ploy for helping to pull off the sleight of hand.

Inception's convoluted narrative ostensibly focuses on Dom Cobb's (Leonardo DiCaprio) quest to return to his estranged children, whom he has been separated from since his then-wife, Mal (Marion Cotillard), supposedly framed him for her murder before killing herself. A mysterious magnate, Saito (Ken Watanabe), subsequently promises to exonerate Cobb if he is able to convince the recent heir of a competing energy conglomerate, Robert Fisher (Cillian Murphy), to break up his empire. Saito seeks out Cobb because of his reputation as the best dream extractor. That is, Cobb is a subconscious thief who specializes in entering the dreams of his marks and stealing their secrets. Despite his acumen in the arts of shared dreaming and subconscious burglary, Saito's request is more difficult than the standard job because it requires Cobb to plant an idea into the mind of his victim—hence inception—rather than to rob it. Complicating things further is Cobb's mysterious history with inception, which he apparently performed on Mal before her death, contributing to her psychological demise. Specifically, he convinced Mal that the two of them were stuck deep in a dream state and that they had to commit suicide to escape. Problems between the two ensue because Cobb is convinced that they are now awake in reality, while Mal believes they are still trapped in a dream and need to kill themselves again to return home. This creates the central retrospective interpretive conundrum for the viewer: who is correct about their ontological state? As a consequence of the guilt he feels from impacting Mal's death by incepting her with suicidal thoughts, she terrorizes his subconscious and invades any dream that he has or shares, jeopardizing Cobb's missions. Eager to complete the proverbial last job that will allow him to go legit, Cobb assembles, in quintessential heist film fashion, a team of elite accomplices, including Saito, the financer; Arthur (Joseph Gordon-Levitt), the planner; Eames (Tom Hardy), the forger; Yusef (Dileep Rao), the chemist; and Ariadne (Ellen Page), the architect. Together aboard a 747 from Sydney to Los Angeles, the team enters the minds of Fisher and each other in a multilayered, shared dreaming escapade, overcoming a series of daunting obstacles to accomplish their lofty objective, or so it seems.

All of this may sound like the stuff of standard classical Hollywood narrative, but it is not so simple or clear-cut throughout the film and, especially, after it ends. It is inaccurate, though, to label *Inception* as "non-classical" because one of the reasons that the film effectively appeals to a mass audience is its strong dependence on Hollywood principles in relation to narrative, form, and genre. The film's classical dual plot structure, which centers on Cobb's quest to return home and his attempt to reconcile with Mal, its compositionally motivated formal decisions that are often heavy-handedly accompanied by familiar classical cues, like dialogue hooks and narratively subservient parallel edits, as well as its reliance on recognizable genre conventions, all function to aid the Hollywood spectator in comprehending the byzantine story easier. Perhaps most notably in this regard is the film's bravura section in which Nolan cross-cuts between multiple levels of the dream and constantly returns to a van plunging off a bridge at the top-layer to anchor viewers in time and space, consistently reminding them how and why what is occurring in the vehicle is impacting the team members accordingly deeper down in the fantasy. Yet, as with other misdirection films that blur the ontological shifts between fantasy and reality, like *Jacob's Ladder*, *Fight Club*, and *Mulholland Dr.*, it is difficult to decipher what "really" happens in *Inception*, even in retrospect, because although the film seems to uphold distinctions between dreaming and waking life, the line separating the two becomes increasingly indistinguishable on closer review.

The primary reason for the film's lingering ambiguity in relation to the difference between fantasy and reality is its changeover, which further complicates, rather than clarifies, what "actually" occurred. Specifically, after Cobb appears to achieve his goals of successfully incepting Fisher, letting go of Mal by forgiving himself for his role in her suicide, and reuniting with his children, the final shot lingers on a close-up of his purported totem—a top that he claims spins endlessly in the dream and only falls when he is awake—that he shockingly turns his back on before viewing its fate so he can instead grab his kids. After Cobb excitedly reunites with his children, the camera then moves to fixate its gaze on the spinning top, which wobbles, but does not actually topple, before the film cuts to the end credits. This edit means that neither Cobb nor the spectator can definitively determine from this sequence of events if he is dreaming this storybook resolution or if it is transpiring in his waking life, even though the preceding scenes have led the viewer to believe that he is no longer asleep.

Thanks to this uncertain conclusion, many fans contend that the top is a red herring, a MacGuffin that distracts viewers from all of the other clues planted throughout the film that may provide better evidence of if it is possible to distinguish between dream and reality. This interpretation has only been bolstered by Nolan's ensuing comments on the issue. To wit, in his 2015 commencement address at Princeton University, Nolan asserted that the film ends with Cobb "in his own subjective reality. He didn't really care anymore, and that makes a statement: perhaps, all levels of reality are valid" (Lee). Such an interpretation can be supported by other textual evidence in relation to the top that suggests it is simply a false clue. Like all totems, the top contains a secret that only its owner is supposed to know to prevent a shared dreamer from manipulating that person's grasp of reality. However, the top's status as Cobb's actual totem is troubled for a number of reasons. First, he informs Ariadne of it, rendering it no longer safe from her potential control. Second, he also reveals that it was really Mal's initially, which is troublesome because totems are not supposed to be handled by others. Finally, it behaves opposite of the way it needs to, as it acts normally in reality (eventually falls) and its special quality (endless spinning) happens in the dream. This last aspect is most crucial because a totem's secret property has to be unique only in waking life to force a dreamer to control it in expected ways in fantasy situations. A top that simply behaves normally in reality, therefore, is a useless totem because others would manipulate it to do the same exact thing in a dream, making it impossible for Cobb to use it to determine if he is actually awake.

As a result of the ambiguity that the open-ended changeover inspires, viewers are encouraged to watch the film repeatedly to decipher the mysteries that precede it, such as the puzzling details of Cobb's totem. Fans have thus competed in games of hermeneutic one-upmanship to convince each other that they have cracked the code most convincingly. A popular counter theory, for example, which is the official explanation that appears on the *Inception* Wiki page for "Dominick Cobb" and relies heavily on textual evidence, is that Cobb's wedding ring is his real totem because it only appears in the scenes coded as in the dream, meaning it is concealed from others in reality. Such activities have helped make the film a hit in the post-theatrical market. In terms of DVD and Blu-ray sales, for example, *Inception* has raked in an additional $160 million to date (the-numbers.com).

The presence of this and other eternal ambiguities that are central to determining the "true" meaning of narrative information is, as Bordwell argues, antithetical to a defining trait of the classical film, which is supposed to leave no primary causal lines of action unresolved at the conclusion. Instead, such an element potentially puts *Inception* closer to Bordwell's art cinema category from *Narration in the Fiction Film* in which narrative incomprehensibility as well as lead characters with uncertain traits and motives are more common. To lessen confusion that arises from the various interpretations that art cinema inspires, Bordwell contends that viewers typically make recourse to real life and authorship. More specifically, these ambiguities are often understood by viewers as existing because of the director's aims to express how chaos reigns off screen, distinguishing art cinema's narrative and associated formal properties from the classical film's valorization of protagonist-driven stories and corresponding representational principles that reassure audiences that the universe abides by a causal logic. Such atypical qualities leave *Inception* particularly open to multiple interpretations, making it a film that would appear likely to alienate classically trained spectators. Yet, it did not struggle with the mass audience partly because of the ways in which it was expertly constructed for middlebrow tastes by combining features typically reserved for "legitimate" art with more accessible elements that are characteristic of mass cultural products.

In addition to its heavy reliance on familiar genre conventions as well as classical narrative and formal devices, much of *Inception*'s mass appeal is attributable to its use of a number of blockbuster standards. First, the film's huge production and marketing budgets are substantially bigger than they are for most Hollywood films. The film's cast is also filled with recognizable stars with broader international origins than is customary, as there are lead performers that hail from the United States, (Tom Berenger, DiCaprio, and Gordon-Levit), Canada (Page), Europe (Caine, Cotillard, Hardy, and Murphy), and are of Asian descent (Watanabe and Rao). The film's global appeal is also linked to location shooting decisions because it is set in exotic destinations, such as Japan, Mombasa, and Paris, that are, according to Itzkoff, actually an amalgamation of diverse production sites across the globe, including Alberta, London, Los Angeles, Paris, Tokyo, and Tangier ("The Man"). These extravagant casting and production decisions can only happen with blockbuster resources and are attractive to an industry that increasingly depends on courting the international market to recover escalating negative costs. It is the film's elaborate, action-packed, spectacle-laden set pieces, though, that situate it most securely in the blockbuster genre. More than anything else, it is these kinds of bombastic sequences that have colloquially come to define the blockbuster film.

Although staples of the blockbuster, like pyrotechnic-filled chase sequences, frequently are used to identify the genre's constituents, determining a film's status as such based on the amount of spectacle it contains is notoriously challenging. As King theorizes, this is tied to the ambiguity of the term "spectacle," which can refer to an array of attributes beyond special effects and similar elements most commonly cited as giving a film the quality. In fact, the exotic locales that serve as backdrops for many of *Inception*'s most dazzling sequences are likely to be counted as spectacular by most observers. To assuage uncertainty associated with identifying this vague trait, King contends that in Hollywood spectacle is most appropriately conceived of as being excessive to the narrative, "as a source of distraction or interruption" from the classical film's primary objective of making its familiar storytelling format easily comprehensible by employing the corresponding invisible style (*New Hollywood* 179). Wisely, he acknowledges that Hollywood's emphasis on spectacle predates the fall of the studio system as well as grants that narrative and spectacle symbiotically coexist in New Hollywood. It is the latter part of this statement that most relates to how spectacle is effectively deployed in *Inception*. Nolan caters to his audience by making spectacle subservient to narrative, as a majority of the film's most astonishing sequences are clearly framed as a product of dream logic, regardless of how spectators reinterpret what actually happened. Consequently, many of the film's most spectacular moments are initially understood as being driven by storytelling demands and do not seem superfluous to the narrative. Even more notably in this regard, one of the most common ways to reinterpret *Inception* is that reality is never represented in the diegesis because the entire film actually solely depicts Cobb's extended dream. This popular reinterpretation of the film's meaning renders *all* of its spectacular moments as narratively explainable in retrospect since viewers are never actually privy to Cobb's waking life.

The theory that the entire film is a portrayal of Cobb's extended dream primarily hinges on a key aspect of Hans Zimmer's score, making the sound design also more narratively relevant and classically driven, in retrospect. Just prior to the opening shot, a musical theme that recurs throughout the film plays. As Itzkoff summarizes in an article for the *New York Times ArtsBeat*, many fans began to read this piece as a dramatically slowed down version of Edith Piaf's "La Vie en Rose" when a YouTube user posted a comparison of the two shortly after the film's release. Specifically, Itzkoff states "When the video's pseudonymous author, camiam321, plays the key musical cue from that score, two ominous blares from a brass section, followed by a slowed-down version of the Piaf song (which the *Inception* characters play at regular speed as a warning to wake up from a dream state), they sound nearly identical" ("Hans"). This evidence compellingly supports the "all a dream" interpretation because, prior to beginning their attempt to incept Fisher, Cobb's team agrees that Piaf's song will be the musical cue that they will play to signal that the kick has to be initiated to wake them from their strong, sedative-induced, multilayered dream state. Crucially, this theme replays at the very conclusion of the film to accompany the final segment of the end credits. In short, according to this explanation, everything that occurs during the film's blockbuster-length two hours and 28 minutes between these two musical cues is actually a representation of Cobb's extended dream while he struggles to stay asleep because he desperately wants the fantasy to continue forever, or is in the final stages of the dream before the kick takes full effect. Such an interpretation is bolstered by the rules conveyed by the dialogue because of how time expands in a dream, especially at multiple levels. Consequently, it is possible to understand the whole film as a portrayal of Cobb's dream, which occurs entirely in the few moments in which he hears the kick being played in reality.

This popular reinterpretation helps to explain the narrative significance of many of the film's most ambiguous and seemingly absurd elements. If it was all just a dream, for instance, then concerns about the veracity of Cobb's totem become irrelevant. It does not matter that it initially belonged to Mal or that others know its secret because it is just a projection of Cobb's subconscious. Additionally, it reveals why

Figure 6.1. The impossible architecture of the hotel room in *Inception* from which Mal commits suicide.

the flashback of Mal's suicide seems nonsensical, as she plunges from a window that is purportedly in their hotel room even though Cobb tries to persuade her not to jump from another window inside of that same room that inexplicably faces her directly. Similarly, the sequences ostensibly coded as depictions of Cobb's waking life that appear too good to be true, like the happy ending, or that are too far-fetched to be realistic, such as the fact that he enters situations in the midst of the action, can be explained as products of dream logic. Most notably in the impractical regard are the chase scenes in Mombasa, where Cobb is pursued mercilessly by agents who act like subconscious projections in dreams, nearly crushed by walls that defy physics by appearing to close in on him, and all-too-conveniently saved by Saito just in time. Accordingly, in retrospect, not even these spectacle-laden, action sequences are forced or narratively irrelevant because they are driven by story demands if Cobb is dreaming the whole time, including the sequences that appear to be coded as reality.

In addition to explaining away *Inception*'s most illogical properties, the extended dream theory helps to dispel many of the other primary critiques of the film. Chief among these disparagements are complaints about the amount of expository dialogue employed to explain the intricate rules of dreaming to the audience, which detractors claim leads to all of Cobb's team members being simplistic characters who lack psychological depth. David Denby of *The New Yorker* typifies this rhetoric by noting "Nolan is working on so many levels of representation at once that he has to lay in pages of dialogue just to explain what's going on." Although this is a fair critique of the film, regardless of how it is interpreted, it becomes a

Figure 6.2. Alley walls appear to close in on Dom Cobb, as he evades being pursued in one of *Inception*'s scenes ostensibly coded as not being part of a dream.

less severe issue if the entirety is understood to be an extended depiction of Cobb's dream. If the members of Cobb's team are just projections of his subconscious that represent different aspects of his personality, then their insufficient character complexity can be explained by the fact that they are supposed to be one-dimensional. As a result, Arthur becomes an embodiment of Cobb's rational side, Ariadne transforms into his creative spirit, and so on. This interpretation, then, can become a totalizing causal logic for comprehending all of the film's ambiguities and shortcomings in a way that resembles the paranoid logic of conspiracy theorists who rely on the discourses of causality and agency to understand more satisfactorily what otherwise remains insufficiently explained. In fact, many fans expand on this theory by claiming that the film is really an extended metaphor for Hollywood filmmaking and the difficulty of planting ideas in the audience's mind, with Cobb standing in for the director and his teammates representing Nolan's collaborators, like an executive producer (Saito), special effects designer (Yusef), and so on.

The interpretation that everything is just a dream also impacts the film's cultural implications. Considering the ways in which *Inception* was marketed and received according to such strong authorial terms, it is unsurprising that critics of Nolan's work often cite it as another example of his disconcerting gender politics. One of the director's most obvious thematic preoccupations is featuring heterosexual, male leads haunted by the tragic deaths of their love interests. Even more troubling to detractors in this regard is how these women cause their bereaved male partners to obsess dangerously about avenging their demise, a theme that is particularly acute in his two previous misdirection films: *Memento* and *The Prestige*. Yet, as with *Memento*, in which considerable ambiguity is raised about whether or not the purportedly dead wife that Leonard Shelby (Guy Pearce) pines for was actually murdered, an interpretation that Cobb dreamed the whole thing unsettles the explanation that Mal's suicide is the root of the protagonist's problems. Of course, if viewers instead think that Cobb is actually awake at the end, then Mal remains the film's unambiguous antagonist because her unwillingness to believe her husband about escaping limbo led to her framing him for murder and subsequently terrorizing his subconscious. In contrast, if the film is all really portraying Cobb's dream, then it becomes possible to interpret Mal's character in a very different fashion, as her theory about them still not being awake and stuck outside of reality might actually be correct.

Fans ascribing to the dream theory have used this as a basis for deriving some of the most outlandish interpretations of the film's "true" meaning. One explanation predicated on it all being a dream that has gained traction in some virtual communities is that Mal is actually the one performing inception on Cobb because he either unwittingly or intentionally refuses to come to terms with the fact that he is stuck in a fantasy. As its proponents contend, this interpretation is backed by the film's discussion about the rules of dreaming, as the limbo state that Cobb and Mal need to escape is the deepest dream level, meaning that it can only happen within another dream. Consequently, when the two commit suicide in limbo they would not have awoken to reality, but instead just entered a shallower level of the dream. Of course, it is possible that this is just a plot hole or a case of classical editorial intelligence in which superfluous information has been omitted for the purpose of privileging narrative propulsion. Nevertheless, some supporters of this reading maintain that Mal is trying to plant the idea of self-forgiveness into Cobb's mind. In particular, she is attempting to convince Cobb that he should not feel guilty for incepting her initially and that all will be well with their family when he finally awakens.

For subscribers of the Mal inception theory, there are many textual clues that can be leveraged to buttress its primary claims. For starters, they posit that Mal is conspiring with others to complete her objective. Cobb's father-in-law, Miles (Michael Caine), for instance, who never appears in the film's sequences ostensibly coded as part of the dream, is reinterpreted to be one of her primary collaborators. Hence, when Cobb conveniently appears in Miles's lecture hall and his father-in-law pleads with him to "come back to reality," he is actually communicating with his son-in-law in the dream state as a member of Mal's incepting team, rather than as simply a concerned family member trying to impart sage advice in reality. Additionally, this interpretation retroactively makes Mal's climactic disagreement with Cobb in limbo about who is right in relation to their ontological state the film's most important dialogue exchange. As Mal explains, it does seem coincidental that Cobb's purported reality is characterized by a persecution complex in which he is chased around the globe by mysterious agents who strikingly resemble the subconscious projections that attack dreamers. Put simply, this interpretation provides a conspiratorial, all-encompassing way to refute claims that Mal is the villain by transforming her into a character benevolently attempting to save her husband from his own guilty conscience.

Despite how such a reading helps to lessen the claims about Nolan's misogynistic tendencies, it does not completely absolve the film from having sexist sensibilities. Even if Mal, whose name in Spanish translates into "bad" in English, is actually a hero and not the antagonist, she is still secretly manipulating her husband's actions behind the scenes. Regardless of whether or not viewers interpret the film as a depiction of only an extended dream, then, Cobb remains the archetypal misdirection film protagonist by being portrayed as emasculated by powerful feminizing forces beyond his control. If it is all just a dream, then Cobb is, at best, trapped in a fantasy that he cannot or does not want to be liberated from or is, at worst, at the mercy of others, most likely his wife, who are incepting him with thoughts that are not his own. In contrast, if the distinctions between dream and reality can actually be sustained, then the film is a representation of his attempts to overcome the seemingly insurmountable obstacles that are attributable to his wife's misguided actions, which stem from her dimwitted inability to discern fantasy from reality, albeit thanks to Cobb's initial and unethical inception of her. Although the latter explanation provides Cobb with greater and more laudable agency than the former interpretation, it still positions him as a wounded man who must surmount Mal's imprudent decision to frame him for her murder because she hoped her suicide threat would also convince him to kill himself.

Such gender dynamics not only align *Inception* with the cultural politics of many misdirection films. They also overlap with the gendered representations contained in most blockbusters. One of the major issues that scholars, like King, have to contend with in their arguments that the seemingly incongruent Hollywood Renaissance and blockbuster-era are more alike than different is the oppositional cultural politics that characterize each production trend. As King details, it is tempting to link each moment to its corresponding zeitgeist because of the overarching political beliefs that are said to define the respective times. This line of thinking makes sense at a cursory level. Whereas the Hollywood Renaissance and its artistic innovation coincided with the countercultural revolution and is known for expressing largely progressive values, the shift to the blockbuster model and its more classically oriented filmmaking was contemporaneous with the Reagan-era and a turn to conservatism in the United States. King counters this simplistic account by highlighting the other contexts, particularly shifting industrial circumstances that influenced these developments as much as, if not more than, changing cultural conditions. He does grant, however, that the transition to blockbuster production did mean largely abandoning the experimentation of the Hollywood Renaissance in favor of a return to traditional classical principles, albeit not primarily because of broader political developments. This shift did have cultural repercussions, though. As King summarizes, since the fall of the studio system, "male audiences have been targeted more heavily" and "male-oriented genres have flourished," which "provides another explanation for the prominence of science fiction and the action film in the contemporary blockbuster economy" (*New Hollywood* 138). Of course, there are examples of constituent films, like *Titanic*, that performed exceptionally with female viewers, and not only men are attracted to the genres most affiliated with blockbuster production. What is clear, though, is that *Inception*, with its heavy science fiction and action film attributes as well as the casting of DiCaprio to appeal to female spectators enamored with his good looks was designed, at least in part, to correspond to the dominant production logic of the blockbuster-era, marking an important moment in the misdirection film's history.

Is It Better to Make a Low- or High-Art Misdirection Film?: The Kafkaesque Genius of *Shutter Island*'s Middlebrow Appeal

In contrast to *Inception*'s clear status as a blockbuster, it is challenging to make a case for *Shutter Island*'s inclusion in the category. The attachment of superstar branded commodities to the project, headlined by the reteaming of DiCaprio and Scorsese, certainly gave it blockbuster potential. Yet, the two's track record at the box office has not netted blockbuster revenues to date. In fact, *Shutter Island* is the duo's most profitable film so far in domestic theaters, garnering approximately $48 million over its estimated $80 million production costs (imdb.com). Such comparatively modest revenues and profit margin, however, are hardly blockbuster material. Even more notable, though, is the film's failure to match the Oscar attention heaped on all of the other collaborations between the two. Each other time the duo has teamed, it resulted in plentiful Academy Award nominations, including 10 for their first collaboration, *Gangs of New York*, 11 for *The Aviator*, five for *The Wolf of Wall Street*, and six for *The Departed*, which finally captured the biggest Oscars that had eluded Scorsese for decades (imdb.com). With zero Academy Award nominations, *Shutter Island* is obviously an outlier. These results cannot be blamed on its status as a misdirection film, however, as *Inception* was well-decorated at the 2011 Oscar ceremony, earning four wins in the technical categories and even garnering a rare nomination for both a blockbuster and misdirection film for Best Picture (imdb.com).

Instead, *Shutter Island*'s anomalous result with the Academy of Motion Picture Arts and Sciences is largely attributable to its distribution strategy. All indications point to the film being initially designed to garner significant Oscar attention. In addition to it being the adaptation of Lehane's follow-up novel to *Mystic River* as well as the first reteaming of Scorsese and DiCaprio since *The Departed*, it was originally slotted for an autumn release, the time the media conglomerates reserve for their strongest Oscar hopefuls to give them momentum for the impending voting process. This distribution tactic has only grown more important economically, as post-theatrical revenues have increased because release window staggering schedules mean that home-video versions are first available near the time of the ceremony, bolstering the potential profits of nominees. Viacom's Paramount film division, however, shockingly decided to delay *Shutter Island*'s initially announced October 2, 2009 domestic theatrical release until February 19, 2010. Paramount's CEO Brad Grey justified the decision by claiming that they made the move "because of the financial pressures associated with the downturn" (qtd. in Finke). It is improbable that the lingering impact of the 2008 U.S. financial crisis was the sole, or determining, factor in the shift. According to rumors, the delay was more likely attributable to DiCaprio's purported unavailability to travel for the international promotional junket and to concerns about rapidly declining profits that DVD sales started producing by then (Finke).

Precipitously declining DVD revenue is a liable culprit for Paramount's decision to alter its distribution plans. By 2010, the downturn in DVD purchases that began a few years earlier had plunged to unforeseen depths. Although the technology had run its course with consumers and consequently started to dip slightly in 2007, total revenues had already plummeted to less than half of what they were at that time by 2010, as DVD sales generated less than $5 billion for the industry in that year (Holden, Wade). This was a sobering statistic for Hollywood executives who had greenlit films due to their potential to perform exceptionally in the aftermarket, especially considering that the 2010 sales figures represented an over $3 billion drop from the nearly $8 billion revenue total of 2009, even though the industry released over 60 more titles on DVD in 2010 than it did in 2009 (Holden, Wade). The goal of constructing *Shutter Island* for the DVD market was central to its production logic, at least according to quotes attributed to Scorsese. James Gilligan, the film's psychiatric advisor, reported that "Scorsese said this film will make double the income because people will have to see it a second time to understand what happened the first time" (qtd. in Cox). Such discursive evidence indicates that the director was keenly aware of how changing revenue streams in the preceding years had altered Hollywood's production tactics. Although Scorsese was right that the industry still eagerly backed films for the DVD market when he joined the project in 2007, the sudden implosion of that line of revenue thereafter helps explain why Paramount unexpectedly postponed the release of a film that once seemed primed for optimal aftermarket performance. By 2010, Hollywood had practically abandoned DVD, preferring to privilege films that would do best on other post-theatrical platforms, such as on-demand and online streaming options, which encourage ephemeral rentals akin to the VCR-era, rather than the permanent purchases inspired by DVD.

Consequently, even though it received no Academy Award consideration, I contend that *Shutter Island* was conceived of as a prototypical prestige product at the outset. Had the film not been subject to industrial circumstances beyond the filmmakers' control, it likely would have been honored with numerous Oscar nominations, especially given the results of all other Scorsese and DiCaprio collaborations. Of course, this is speculative in spite of the corroborating evidence that suggests its poor fate with Oscar voters was virtually sealed when its release was pushed back to February since few films that hit theaters during the first months of the calendar year are ultimately recognized by the Academy. Yet, an examination of the ways in which the film was marketed and constructed illustrates that it was originally created with a middlebrow sensibility designed to maximize its profit and cachet.

Small distinctions between the first trailer made for *Shutter Island* and a subsequent one cut after the release date was delayed begin to highlight how high- and low-art elements were combined in the film. As is standard for New Hollywood advertising, the two trailers strongly foreground generic hybridity, as both accentuate its affiliations with film noir, the psychological thriller, horror, and the misdirection film. In the first trailer, the psychological thriller elements are prioritized in the presentation of the film's quest narrative, the film noir aspects are explicit in formal aspects, particularly in the *mise-en-scène*, while facets of horror and misdirection are peppered in, such as when a disturbingly disfigured prisoner stares at the camera and indirectly tells the spectator that "This is a game. You're a rat in a maze." What differentiates the second similar, but slightly re-edited, version of the preview, which advertises the belated February release date, is its greater emphasis on the film's horror properties. Images featuring gore absent from the initial trailer are present in the revised one, including shots of a character's face covered in blood. Additionally, the preview ends with a prototypical jump scare when a mysterious character leaps out of the darkness onto another one. These minor changes indicate that producers knowingly shifted their marketing approach to accentuate the film's more traditionally debased aspects after it was clear that it was now likely out of serious Oscar contention.

One reason why *Shutter Island* contains many horror facets and elements of other genres that are often degraded is because evidence suggests it was partly designed as Scorsese's extended homages to those films. Such properties are unsurprising because references to film history are one of the director's authorial calling cards, a fact made even more evident in his follow-up to *Shutter Island*, *Hugo* (2011), his love letter to Georges Méliès and early cinema, which returned Scorsese to familiar Academy Award fame by garnering 11 nominations and five wins (imdb.

com). Framing the film for readers of a promotional interview the director did for *TimeOut London* magazine, Dave Calhoun describes *Shutter Island* as a "1950s-set thriller with Hitchcockian B-movie flavor." As this illustrates, the film was received by some critics as an amalgamation of low- and high-art elements. The combination of B-movie allusions with direct references to Hitchcock, a filmmaker once considered to be little more than a commercial entertainer, whose reputation has since transformed into that of a revered artist, epitomizes reviewers' reactions. For some critics, the B-movie traditions hampered the film. Joe Neumaier of the *New York Daily News*, for instance, complains about the script and DiCaprio's consequent performance by noting the actor "often simply mouths questions and waits for some B-movie tradition (the jabbering madman, the German doctor, the mystery woman) to provide answers."

Other reviewers, though, considered *Shutter Island*'s many homages to film history to be a strength, especially if they could be linked to Hitchcock, arguably the most important progenitor of the contemporary misdirection film. In an article for *The Guardian*'s website, entitled "Martin Scorsese: Master of the Hitchcock Tribute," Andrew Pulver writes that Scorsese "has taken the Hitchcock atmosphere of murderous insanity and run with it, shoehorning in one Hitchcock bit after another." He subsequently provides YouTube clip evidence of how *Shutter Island* references many of Hitchcock's films, including *Psycho* (1960), *Spellbound* (1945), *Marnie* (1964), *Vertigo* (1958), and *Notorious* (1946). There is a shot, for instance, that exactly replicates the one of the showerhead in *Psycho* and a scene of a run up a twisty, lighthouse staircase that evokes the treks up the bell tower stairs in *Vertigo*. The fact that Scorsese was thinking of Hitchcock while making the film is supported by his thematic preoccupations and the production history. As he told Calhoun, he "showed his colleagues *The Wrong Man* [1957]" to prepare for *Shutter Island* because "The main character in that is innocent but he feels guilty for who he is . . . I was raised a Catholic and I'm interested in that aspect of ourselves."

Shutter Island similarly focuses on a tormented protagonist, who is referred to as Edward "Teddy" Daniels or Andrew Laeddis (Leonardo DiCaprio), and has been committed to Ashecliffe mental institution for the criminally insane on Shutter Island. He is sentenced for his inability to cope with the guilt associated with his murder of his wife, who is called both Rachel Solando and Dolores Chanal (Michelle Williams), after he purportedly both denied her insanity and found she drowned their three children. Complicating things for the viewer is the fact that Teddy's (the name I use to refer to him as for clarity's sake) status as a patient is neither evident to him nor the spectator until the changeover, which is highly indebted to *The Cabinet of Dr. Caligari*'s (1920) similar epiphany. The changeover exposes why it is difficult to know what "really" happened because it reveals that Teddy is the subject of Dr. Cawley's (Ben Kingsley) conspiratorial scheme. For the radical psychological experiment, the doctors pretend that Teddy is a U.S. Marshall, partnered with his primary psychiatrist, Dr. Sheehan (Mark Ruffalo), in disguise. Teddy is tricked into believing the two are investigating an escaped patient, Rachel Solando (Emily Mortimer). This is intended to make him realize he is living a lie to save him from a lobotomy, a ploy that initially seems to work. As Cawley explains during the changeover that leads to Teddy's cognitive crisis, for example, his and his wife's alter-egos are anagrams for the elaborate ruse. Like *Inception*, which also centers on DiCaprio's character's overcoming the guilt of his wife's apparent death, though, it is difficult to know what "actually" happened despite the revelation. Although Cawley seems to give a totalizing account during the changeover, its veracity depends on the viewer's beliefs about the doctors' motives and Teddy's mental state. This is because, as with *Memento*, the narrative is focalized through an unreliable protagonist with psychological issues, rendering him a potential pawn and his traits, such as his employment as a U.S. Marshall, open to scrutiny. Textual evidence that precedes the changeover bolsters this vagueness because Cawley goes to ethically dubious extremes to prove that his psychological methods are superior to alternatives he deems outmoded. It is also possible, however, that Cawley seems that way because the viewer learns about him through a delusional protagonist, or because it is just a cover for a more nefarious plot, making it hard to delineate fact from fiction.

Figure 6.3. Edward "Teddy" Daniels walks away from Dr. Sheehan in *Shutter Island* after uttering his ambiguous final line of dialogue.

Such ambiguity is compounded by what follows the changeover, as Teddy's last line of dialogue in which, after appearing to regress back into insanity, he waxes poetic about if it would be "worse to live as a monster, or to die as a good man?" This unexpected ending indicates that he is likely faking his relapse to submit to brain surgery, rather than either to continue to face what he now perceives to be true about his identity, or to fight the doctors futilely. Such a reading is supported by the film's ensuing, final shot of a lighthouse, the location where Teddy suspects the lobotomies happen. On cursory review, this implies that Teddy has consciously sabotaged Cawley's plan to convince the Board of Overseers and the doctor's supposed rival, Dr. Naehring (Max von Sydow), that his mental illness can be treated without brain surgery. Cawley informs Teddy during the changeover, though, that he relapsed after they had a previous breakthrough, suggesting that his current regression could be genuine. As Cox summarizes, this uncertainty has helped the film to be discussed intently by fans since its release. He also notes that, like *Inception*, Scorsese and DiCaprio have refused to provide further detail about the "correct" interpretation, only fueling more fan activity. This is exacerbated by the fact that Teddy's final line of dialogue is original to Laeta Kalogridis's screenplay, making Lehane's source novel a dead end. As Caine did in relation to *Inception*, however, Cox claims that Gilligan reported that the ending is unambiguous because it unequivocally reveals that Teddy was "too guilty to go on living," meaning that he is "going to vicariously commit suicide by handing [him]self over to the people who're going to lobotomise [him]." According to the film's psychiatric advisor, this reading is crucial because lobotomies are now threatening to return to the actual field. Like Cawley's explanation, then, Gilligan's declaration about his interpretation being definitive is questionable largely because of his vested interest in making the assertion.

Many spectators refuse to accept this simple explanation as absolute and instead leverage the film's lingering ambiguity to interpret it in numerous other ways, regardless of what Teddy's final rhetorical question and the concluding shot of the lighthouse insinuate. Again, recourse to authorship is a driving force in this regard because Scorsese has used eternal narrative uncertainty to probe the thin line separating sanity and insanity before, most famously in *Taxi Driver*. For most of these fans, *Shutter Island*'s ending resembles *Taxi Driver*'s unclear resolution of its protagonist's mental state and *Inception*'s spinning top. The question of whether Teddy has regressed is thus irrelevant to them. Rather, these viewers begin from the premise that Teddy has consciously elected brain surgery and instead focus on the "real" reasons for that choice. These theories largely hinge on deciphering the doctors' objectives, rejecting Cawley's explanation during the changeover as truth. One such compelling interpretation is housed on an anonymous, amateur website, the *Wistful Writer*, which contains posts about the male author's (he uses male pronouns to describe himself) assorted interests, including film and literature. When I retrieved his "The *Shutter Island* Mystery" essay in August 2015, the site's listings of the month's top posts clearly revealed that this entry was its primary draw and had resonated with readers, as it had over 5,000 views, dwarfing the second-place finisher, which had under 400 hits. Importantly, he frames his sophisticated analysis as just one interpretation, claiming that he does not intend "to impose it on others." His reading, then, is predicated on the notion that the film's meaning cannot be understood definitively, a position that differs from standard misdirection film reception and typical readings of *Shutter Island*. Most participants on the film's *Internet Movie Database* "Message Board," for example, make absolute claims about the film's meaning, such as is if the protagonist is "actually" Teddy or Andrew. In contrast, this author reiterates the film's lasting ambiguity even in relation to his own account by noting "there are many issues with all interpretations of the story, including mine."

One aspect that makes the interpretation on the *Wistful Writer*'s site compelling is its interesting overlaps with *Inception*. In particular, he argues that Cawley is anything but a benevolent psychiatrist because he is instead trying to plant false memories in Teddy's mind for malevolent purposes. Such a reading begins not only to explain the questionable ethics of Cawley and his associates, but it also imbues the film's many conspiratorial references to Ashecliffe actually being a government-funded facility run by the military to conduct clandestine tests with greater narrative significance. According to this interpretation, Ashecliffe is "really" comprised of doctors testing Nazi-inspired mind control experiments on patients to create more adept special soldiers to fight communism during the Cold War. Consequently, the seemingly paranoid beliefs that Teddy has and learns about what transpires on Shutter Island behind the scenes might not be delusions. That is not to say that all of his speculations are accurate, as even this theory's author grants that "maybe Teddy is just a conspiracy theorist obsessed with intelligence agencies." As he also notes, however, it is strange that the facility is policed by guards with military vehicles and guns, that an orderly does not dispute Teddy's claim that the Warden (Ted Levine) is "an ex-military prick," as well as that Cawley is renowned for his work with "Scotland Yard, MI5, and the OSS." This interpretation, then, aligns the film more closely with

Figure 6.4. Visual evidence of *Shutter Island's* Ashecliffe Hospital being run and guarded by the U.S. military.

Arlington Road (1999) and, especially, with *Jacob's Ladder* than with any other misdirection film because of how it depicts agency panic about a protagonist made into a patsy by a powerful organization that transforms him into a warrior for their cause. Most importantly, like *Jacob's Ladder*, if Teddy is "actually" a test patient, it is difficult to determine what, if anything, is factual. This renders its mix of low- and high-art more narratively meaningful retrospectively because those elements can all be understood as fabrications for the ruse.

The theory forwarded by the author of the *Wistful Writer* site hinges primarily on challenging the claims that Cawley and his associates make about Teddy's "true" identity and his personal history by countering that they are "actually" part of the cover story. To wit, he contends that Teddy was never a U.S. Marshal, Andrew Laeddis (Elias Koteas) is a product of his dissociative identity disorder, and that he did not kill his wife for murdering their kids because they were actually childless. He instead posits that Teddy was committed to Ashecliffe for being a pyromaniac, who killed his wife when he burned their apartment building. To repress the crime, he creates the Laeddis alter-ego and constructs an alternative past. Thus, he is ideal for the conspiratorial ploy because he has already lost grasp of reality and his history. Hence the reason he identifies Laeddis as the "firebug" who killed his wife and why, when the manifestation of his dissociative identity disorder appears, he looks evil and deformed. As he also speculates, Andrew Laeddis seems much more like a fictional name than Edward Daniels. The contention that Teddy is "actually" an arsonist is supported by how he blows up Cawley's car with only his tie and a pebble, a feat the doctor seems to confirm during the changeover, as well as how he and Laeddis are shown in close-ups lighting matches the same way. In contrast, he reconstructs his Teddy identity as heroic, explaining why the doctors make him into a fake U.S. Marshall, complete with the film noir traits for the role play. Although this reading might be far-fetched, it explains ambiguities unresolved by the changeover's account. For starters, it highlights why Teddy is adamant that "it was the smoke that got her" in the fire that kills his wife and never mentions his children until Cawley prompts him, even though he says that "four people died" in the blaze. It also reveals why the doctors act unethically by having a nurse impersonate Rachel, patients submit to Teddy's interrogations, and Teddy fight other patients.

These inconsistencies are just the beginning because the interpretive possibilities created by such a theory potentially make all of *Shutter Island*'s ambiguities narratively meaningful, in retrospect. Most significantly, they transform all of the B-film and high-art references from being potentially read as primarily artistic flourishes or authorial signatures into narratively relevant aspects. That is, these ostensibly outlandish elements become more plausible in relation to the story if they are reinterpreted as beholden to an evil mind-control scheme, as opposed to a compassionately curative plan. Indeed, the high- and low-art properties can now be understood as Hollywood-inspired creations that make the fakery more dramatic and believable for Teddy and the viewer, albeit often anachronistically, as the references to Hitchcock's post-1954 films demonstrate. When the viewer first sees Shutter Island through Teddy's eyes as he nears it on the boat he has been placed on, for example, the foreboding shot, accompanied by the ominous soundtrack, directly evoke Skull Island in the monster film, *King Kong* (1933). Likewise, the film noir qualities, such as the ubiquitous fedoras, trench coats, and chain-smoking, can be reinterpreted as conscious decisions by the scheming doctors that are even more related to that genre's convention of the protagonist's inescapable past haunting him because they manufactured that history. The conspiratorial story that Sheehan feeds Teddy in the creepy mausoleum also makes more sense if it is understood as designed by the doctors to spook their mark. Similarly, Naehring's amplification of his German heritage takes on greater meaning if it is comprehended as helping to convince Teddy about what "really" transpired during his military service and his associated memories of the liberation of Dachau. Obviously, the B-film references extend beyond these examples, but what is relevant is how the mind-control explanation retrospectively makes them more narratively significant for Teddy and the viewer.

The same is true of the high-art elements, which are most evident during Naehring's introduction. Teddy seamlessly exchanges German dialogue about concentration camps with Naehring, which is uncharacteristically not subtitled for classical viewers, encouraging them to search for a translation. Teddy also displays his knowledge of German culture by correcting Sheehan's likely purposeful misidentification of diegetic music as being composed by the Austrian Mahler, whose music would have been banned by the Nazis because he was a Jew, and not by the German Brahms, as his fake partner claims. These two seemingly benign moments are important retrospectively, according to the *Wistful Writer*, who argues that although Teddy was a soldier during WWII, it is difficult to know what he "actually" experienced. Cawley claims during the changeover that Teddy was "at the liberation of Dachau," but it is unknown if he killed any guards. Yet, during Teddy's flashback-inspired memory of Dachau, he murders German soldiers and makes the *Kommandant* suffer a slow death from a botched suicide. Crucially, then, the thoughts the doctors implant differ from Teddy's memories. The issue of Teddy's violence is frequently broached, most memorably during his disconcerting exchange with the sadistic Warden, who is costumed like an SS officer and unethically tries to incite the patient's ferocity. This is significant in light of the fact that the girl who haunts his memories from the mass of bodies at Dachau for not being able to save her becomes his daughter, Rachel Laeddis, in Cawley's revised explanation. As the *Wistful Writer* contends, however, she is the only of Teddy's supposed children who communicates with him in his delusions, raising doubt about him being a father at all. The doctors' alteration of the Dachau account, then, can be read as part of the effort to convince Teddy that his wife did not die in the fire he lit because he instead reverted to his "violent nature" after discovering she murdered their kids.

As the Rachel Solando (Patricia Clarkson), whom Teddy discovers hiding in the cave and provides much of the source material for the mind-control reinterpretation, such as how the patient has been surreptitiously fed psychotropic drugs by the doctors to instigate his delusions since the role play began, claims, this is the film's "Kafkaesque genius." Once Teddy is declared insane by the doctors, any of his attempts to refute their diagnosis can be used against him as further proof of his mental illness. Although she is almost certainly just a manifestation of Teddy's paranoid visions, her high-art reference to Franz Kafka's literature is perhaps the biggest clue to deciphering *Shutter Island* in this way. As the Kafkaesque allusion connotes, the author became renowned for expressing the confusion associated with the bureaucratic madness of modernity in his novels, especially *The Trial*. Like that book's protagonist, Josef K., who is unable to determine what he has been arrested for, or how to mount an appropriate defense in response, both Teddy and the viewer are left to ponder eternally what crimes he "actually" committed and what the doctors are "really" doing to him as a result. Again, such an intertextual connection only becomes possible if viewers accept that the changeover and what ensues, particularly Teddy's last line of dialogue, open more questions than provide definitive answers about the narrative's "true" meaning and have knowledge of Kafka's output.

This lingering ambiguity is further supported by the film's *mise-en-scène*, which, like *Memento*'s, a film that it is also similar to, is itself unreliable. This becomes most evident during the scene when Teddy interrogates Mrs. Kearns (Robin Bartlett), in which she asks for a glass of water that appears to be there initially, disappears when she goes to drink it, and then reappears on the table when she sets it down. This is not the only instance when such visual unreliability occurs, as, for example, a liquor bottle initially seen in Teddy's wife's hand during a dream sequence disappears subsequently. Obviously, this impossibility can be attributed to the irrationality of dream logic; however, a similar discontinuity in relation to the lighthouse is less easy to explain. Although Deputy Warden McPherson (John Carroll Lynch) indicates that the lighthouse is a "sewage treatment facility," Teddy eventually believes that it is where the brain surgeries are conducted. When he finally arrives there, though, he discovers it is practically empty, aside from a small office where Cawley is waiting for him to provide the explanation that serves as the changeover. Yet, the lighthouse shown in the final shot does not exactly match the one he initially sees or visits because, as the *Wistful Writer* shows, it is not bordered by the same fence, raising the possibility that something

Figure 6.5. *Shutter Island*'s final shot presents a seemingly distinct lighthouse from the previous one, as the long fence extending beyond the small one bordering it alone has vanished.

underhanded is actually occurring in the alternate lighthouse that Teddy never actually finds. Cawley himself insinuates what might be occurring there when he taunts Teddy during the changeover by asking him "where are the Nazi experiments . . . the Satanic O.R.s?" The viewer, like Teddy, can never know because the insides of the possible second lighthouse remain forever undisclosed.

In contrast to the liquor bottle inconsistency, but like the lighthouse discrepancy, it is difficult to attribute the water glass issue to delusion, though, the retrospective knowledge that Teddy is experiencing psychological issues potentially explains its rationale in that way. How viewers ultimately interpret the scene's meaning, then, is again ultimately contingent on what they believe about the doctors' motives. Importantly, the scene initially seems to be a quintessential misdirection film moment because, in retrospect, it highlights how classical formal devices disguise the impending changeover at the same time that they flaunt it for viewer discovery. Specifically, when Teddy presses Mrs. Kearns about the purportedly absent Sheehan, the camera cuts numerous times, in prototypical shot/reverse shot fashion, to the psychiatrist's facial reactions, practically giving away a big secret, as both Teddy and the audience still believe he is also just a U.S. Marshall investigating the mystery. The way the water glass sequence is formally constructed, however, complicates this standard misdirection film reading. Although its illogical properties could be the product of a continuity error or an indication of Teddy's increasingly delusional perception, neither of those is the only possible, nor necessarily most convincing, explanations. This is because the full glass is clearly visible in Sheehan's hand, until the film cuts to a close-up of Mrs. Kearns imaginarily drinking it, before it cuts again to a birds-eye view of her placing the now empty cup on the table. What is most relevant about the three shots is that none of them are unquestionably framed as being from Teddy's perspective, though, the one with nothing in her hand can certainly be interpreted as portraying his vision; however, Sheehan is situated directly behind Teddy at that moment, making it as likely that the viewer could be getting the information from his perspective since he also frequently exchanges gazes with Mrs. Kearns during the discussion.

The point is that it is impossible to tell what "actually" happened or why it "really" occurred in that scene and in relation to the lighthouse, which makes them both fitting microcosms for how the viewer seems to be encouraged to interpret the entire film. The film's *mise-en-scène*, then, may ultimately be a red herring, too, suggesting that, more than anything else, *Shutter Island* is likely an unsolvable Kafkaesque narrative that does not provide a definitive answer about who Teddy is or what the doctors are doing to him. As many fans have pointed out, water and fire are deployed throughout the film constantly to signal the unreliability of Teddy's perceptions. In relation to water, there are many clues, in addition to the aforementioned glass, that suggest its significance, including the opening scene when Teddy splashes water on his face after expressing his dislike of it from getting sick on a boat in which the shackles that held him before the role play began are visible, the torrential rains that consistently obscure his ability to discern reality, and the water leaking from the fake revolver that he breaks during the changeover. Similarly, fire is also associated with his delusions, as the same roaring fire that demonically appears behind Naehring during his introduction rages behind the also sinister Laeddis, and a campfire is the only source of light when he encounters the cave-dwelling Rachel. Both elemental symbols, then, are not only linked to Teddy's unreliability; they are also connected to the two most plausible explanations given for his psychological instability: his inability to cope with his wife's death from his arson, or murdering her after she drowned their children. Either way, it is clear that Teddy is delusional and has been the subject of an elaborate role play. The ambiguity about what killed his wife, then, does little to change the viewer's conception of Teddy's condition and his lack of agency. Instead, it creates considerable uncertainty about why he is mentally ill and what the doctors are doing about it. That is, the film ultimately leaves it to the viewer to decide if Cawley conducted the role play in a last ditch effort to save Teddy from a lobotomy, or if the doctors conspired to manipulate the patient by drugging him and then subjecting him to brain surgery to complete his transformation.

Regardless of how the viewer interprets *Shutter Island* as a result of this lingering ambiguity, its connections to the broader thematic concerns and stylistic tendencies of *Inception*, particularly, and the misdirection film genre, generally, are clear. Whichever way it is read, it depicts a protagonist who lost his autonomy because of a traumatic event linked to his wife. His inability to exert traditional masculine control over his family caused him either to commit familicide by killing his wife because of his unhealthy obsession with fire or to murder her out of revenge for drowning their kids. This act resulted in him having to submit to the will of the doctors who now either benevolently or nefariously control his fate. As the last line of dialogue reveals, the only possible agency that remains for Teddy is faking his regression to save himself from guilt or giving in to the doctors' plans for brain surgery. Like the viewer of the misdirection film, then, Teddy knows he is being manipulated, but cannot do anything about it. This inability to know what the doctors are "really" doing is largely a product of storytelling and representational decisions to focalize the film through an unreliable protagonist, afflicted with "actual" or manufactured delusions. These indisputably paranoid visions make the film's expert combination of high- and low-art elements more narratively significant, in retrospect, because they can be read as products of Teddy's imaginings that are heightened either by the compassionate role play, or the doctors' drugging him as part of an evil plot to fulfill their sinister agenda. Such qualities align the film closely with *Inception*, which also presents an irresolvable puzzle that puts the viewer in the position of its broken protagonist who struggles to maintain a fading grasp on reality because of a tragedy related to his wife. That film's eternal uncertainty about the distinction between what is real and imaginary renders its many blockbuster elements more narratively relevant. Both films' similar presentation of the ontological blurring between reality and fantasy made them ripe for examination in virtual communities. These two films, therefore, are the contemporary misdirection film's apotheosis because they successfully attracted wide audiences by crystalizing the genre's formal tendencies and thematic concerns in Hollywood's most expensive and prestigious packages.

Conclusion

The 2010 cultural and industrial zenith of the genre was short-lived, as comparatively few misdirection films have been released since then. Instead, narrative complexity has become more associated with commercial American television than it has with Hollywood film since at least that time, especially on premium cable. Although they were slower to seize the opportunity, television producers have also attempted to augment their bottomlines and authorial reputations by creating shows, which contain narratives that encourage viewers to watch them repeatedly and discuss them fervently in virtual communities. This evidence suggests that changing cultural, industrial, and technological conditions have similarly impacted the narrative strategies that have been deployed of late in commercial, moving-image media forms other than film. The proliferation of computer role-playing games since the 1990s, for instance, has been triggered by industrial motives and audience desires that resemble those that contributed to the rise in contemporary Hollywood misdirection films. Popular role-playing videogame franchises, such as the *Final Fantasy* series, which began as console games and have developed into massively multiplayer online games, similarly require gamers to devote considerable time and energy to solving their mysteries by sharing resources in virtual communities to unearth their secrets. My brief examination of recent narrative developments on television in this Conclusion, then, indicates potential areas for further study by showing that Hollywood was at the forefront of a trend that has subsequently become more common across the U.S. media industries.

Shows containing complex narratives that prompt audiences to watch them obsessively and go online to unravel their mysteries have indeed become more customary of late on U.S. television. Even a reality show that has become a cross-cultural phenomenon, like *Survivor* (2000–), appeals to producers and spectators partly for reasons that are similar to those associated to the contemporary Hollywood misdirection film. Henry Jenkins contends that *Survivor* is "television for the Internet age—designed to be discussed, debated, predicted, and critiqued" (*Convergence* 25). As his analysis of the online message boards devoted to the show demonstrates, it was initially successful in attracting an ardent fan base dedicated to cracking its code. This transpired largely because the show coaxed viewers into guessing its most significant outcomes. Participants on these sites rely on evidence gleaned from the episodes themselves and their paratexts to draw conclusions before they air, such as who is going to be voted off the island each week, who makes it to the final four, and who will eventually be the winner. These hypotheses are difficult to make, however, because Mark Burnett, the U.S. version's executive producer, admits to monitoring message boards to edit the show in ways that provoke viewers to draw incorrect conclusions. Fan discourse, Jenkins writes, suggests that Burnett's efforts effectively positioned the show as a competition between producers and viewers, buttressed by "a belief that through a contest over information, some ultimate truth will emerge" (*Convergence* 43). These interpretive activities, therefore, resemble the behaviors of conspiracy theorists, who compete to derive superior alternative explanations. Like conspiracy theories, though, fan predictions are not necessarily intended to reveal the "truth." As Jenkins notes, viewers are generally disappointed by the premature exposure of secrets because they revel in continually battling Burnett. In sum, *Survivor* has appealed to a loyal audience who enjoys outwitting, outsmarting, and outlasting its purported mastermind, who strives to conceal the "truth."

The lingering ambiguity that remains unresolved in each episode of *Survivor* is not uncommon in commercial U.S. television programming. For decades, serialized television shows, which were once relegated primarily to daytime soap operas and primetime dramas, have contained ongoing storylines that extend for full seasons and beyond. As Michael Newman notes, however, this trend has migrated to other types of shows not traditionally affiliated with seriality. Newman claims, for instance, that *Survivor* and *Arrested Development* (2003–2006) exemplify how genres, like reality programming and the sitcom, now have narratives that are "thoroughly serialized" ("From Beats" 16). In contrast to the episodic format that once dominated fictional television programming, a wider variety of shows have recently relied on devices typically central to the serial, including open-ended storylines, long narrative arcs, and a sustained focus on character development. *Survivor*, for instance, helped inspire a litany of game-show-themed, reality programs that are highly invested in character and in which many narrative ambiguities remain unresolved after an episode or season's end. The growing popularity of the serial on television was perhaps best evidenced by the success of expensive dramas, like *24* (2001–2010), *Lost* (2004–2010), and *Heroes* (2006–2010), three of the most narratively complex shows ever to air on the traditional powerhouses at the time, that were uncharacteristically greenlit by historically risk averse network television executives. Of course, as I demonstrate in chapter 4, a show like *Twin Peaks* (1990–1991) indicates that programs requiring spectators to re-watch them and discuss their meanings in virtual communities to appreciate them deeply are not new. Since the early 2000s, however, shifting industrial and technological contexts have made these kinds of shows more attractive to producers and some spectators, suggesting that they are enticing in part because of how they respond similarly to the cultural paranoia that made the misdirection film appealing.

Although *Twin Peaks* lasted only two seasons, despite generating a small, yet loyal fan base, shows, such as *24*, *Lost*, and *Heroes*, remained on the air for longer periods even though their intricate narratives alienated some viewers. This is largely because television, like the film industry, benefits from the additional revenue streams created by DVD and amplified by subsequent platforms, like direct-for-purchase streaming video. As Derek Kompare details in "Publishing Flow," the success of the DVD player changed the economic strategies of television executives. Prior to the VCR, it was difficult for viewers to re-watch their most beloved programs; audiences usually had to wait for reruns or hope their favorite shows would go into syndication to view them more times. Accordingly, television executives once solely aimed to create content that produced the greatest number of targeted viewers for advertisers because that was the industry's lone source of income. As Kompare documents, however, DVD was the first technology that allowed the television industry to adopt a "publishing" model in which it could sell its product directly to consumers, enabling the industry to turn profits from shows that built niche audiences at a slower rate. Of course, the VCR provided viewers the ability to record and replay programs at their leisure before the DVD player existed. However, the VCR was primarily embraced by consumers because it enabled them to view Hollywood films in the home. Additionally, the size, cost, and approximately two-hour capacity of the VHS tape made it virtually impossible for either retailers or consumers to devote the money and shelf-space necessary to obtain even a single season's worth of episodes. Consequently, most serialized programs were not transferred to VHS because their long narrative arcs did not translate well to the best-of format that was standard on the technology. The DVD, in contrast, could be hawked straight to consumers in a high quality, user-friendly, and comparatively cost-effective package.

Yet, the television industry did not capitalize on the DVD player when it became available to consumers in 1997 because it was initially perceived to be an extension of the VCR. During its first few years on the market, television executives remained unconvinced that there was the same kind of home-video customer base for their products as there was for Hollywood films. However, when the television DVD box set became available in 2000, it rapidly changed the industry's strategy. As Kompare writes, the DVD box set "brought television's home video practices more in line with film's and indicates how new technologies can prompt new uses and new practices while preserving old goals" ("Publishing" 338). It is still important for television producers to please advertisers because they remain the financial lifeblood of the industry. The additional revenue streams created by DVD technology and ensuing platforms, though, have undeniably altered the television industry's production tactics. In an age dominated by corporate consolidation and the logic of synergy, it has provided the media conglomerates that now control commercial U.S. television the chance to reap enormous profits from the sale of shows on DVD. As early as fall 2002, for example, "Fox chairman Peter Chernin reportedly claimed that television on DVD had already generated $100 million of revenue for his studio" (qtd. in Kompare "Publishing" 352). This staggering figure begins to illustrate why television executives eagerly backed shows that contain complex narratives that appealed to narrower, but loyal, audiences attracted to how those programs tap into desires and anxieties about the status of the "truth" in ways that resemble the misdirection film's expressions.

Interestingly, the first series ever to be manufactured in the box-set format was *The X-Files* (1993–2002), a narratively convoluted show that initially appealed to a cult audience, but eventually became one of the highest rated programs on television. As I argued in chapter 2, *The X-Files* can be read as being akin to the misdirection film even though it does not contain a narrative that inspires viewers to reinterpret a majority of narrative information retrospectively. More specifically, like the misdirection film, which encourages audiences to reread it conspiratorially, irrespective of its content, *The X-Files* engenders paranoia in viewers by forwarding a narrative that depicts an unending search for an elusive "truth" concealed from view by powerful agents. Even though a majority of its episodes aired before the DVD box set became available, then, its nine-season-long, serialized narrative appears tailor-made for the technology. Its focus on central narrative enigmas that seem to remain perpetually unsolved exemplifies the kind of storytelling tactics that now appear with greater regularity on commercial U.S. television because of changing cultural, industrial, and technological conditions. The success of

The X-Files and other shows subsequently released in DVD box set form have revealed that a solid core of ardent fans can be enough to make a show appealing to producers even if it does not perform particularly well in the Nielsen ratings during its first few seasons. As Jason Mittell documents, for instance, shortly after Fox decided to end *Family Guy* (1999–) because of low ratings, the show's DVD box sets "sold so well that Fox reversed its cancellation by returning the series to its lineup" (*Television* 424). Whereas television shows that appealed to only loyal fans were once viewed with skepticism by an industry that aimed for the highest ratings possible, programs targeted at potentially profitable and smaller target markets have become increasingly desirable at a time in which alternative revenue streams can now return hefty profits in the long run.

Just a few short years after the DVD box set became dominant, the television industry began to alter its narrative strategies in response to these new conditions of reception. Disney subsidiary ABC's *Lost* is perhaps the best example of the kind of storytelling that has become more common on television as a result of these changes. As Mittell and Jonathan Gray summarize, the interpretive activities that the show inspires demand that scholars reassess "what 'normal' narrative engagement might look like in the digital age." *Lost* depicts the adventures of a group of plane crash survivors, marooned on a mysterious island that is governed by supernatural forces. Its narrative is propelled by the perplexing events that occur on, or as a consequence of, the island. It thus centers on a search for answers to the island's most baffling enigmas, such as its specific location, the reasons that strange events consistently occur there, why the survivors have each ended up there, and so on. Consequently, each week fans were encouraged to try to solve the show's dizzying web of puzzles, which only became more elaborate and befuddling as the narrative unfurled in successive seasons.

Crucially, the information that is necessary to begin figuring out these mysteries was often presented during extended flashback, flash-forward, and even flashsideway scenes. These sequences are usually of the utmost narrative importance because they typically inspire viewers to reinterpret the significance of what has come before. During season one, for instance, a flashback shockingly reveals that one of the most ostensibly virile survivors—John Locke (Terry O'Quinn)—was a paraplegic prior to the plane crash. As Locke's name epitomizes, the show also contains many high-culture references, as other characters are similarly inspired by famous philosophers, including Hume, Faraday, and Rousseau, coupled with low-culture staples, such as its soap opera inspired love triangles and supernatural, B-movie elements. Such a mix of references as well as its combination of artistic innovation and convention gives it a quintessential middlebrow sensibility similar to the one contained in *Shutter Island* (2010) and other misdirection films. This amalgamation of high- and low-culture facets helped bring the show great critical acclaim, as it won the 2006 Golden Globe for Best Television Drama and compiled 11 Emmy Award wins over its six-year run (imdb.com). In regard to its narrative innovations, after it is revealed that the island has restored Locke's ability to walk, it becomes possible to reassess the meaning of why previous episodes showed that he wants to remain there. This kind of drastic epiphany that requires retrospective reinterpretations occurs regularly. During season one, a number of other flashbacks also reveal that characters, such as Kate Austen (Evangeline Lilly) and James "Sawyer" Ford (Josh Holloway), similarly hope to stay on the island because of their unhappy pasts off of it. Complicating things further, these frequent temporal shifts are not always blatantly framed as such, making it more difficult than normal for television spectators to orient themselves in time and space as well as determine how the information imparted relates to larger narrative meaning. Moreover, the sequences are generally not explicitly referenced in subsequent episodes because they are designed to elicit suspense by giving loyal viewers privileged information about the obstacles facing the characters, at the same time that they give enough away not to alienate casual viewers more accustomed to the episodic series format.

The increasing prevalence of these once unconventional storytelling strategies on television have been inspired by changing viewing practices and the new revenue streams associated with them. *Lost* is well-suited for a time in which spectators routinely use new technologies, such as DVRs, on-demand, DVD players, and the Internet, to re-watch episodes of their favorite shows after they have initially aired. Additionally, as scholars like Jenkins argue, in an age of media convergence and synergy, fans now expect to be able to gain access to a wealth of extra information related to these narratively complex media texts on a variety of platforms, such as books, videogames, DVDs, and the web. The DVD box set for the second season of *Lost*, for instance, contains a chart entitled "Lost Connections" that maps the intricate web of relationships that exist between the characters. Similarly, ABC created "The Lost Experience," a website that both provided a space for fans to solve the show's mysteries and advertised the network's other programs. The decision to produce shows with narratives that strongly encourage viewers to engage in these interpretive activities, then, is backed by a dramatic change in the industry's economic logic, precipitated by shifting conditions of television reception.

The success of the DVD box set, though, does not mean that the Nielsen ratings became unimportant to the industry. Like the domestic theatrical runs of Hollywood films, television shows are likely to be most profitable in ancillary markets if they capture a mass audience when initially broadcast. The series *24*, *Lost*, and *Heroes* each performed admirably in the Nielsen ratings, at least for some of their runs. However, their popularity generally dipped in the ratings after their maiden seasons, as their increasingly convoluted narratives in subsequent years turned off some spectators. The average number of viewers per episode during the third season of *Heroes*, for instance, was approximately 10 million, down substantially from the 14.3 million who watched the pilot. Likewise, ensuing season premieres of *Lost* never matched the 15.7 million viewers who tuned in for the show's highly publicized and expensive pilot in 2004 ("Season"). The atypically high production values of *Lost*'s pilot are noteworthy because it was often received as having blockbuster film qualities. Stacey Abbott, for example, theorizes that the first episode, with its then astronomical $10 million production budget, as well as its extravagant marketing campaign and unprecedented Comic-Con premiere before it aired on television, gave it blockbuster attributes (13–14). Like *Inception*, these unconventional, blockbuster facets were palatable to fans largely because the show's fantasy attributes made them narratively subservient, in retrospect. Despite this retroactive classical structure, the audience for *Lost* dwindled to 13.4 million viewers for the first episode of season four in 2008 and 12.2 million viewers for the opening installment of season five ("Season"). Even *Lost*'s much ballyhooed series finale attracted only 13.5 million viewers, according to the Nielsen ratings (Ross). Undoubtedly, the shrinking numbers for these shows are partly attributable to how they repel viewers who are unwilling or unable to put forth the effort necessary to decipher their narrative puzzles.

In spite of such discouraging trends in the ratings, shows with similarly complex narratives recently have been and continue to be key constituents of current television programming dockets. The tremendous success of subsequent programs, like *Breaking Bad* (2008–2013) and *Mad Men* (2007–2015), demonstrates that their predecessors were not anomalous on non-premium cable outlets. Undeniably, though, premium cable and streaming content providers have made those venues an ideal place for these kinds of shows because their lack of advertising-backed financing for original programming means that they require unconventional commitments from executives to survive on the networks or basic cable. As Mittell notes, in the face of falling audience numbers in 2007, ABC surprisingly agreed to producers' requests to extend *Lost* through six seasons, to an end date of 2010 (*Television* 266). *Lost*'s atypical narrative structure practically demanded such a declaration. As my summary of *Twin Peaks* in chapter 4 exhibited, that show failed partly because critics and spectators grew concerned that its central mystery could never be resolved satisfactorily. Fans of *Lost* similarly expressed anxiety early in the show's run that its creators did not have a grand narrative plan. However, two of the show's most prominent creative personnel—Damon Lindelof and Carlton Cuse—made explicit efforts to refute those claims publicly. Specifically, in a press release, they noted that it was such a win to get the network to agree to sign on for six full seasons because they "always envisioned *Lost* as a show with a beginning, middle and end," which means that viewers "will now have the security of knowing that the story will play out as [they] intended" ("ABC").

It is a bit strange, however, that Lindelof and Cuse made this statement in spite of the credit they are often given for being *Lost*'s primary showrunners. Although a number of individuals share the show's executive producer and writing credits, J. J. Abrams, who rose to fame as a writer/producer of *Felicity* (1998–2002) and the similarly narratively puzzling *Alias* (2001–2006), was typically cited in the popular press initially as the creative genius behind *Lost*. Abrams leveraged the critical success of *Lost* to become a marketable commodity in the commercial U.S. media industries. For example, *Fringe* (2008–2013), his subsequent narratively complex television project, featured the most expensive pilot episode ever to air on the medium at the time, eclipsing the exorbitant one produced for *Lost* (Schweitzer). Furthermore, his burgeoning reputation as an auteur gave Paramount enough faith in his brand name to make him the director of the $150 million first installment of the latest iteration of the *Star Trek* (2009) franchise, which also contains an unconventionally convoluted narrative that depicts time travel and alternate realities (imdb.com). Perhaps most notably, he was then given the chance to direct *Star Wars: The Force Awakens* (2015). As with promotional efforts for the misdirection film that foreground the director as the mastermind, the attachment of Abrams's name to *Lost* was important to its success because it originally provided fans a recognizable adversary with whom they could compete from week-to-week, even if other creative personnel ultimately became more visibly associated with orchestrating the narrative. It also helped Abrams construct an authorial reputation that, like Nolan, he has been able to leverage into a superstar image that mixes artistic innovation with blockbuster credibility as well as can be transported across genres and media.

The programming and production strategies related to *Lost* are thus relevant to this book for a number of reasons. For starters, they indicate that, in spite of popular discourses to the contrary, media industry executives do not necessarily still use traditional instruments to measure the success of their products. Now that many venues exist for a show to turn a profit after it is broadcast, the Nielsen ratings, like domestic box-office returns, no longer exert as much influence on the industry as they once did. The season two box set of *Lost*, for example, was the best-selling DVD on the market when it became available in September 2006, topping all Hollywood films released on DVD at the time (Arnold 18). Its strong performance in ancillary markets exemplifies why it is misguided to continue to think of the economic incentives that drive the U.S media industries in outdated terms. New media and communication technologies deeply influence the ways that many audiences now commonly interact with media texts, which, in turn, impact the production and promotional tactics of industry executives and creative personnel.

The success of contemporary Hollywood misdirection films and recent television shows that inspire analogous interpretive practices, though, cannot simply be explained by technological developments and the media industries' economic motives. New media technologies and changing industrial motives alone do not account for the specific ways that these similarly structured atypical narrative forms have come into fruition and why they have resonated strongly with some viewers. The kinds of duplicitous narratives that appear in these programs and misdirection films consistently tap into shared cultural anxieties and desires in relation to the status of the "truth." In particular, although they suggest that the "truth" is difficult to determine because it is hidden from view by powerful forces, they do not usually suggest that it is perpetually in flux. Instead, devoted spectators of most of these films and shows are ultimately assured that it is possible to know what "actually" occurred and who "really" made things happen. Of course, fans have to be up to the tasks of enduring the perpetual slew of convoluted narrative machinations and unearthing the secrets that they deem to be concealed by their makers to gain access to this privileged information. In misdirection films and these shows alike, then, a discovery of the "truth" is typically the ultimate payoff because it is usually either explicitly revealed, or perceived to have been deliberately buried for discovery by their creators.

Returning briefly to the *Lost* example to illustrate this phenomenon, the search for the "truth" is the show's central thematic concern. Not only did the show's creators deliver on their promise to dedicated fans willing to conduct the labor necessary to interpret the meaning that it would all make sense in the end, the existential search for "truth" was also depicted explicitly by the narrative, articulated most clearly by the ongoing thematic struggle for supremacy between faith and science. The characters closely linked to these competing philosophies shifted throughout the show's run; however, for a majority of it, Dr. Jack Shephard (Matthew Fox) represented science and faith was embodied by

Locke. Although the cast of *Lost* is deliberately peppered with women and racial minorities to appeal to a diverse audience and inoculate the show from charges of racism and sexism, it is significant that Jack and John are the show's primary protagonists. Indeed, it does not take long before the survivors split into two separate camps on the island because they are drawn to the competing philosophies of their respective leaders. These two white, heterosexual men, therefore, are able to reclaim the traditional manhood on the island that they were previously stripped of off of it by being the individuals who are perceived as being capable of eventually bringing order out chaos.

As I discussed in chapter 3, then, *Lost* can be understood as expressing similar gender politics as many contemporary misdirection films because it depicts a culture in which purportedly emasculated male heroes are ultimately able to regain their masculine authority. In the case of Locke, for instance, the island revitalizes his manhood by enabling him to reuse his legs. The supernatural turn of events allows him to leverage his skills as a hunter to provide food for the other survivors, establishing him as a powerful figure on the island. Additionally, the show's complex narrative also often expressed nervous concern about the possibility that the actions of these two leaders may ultimately be irrelevant because a series of even more powerful white, heterosexual, male characters, including Benjamin Linus (Michael Emerson), Charles Whidmore (Alan Dale), Sawyer, and Jacob (Mark Pellegrino), were periodically shown to be the ones who may really be in control of the fates of the survivors. In the end, *Lost* did reveal that individual agency is restricted for Jack, the character who turned out to be the unequivocal protagonist, as the final changeover showed that he was dead and that the island was purgatory. *Lost* thus also expresses a panic about the viability of individual autonomy, which, as I claimed in chapter 2, has been a key factor driving the recent rise of conspiratorial narratives in both U.S. political and popular culture. As with the misdirection film, *Lost*'s narrative is ultimately appealing to many viewers partly because it assures them that concepts associated with modernity, including the existence of absolute "truth" as well as the persistence of racial and gender hierarchies, have not been supplanted by tenets associated with postmodernity, such as relativity and multiculturalism.

As a result of these tendencies, the cultural implications of the contemporary Hollywood misdirection film will be generally disappointing to progressive critics who correctly argue that the industry still usually deploys its time-tested practices and conveys dominant ideologies to make its products attractive to a wide audience. Although it is true that many of these films are targeted at a smaller cohort than most Hollywood films once were, they are still constructed in ways that appeal to the market segment with the greatest profit potential. As I contended in chapter 4, contemporary misdirection films are often designed to capture a niche audience of predominantly young, white, male spectators, who derive pleasure from sorting out the clues that they believe have been laid out for their discovery by their male creators. Consequently, these films usually end up supporting traditional ways of thinking even though their unconventional narrative structures are particularly well-suited to challenge Hollywood's typically conservative agenda. Their duplicitous narratives, for instance, are uniquely positioned to expose the artificiality of narrative closure. Rather than attribute narrative causality to random or inexplicable forces, though, the alternative narrative explanation most often reveals that events were actually orchestrated by identifiable agents, who are almost inevitably male. Such retrospective reinterpretations appeal to audiences who have grown comfortable with Hollywood conventions. In the end, dedicated spectators are rewarded with the evidence necessary to transform films that initially appear to represent departures from the norm into ones that both adhere to the classical paradigm and express dominant American ideologies.

The presence of an alternative narrative explanation that renders these films comprehensible and comfortable to many viewers demonstrates why they exhibit the attributes that critics, like David Bordwell, identify as being embodied by the classical Hollywood film. The exposure or discovery of the revelatory information often makes these films hyper-classical because spectators can reinterpret their narratives according to a revised causality that is tied to the actions of clearly identifiable agents. Moreover, it is true that misdirection films rely heavily on Hollywood's generic, formal, ideological, and narrative conventions to work their deceptive magic. In fact, these very standards are what typically encourage viewers to draw the incorrect conclusions about the causal relationship of events. Although they are highly dependent on classical devices, however, it is difficult to claim that these films are simply constituents of that particular mode of narration. Even though fans often go to great lengths to try to make them narratively coherent, some of these films violate the most basic tenets of the classical film by lingering on perpetual ambiguity, presenting primary characters with indeterminate motives, making it impossible to distinguish fantasy from reality, and so on. These examples similarly respond to nervous concerns about the existence of absolute "truth," but amplify that anxiety by suggesting that it might be unknowable. This does not prevent most fans, though, from doggedly trying to find ways to reassess narrative meaning coherently. Regardless of how they respond to this broader and irreconcilable cultural conflict, misdirection films depart from the classical film by alerting audiences to their status as a construction, rendering the narrative and formal mechanics of the Hollywood film highly visible, in retrospect. Misdirection films, then, require multiple viewings and/or the shared knowledge of fans to be appreciated most deeply, which are interpretive behaviors that are not supposed to be expected of the classical spectator.

The constituent films of the genre suggest that Hollywood does not simply employ a simplistic production formula that has remained constant throughout its history. Rather, these films reveal that, when associated conditions are optimal, Hollywood is willing to design products that can be distinguished from its other fare precisely because they contain non-classical tendencies, at the same time that they continue to abide by some classical principles. The creation of a purely classically constructed narrative, therefore, is not and has never been Hollywood's primary concern. The misdirection film is a viable genre that discursive evidence reveals has existed throughout most of cinema history, but became more popular with many audiences and producers from 1990 to 2010 by effectively combining a specific blend of sameness and difference in response to its particular cultural, industrial, and technological contexts.

Works Cited

Abbott, Stacey. "How *Lost* Found its Audience" in *Reading Lost: Perspectives on a Hit Television Show*. Ed. Roberta Pearson. London: I. B. Tauris, 2009. 9–26.

"ABC Gives Viewers 48 More Original Episodes of the Hit Drama *Lost* Culminating in an Exciting Series Conclusion (Press Release)." *ABC Medianet*. <http://web.archive.org/web/20070510030616/http://www.abcmedianet.com/assets/pr%5chtml/050707_01.html>. Accessed 20 February 2009.

Altman, Rick. *Film/Genre*. London: BFI Publishing, 1999.

"America's Greatest Movies (2007)." *The American Film Institute* <http://www.afi.com/tvevents/100years/movies10.aspx>. Accessed 18 December 2007.

Anderson, Benedict. *Imagined Communities: Reflections on the Origins and Spread of Nationalism* (Revised Edition). London and New York: Verso, 1991.

Arnold, Thomas K. "*Lost* Makes Trek to Number One in DVD Sales." *The Hollywood Reporter*. 14 September 2006. 18.

Atkinson, Michael. "The Dead Pool." *The Village Voice.com*. 11 July 2006. <http://www.villagevoice.com/film/the-dead-pool-6427356>. Accessed 23 February 2015.

Bamberger, Michael. *The Man Who Heard Voices: Or, How M. Night Shyamalan Risked His Career on a Fairy Tale*. New York: Gotham Books, 2006.

Barlow, Aaron. *The DVD Revolution: Movies, Technology, and Culture*. Westport, CT: Praeger Publishers, 2005.

Barnes, Elizabeth. "Loving with a Vengeance: *Wieland*, Familicide, and the Crisis of Masculinity in the Early Nation" in *Boys Don't Cry: Rethinking Narratives of Masculinity and Emotion in the U.S.* Eds. Milette Shamir and Jennifer Travis. New York: Columbia University Press, 2002. 44–63.

Berardinelli, James. "*Lady in the Water* (Film Review). *Reel Views.net*. <http://www.reelviews.net/reelviews/lady-in-the-water-the>. Accessed 23 February 2015.

———. "*Magnolia* (Film Review). *Reel Views.net*. <http://www.reelviews.net/reelviews/magnolia>. Accessed 25 June 2013.

———. "*Unbreakable* (Film Review)." *Reel Views.net*. <http://www.reelviews.net/movies/u/unbreakable.html>. Accessed 15 March 2008.

Bing, Jonathon. "*Fight Club* Author Books Pair of Deals." *Variety*. 11 April 2001. <http://www.variety.com/article/VR1117796888.html?categoryid=1007&cs=1>. Accessed 23 November 2008.

Birchall, Clare. *Knowledge Goes Pop: From Conspiracy Theory to Gossip*. Oxford and New York: Berg, 2006.

Bly, Robert. *Iron John: A Book About Men*. Reading, PA: Addison-Wesley, 1990.

Boggs, Carl, and Tom Pollard. *A World in Chaos: Social Crisis and the Rise of Postmodern Cinema*. Lanham, MD: Rowan & Littlefield Publishers, Inc., 2003.

Booker, M. Keith. *Strange TV: Innovative Television Series from* The Twilight Zone *to* The X-Files. Westport, CT, and London: Greenwood Press, 2002.

Booth, Michael. "Director Works His Magic." *The Denver Post.com*. 20 October 2006. <http://www.denverpost.com/movies/ci_4511972>. Accessed 4 March 2015.

———. "*Lady in the Water* is a Murky Fairy Tale." *The Denver Post.com*. 20 July 2006. <http://www.denverpost.com/movies/ci_4071453>. Accessed 23 February 2015.

Bordwell, David. *Narration in the Fiction Film*. Madison: University of Wisconsin Press, 1985.

———. *The Way Hollywood Tells It: Story and Style in Modern Movies*. Berkeley: University of California Press, 2006.

Bordwell, David, Janet Staiger, and Kristin Thompson. *The Classical Hollywood Cinema*. New York: Columbia University Press, 1985.

Bourdieu, Pierre. "The Market of Symbolic Goods" in *The Field of Cultural Production*. Ed. Randal Johnson. Cambridge, UK: Polity Press, 1993.

Bowles, Scott. "DiCaprio is Choosy When it comes to Roles, Directors." *USA Today.com*. 24 December 2012. <http://www.usatoday.com/story/life/movies/2012/12/23/django-leonardo-dicaprio/1749703/>. Accessed 6 March 2015.

Box Office Mojo. <http://www.boxofficemojo.com/>.

Brevert, Brad. "Michael Caine Explains the End of *Inception*, but should He have?" *Ropes of Silicon.com*. 5 October 2010. <http://www.ropeofsilicon.com/michael-caine-explains-the-end-of-inception-but-should-he-have/>. Accessed 7 March 2015.

"The Briefcase & The Band-Aid." *PulpFicton.com*. 14 November 2000. <http://www.pulpfiction.com/brief-case-and-band-aid>. Accessed 31 May 2013.

Bruzzi, Stella. *Bringing Up Daddy: Fatherhood and Masculinity in Post-War Hollywood*. London: BFI Publishing, 2005.

Buckland, Warren. *Directed by Steven Spielberg: Poetics of the Contemporary Hollywood Blockbuster*. New York and London: Continuum, 2006.

Burgess, Adrienne. *Fatherhood Reclaimed: The Making of the Modern Father*. London: Vermillion, 1997.

Butler, Jeremy. "The Internet and the World Wide Web" in *The New Media Book*. Ed. Dan Harries. London: BFI Publishing, 2004. 40–51.

Butler, Judith. *Gender Trouble: Feminism and the Subversion of Identity* (Routledge Classics Edition). London and New York: Routledge, 2006.

Calhoun, Dave. "Martin Scorsese Talks *Shutter Island*." *TimeOut.com*. <http://www.timeout.com/london/film/martin-scorsese-talks-shutter-island-1>. Accessed 13 March 2015.

Capps, Robert. "Q&A: Christopher Nolan on Dreams, Architecture, and Ambiguity." *Wired.com*. 29 November 2010. <http://www.wired.com/2010/11/pl_inception_nolan/>. Accessed 7 March 2015.

Caro, Mark. "Abundance of Symbols in *Magnolia* has Filmgoers Searching for Clues." *Chicago Tribune*.com. 23 January 2000. <http://articles.chicagotribune.com/2000-01-23/news/0001230275_1_movie-magnolia-frog>. Accessed 7 January 2015.

Carver, Terrell. "*Fight Club*: Dramma Giocasa." *International Journal of Feminist Politics*. 4.1 (April 2002): 129–35.

Chhabra. Aseem. "The Myth about Shyamalan." *Mumbai Mirror.com*. 9 June 2013. <http://www.mumbaimirror.com/columns/columnists/aseem-chhabra/The-myth-about-Shyamalan/articleshow/20498159.cms>. Accessed 27 February 2015.

Clark, J. Michael. "Faludi, *Fight Club*, and Phallic Masculinity: Exploring the Emasculating Economics of Patriarchy." *Journal of Men's Studies*. 11.1 (Fall 2002): 65–76.

Clark, Mike. "Surprising, Sensitive *Sixth Sense*: Willis Goes Deep in Ghost Story." *USA Today*. 6 August 1999. 10E.

Cohan, Steven. *Masked Men: Masculinity and the Movies in the Fifties*. Bloomington and Indianapolis: Indiana University Press, 1997.

Corliss, Richard. "Shyamalan's Lost Sense." *Time.com*. 12 June 2008. <http://content.time.com/time/arts/article/0,8599,1813911,00.html>. Accessed 25 February 2015.

Corrigan, Timothy. "Auteurs and the New Hollywood" in *The New American Cinema*. Ed. Jon Lewis. Durham, NC: Duke University Press, 1998. 38–63.

Covert, Colin. "*The Master* is a Cult Hit." *Star Tribune.com*. 21 September 2012. <http://www.startribune.com/the-master-is-a-cult-hit/170535026/>. Accessed 25 July 2013.

Cowie, Elizabeth. "Storytelling: Classical Hollywood Cinema and Classical Narrative" in *Contemporary Hollywood Cinema*. Ed. Steve Neale and Murray Smith. London and New York: Routledge, 1998. 178–90.

Cox, David. "*Shutter Island*'s Ending Explained." *The Guardian.com*. 29 July 2010. <http://www.theguardian.com/film/filmblog/2010/jul/29/shutter-island-ending>. Accessed 13 March 2015.

DeFalco, Tom. "1960s" in *Marvel Chronicle: A Year by Year History*. Ed. Laura Gilbert. New York: DK Publishing, 2008.

Deleuze, Gilles. *Cinema II: The Time Image*. Minneapolis: University of Minnesota Press (Sixth Edition), 2001.

Denby, David. "Dream Factory." *The New Yorker.com*. 26 July 2010. <http://www.newyorker.com/magazine/2010/07/26/dream-factory>. Accessed 7 March 2015.

Dillman, Joanne Clarke. "*Magnolia*: Masquerading as Soap Opera." *Journal of Popular Film and Television*. 33.3 (Fall 2005): 142–50.

"Dominick Cobb." *The Inception Wiki*. <http://inception.wikia.com/wiki/Dominick_Cobb>. Accessed 7 March 2015.

Dreher, Rod. "It'll Scare you 'Sense'-less." *New York Post*. 6 August 1999, 43.

Duckner, Johannes. *The Unofficial Christopher Nolan Web Site*. <http://www.christophernolan.net/memento_mem.php>.

Dyer, Richard. *Heavenly Bodies: Film Stars and Society* (Second Edition). London and New York: Routledge, 2004.

Ebert, Roger. "*Fight Club* (Film Review)." *Chicago Sun-Times*. 15 October 1999, 31.

———. "*Inception* (Film Review). *Roger Ebert.com*. 14 July 2010. <http://www.rogerebert.com/reviews/inception-2010>. Accessed 7 March 2015.

———. "*Lost Highway* (Film Review)." *Chicago Sun-Times*. 28 February 1997, 35.

———. "*Magnolia* (Film Review)." *Roger Ebert.com*. 7 January 2000. <http://www.rogerebert.com/reviews/magnolia-2000>. Accessed 2 August 2013.

———. "*Memento* (Film Review). *Roger Ebert.com*. 13 April 2001. <http://www.rogerebert.com/reviews/memento-2001>. Accessed 22 February 2015.

———. "*Mulholland Dr.* (Film Review)." *Chicago Sun-Times*. 12 October 2001, 31.

———. "*The Village* (Film Review). *Roger Ebert.com*. 19 July 2004. <http://www.rogerebert.com/reviews/the-village-2004>. Accessed 23 February 2015.

Elsaesser, Thomas. "The Mind-Game Film" in *Puzzle Films*. Ed. Warren Buckland. Malden and Oxford: Blackwell Publishers, 2009. 13–41.

Faludi, Susan. *Stiffed: The Betrayal of the American Man*. New York: William Morrow and Company, 1999.

Fenster, Mark. *Conspiracy Theories: Secrecy and Power in American Culture*. Minneapolis: University of Minnesota Press, 1999.

"The 50 Essential DVDs." *Entertainment Weekly*. <http://www.ew.com/ew/article/0,,279415,00.html>. Accessed 22 November 2008.

Fleming, Michael. "Scorsese, DiCaprio Team for *Shutter Island*." *Variety.com*. 22 October 2007. <http://variety.com/2007/film/markets-festivals/scorsese-dicaprio-team-for-island-2-1117974525/>. Accessed 6 March 2015.

Finke, Nikki. "Shocker! Paramount Moves Scorsese's *Shutter Island* to February 19, 2010." *Deadline Hollywood.com*. 21 August 2009. <http://deadline.com/2009/08/shocker-paramount-moving-scorsesedicaprios-shutter-island-to-february-2010-12459/>. Accessed 12 March 2015.

Fradley, Martin. "Maximus Melodramaticus: Masculinity, Masochism and White Male Paranoia in Contemporary Hollywood Cinema" in *Action and Adventure Cinema*. Ed. Yvonne Tasker. London and New York: Routledge, 2004. 235–51.

Friedman, Seth. "Misdirection in Fits and Starts: Alfred Hitchcock's Popular Reputation and the Reception of His Films." *Quarterly Review of Film and Video*. 29.1 (January 2012): 76–94.

Fritz, Ben. "Movie Projector: *Inception* Headed for No. 1, *Sorcerer's Apprentice* to Open in Third." *LA Times.com*. 15 July 2010. <http://latimesblogs.latimes.com/entertainmentnewsbuzz/2010/07/inception-sorcerers-box-office.html>. Accessed 12 September 2014.

Fritz, Ben, and Claudia Eller. "Warner Gambles on an Unproven Commodity." *LA Times.com*. 13 July 2010. <http://articles.latimes.com/2010/jul/13/business/la-fi-ct-inception-20100713>. Accessed 6 March 2015.

Gates, Philippa. *Detecting Men: Masculinity and the Hollywood Detective Film*. Albany, NY: SUNY Press, 2006.

Giles, Jeff. "Out of this World." *Newsweek*. 140.1 (5 August 2002): 48–56.

Gilmore, Mikal. "The Lost Boys." *Rolling Stone*. 6 March 1997 (Issue 755). 36–46.

Giroux, Henry A. "Private Satisfactions and Public Disorders: *Fight Club*, Patriarchy, and the Politics of Masculine Violence." Henry A Giroux: Global Television Network Chair in Communication Studies. 3 July 2003. <http://www.henrygiroux.com>. Accessed 4 March 2008.

Goffman, Erving. *Frame Analysis: An Essay on the Organization of Experience*. Boston: Northeastern University Press, 1974.

Gomery, Douglas. *Shared Pleasures: A History of Moviegoing in the United States*. Madison: University of Wisconsin Press, 1992.

Goodykoontz, Bill. "*Inception* (Film Review)." *AZ Central.com*. 14 July 2010. <http://www.azcentral.com/thingstodo/movies/articles/2010/07/14/20100714inception.html>. Accessed 7 March 2015.

Gray, Jonathan, and Jason Mittell. "Speculation on Spoilers: *Lost* Fandom, Narrative Consumption and Rethinking Textuality." *Participations*. 4.1 (May 2007).

Greven, David. *Manhood in Hollywood from Bush to Bush*. Austin: University of Texas Press, 2009.

Halberstam, Jack (Judith). *Female Masculinity*. Durham, NC: Duke University Press, 1998.

Harper, Graeme. "DVD and the New Cinema of Complexity" in *New Punk Cinema*. Ed. Nicholas Rombes. Edinburgh: Edinburgh University Press, 2005. 89–101.

Harrison, Eric. "Breaking Point: Willis, Jackson Bring Quality Acting to Recycled *Unbreakable*." *The Houston Chronicle*. 22 November 2000, Houston 1.

Hartl, John. "Adrian Lyne Met a Metaphysical Challenge." *The Seattle Times.com*. 1 November 1990. <http://community.seattletimes.nwsource.com/archive/?date=19901101&slug=1101695>. Accessed 15 January 2015.

Hawkins, Joan. "'See it From the Beginning:' Hitchcock's Reconstruction of Film History" in *Framing Hitchcock*. Eds. Sidney Gottlieb and Christopher Brookhouse. Detroit, MI: Wayne State University Press, 2002. 373–86.

Hellinger, Daniel. "Paranoia, Conspiracy, and Hegemony in American Politics" in *Transparency and Conspiracy: Ethnographies of Suspicion in the New World Order*. Eds. Harry West and Todd Sanders. Durham, NC: Duke University Press, 2003. 204–32.

Hellinger, Daniel, and Dennis Judd. *The Democratic Façade*. Belmont, CA: Wadsworth Publishing Company, 1994.

Hicks, Heather. "Hoodoo Economics: White Men's Work and Black Men's Magic in Contemporary American Film." *Camera Obscura*. 18.2 (Summer 2003): 27–54.

Higson, Andrew. "Film Acting and Independent Cinema" in *Movie Acting, the Film Reader*. Ed. Pamela Robertson Wojcik. London and New York: Routledge, 2004. 145–64.

Hirschberg, Lynn. "His Way." *New York Times*. 19 December 1999, SM 52–56.

Hiscock, John. "M. Night Shyamalan Interview for *After Earth*: 'I Offer Originality.' " *The Telegraph.com*. 31 May 2013. <http://www.telegraph.co.uk/culture/film/10077922/M-Night-Shyamalan-interview-for-After-Earth-I-offer-originality.html>. Accessed 27 February 2015.

Hofstadter, Richard. *The Paranoid Style in American Politics*. New York: Knopf, 1965.

Holden, Stephen. "A Boy Who Sees the Dead, and a Psychologist Determined Not to Fail Him." *New York Times*. 6 August 1999, E14.

Holden, Wade. "Wholesale DVD Revenue Drops in 2010." *SNL Kagan.com*. 10 May 2011. <https://www.snl.com/InteractiveX/article.aspx?CDID=A-12741319-13614&KPLT=2>. Accessed 13 March 2015.

Holmlund, Chris. "Masculinity and Multiple Masquerade: The 'Mature' Stallone and the Stallone Clone" in *Screening The Male: Exploring Masculinities in Hollywood Cinema*. Eds. Steve Cohan and Ina Rae Hark. London and New York: Routledge, 1993. 213–44.

Horne, Philip. "M. Night Shyamalan Interview: A New Sense of the Spectacular." *The Telegraph.com*. 11 August 2010. <http://www.telegraph.co.uk/culture/film/7930719/M-Night-Shyamalan-interview-a-new-sense-of-the-spectacular.html>. Accessed 25 February 2015.

Hunter, Stephen. "*The Village*: Right on the Beaten Path." *The Washington Post*. 30 July 2004, C1.

"In *Fight Club* is Marla Singer a Second Figment of Jack's Imagination?" *Movies & TV Stack Exchange.com*. <http://movies.stackexchange.com/questions/10421/in-fight-club-is-marla-singer-a-second-figment-of-jacks-imagination>. Accessed 8 July 2013.

Internet Movie Database. <http://www.imdb.com/>.

Iocco, Melissa. "Addicted to Affliction: Masculinity and Perversity in *Crash* and *Fight Club*." *Gothic Studies*. 9.1 (May 2007): 46–56.

Isaacs, Bruce. "Non-linear Narrative" in *New Punk Cinema*. Ed. Nicholas Rombes. Edinburgh: Edinburgh University Press, 2005. 126–38.

Itzkoff, Dave. "A Man and his Dream: Christopher Nolan and *Inception*." *NY Times.com (Arts Beat Blog)*. 30 June 2010. <http://artsbeat.blogs.nytimes.com/2010/06/30/a-man-and-his-dream-christopher-nolan-and-inception/?_r=0>. Accessed 3 March 2015.

———. "Hans Zimmer Extracts the Secrets of *Inception*'s Score." *NY Times.com (Arts Beat Blog)*. 28 July 2010. <http://artsbeat.blogs.nytimes.com/2010/07/28/hans-zimmer-extracts-the-secrets-of-the-inception-score/>. Accessed 3 March 2015.

———. "The Man Behind the Dreamscape." *NYTimes.com*. 30 June 2010. <http://www.nytimes.com/2010/07/04/movies/04inception.html>. Accessed 3 March 2015.

Jameson, Fredric. "Cognitive Mapping" in *Marxism and the Interpretation of Culture*. Eds. Cary Nelson and Lawrence Grossberg. Urbana and Chicago: University of Illinois Press, 1988. 347–357.

———. *Postmodernism: or the Cultural Logic of Late Capitalism*. Durham, NC: Duke University Press, 1991.

Jeffords, Susan. *Hard Bodies: Hollywood Masculinity in the Reagan Era*. New Brunswick, NJ: Rutgers University Press, 1994.

Jenkins, Henry. *Convergence Culture: Where Old and New Media Collide*. New York: New York University Press, 2006.

———. "'Do You Enjoy Making the Rest of Us Feel Stupid?'": alt.tv.twinpeaks, the Trickster Author, and Viewer Mastery" in *Full of Secrets: Critical Approaches to Twin Peaks*. Ed. David Lavery. Detroit, MI: Wayne State University Press, 1995. 51–70.

———. *Textual Poachers*. New York and London: Routledge, 1992.

Kafalenos, Emma. "Functions after Propp: Words to Talk about How We Read Narrative." *Poetics Today*. 18.4 (Winter 1997): 469–94.

Kapsis, Robert. *Hitchcock: The Making of a Reputation*. Chicago and London: The University of Chicago Press, 1992.

Kellner, Douglas. *Media Culture: Cultural Studies, Identity and Politics between the Modern and the Postmodern*. London and New York: Routledge, 1995.

Kimmel, Michael. *Manhood in America: A Cultural History* (Second Edition). Oxford and New York: Oxford University Press, 2006.

King, Geoff. *American Independent Cinema*. London: I. B. Tauris, 2005.

———. *New Hollywood Cinema: An Introduction*. London: I. B. Tauris, 2002.

Klecker, Cornelia. "Mind-Tricking Narratives: Between Classical and Art-Cinema Narration." *Poetics Today*. 34.1–2 (Spring/Summer 2013): 119–46.

Klein, Amanda Ann. *American Film Cycles: Reframing Genres, Screening Social Problems, and Defining Subcultures*. Austin: University of Texas Press, 2012.

Klein, Andy. "Everything You Wanted to Know about *Memento*." *Salon.com*. 28 June 2001. <http://www.salon.com/2001/06/28/memento_analysis/>. Accessed 28 June 2008.

Klinger, Barbara. *Beyond the Multiplex: Cinema, New Technologies, and the Home*. Berkeley: University of California Press, 2006.

———. "Film History Terminable and Interminable: Recovering the Past in Reception Studies." *Screen*. 38.2 (Summer 1997): 107–28.

Kompare, Derek. "Publishing Flow: DVD Box Sets and the Reconception of Television." *Television and New Media*. 7.4 (November 2006): 335–60.

———. *Rerun Nation: How Repeats Invented American Television*. London: Routledge, 2004.

Kramer, Peter. "The Lure of the Big Picture: Film, Television, and Hollywood" in *Big Picture, Small Screen: The Relations between Film and Television*. Ed. John Hill and Martin McLoone. Luton: John Libbey, 1996. 9–46.

LaSalle, Mick. "Batman: The Caped Crusader has come Back. He's Brawnier, but He Still has Brains." *SFGate.com*. 14 June 2005. <http://www.sfgate.com/movies/article/BATMAN-The-caped-crusader-has-come-back-He-s-2662591.php>. Accessed 4 March 2015.

———. "Boy is Dead-On Amazing in *Sixth Sense* Thriller." *San Francisco Chronicle*. 6 August 1999, C1.

———. "*Lady* Hints at Message that's Never Delivered." *SFGate.com*. 21 July 2006. <http://www.sfgate.com/movies/article/Lady-hints-at-message-that-s-never-delivered-2515768.php>. Accessed 23 February 2015.

Lavik, Erlend. "Narrative Structure in *The Sixth Sense*: A New Twist in Twist Movies." *The Velvet Light Trap*. 58.3 (Fall 2006): 55–64.

Lee, Ashley. "Christopher Nolan Talks *Inception* Ending, Batman, and 'Chasing Reality' in Princeton Grad Speech." *Hollywood Reporter.com*. 1 June 2015. <http://www.hollywoodreporter.com/news/christopher-nolan-princeton-graduation-speech-799121>. Accessed 8 July 2015.

Lost on Mullholand Dr. <http://www.mulholland-drive.net>.

Lumenick, Lou. "*Unbreakable* Keeps the Faith." *New York Post*. 22 November 2000, 47.

Macdonald, Moira. "*Inception* (Film Review)." *The Seattle Times.com*. 15 July 2010. <http://www.seattletimes.com/entertainment/movies/inception-leonardo-dicaprio-takes-a-dizzyingly-inventive-trip-into-world-of-dreams/>. Accessed 7 March 2015.

Malin, Brenton J. *American Masculinity Under Clinton: Popular Media and the Nineties "Crisis of Masculinity."* New York and Washington DC: Peter Lang Publishers, 2005.

Maltby, Richard. *Hollywood Cinema* (Second Edition). Malden, UK: Blackwell Publishing, 2005.

Marshall, Rick. "Bruce Willis Says M. Night Shyamalan 'Still Thinking' about *Unbreakable 2*." *Mtv.com*. <http://splashpage.mtv.com/2010/02/22/bruce-willis-says-m-night-shyamalan-still-thinking-about-unbreakable-2/>. Accessed 16 August 2013.

Maslin, Janet. "*Magnolia* (Film Review)." *New York Times.com*. 17 December 1999. <http://www.nytimes.com/movie/review?res=940CE3DD1430F934A25751C1A96F958260>. Accessed 3 August 2013.

McKenzie, Rob. "Surprise! When One Twist Ending Isn't Enough." *National Post* (Canada). 31 May 2003, SP7.

McMillan, Graeme. "Beyond Batman: Christopher Nolan Really is Hollywood's Best New Talent." *Time.com*. 18 July 2012. <http://entertainment.time.com/2012/07/18/i-admit-it-ii/>. Accessed 22 February 2015.

Melley, Timothy. *Empire of Conspiracy: The Culture of Paranoia in Postwar America*. Ithaca, NY: Cornell University Press, 2000.

Memento (Official Web site). <http://www.otnemem.com>.

Mendelson, Scott. "Why Sony was Wrong to Hide M. Night Shyamalan while Marketing *After Earth*." *Forbes.com*. 5 June 2013. <http://www.forbes.com/sites/scottmendelson/2013/06/05/why-sony-was-wrong-to-hide-m-night-shyamalan-while-marketing-after-earth/>. Accessed 22 February 2015.

Mittell, Jason. "Forensic Fandom and the Drillable Text." *Spreadable Media.org*. <http://spreadablemedia.org/essays/mittell/#.VdXZ5Zcl9v4>. Accessed 23 June 2015.

———. *Genre and Television: From Cop Shows to Cartoons in American Culture*. London: Routledge, 2004.

———. *Television and American Culture*. Oxford and New York: Oxford University Press, 2010.

Naglazas, Mark. "I See 3D People." *The West Australian*. 16 September 2010. TOD 6.

Naremore, James. *Acting in the Cinema*. Berkeley: University of California Press, 1988.

———. *More Than Night: Film Noir in Its Contexts*. Berkeley: University of California Press, 1998.

Neale, Steve. *Genre and Hollywood*. London and New York: Routledge, 2000.

Neumaier, Joe. "*Shutter Island* (Film Review)." *NY Daily News.com*. 18 February 2010. Accessed 14 March 2015.

Newman, Michael Z. "From Beats to Arcs: Toward a Poetics of Television Narrative." *The Velvet Light Trap*. 58 (Fall 2006): 16–28.

———. *Indie: An American Film Culture*. New York: Columbia University Press, 2011.

The Numbers.com. <http://www.the-numbers.com/>.

O'Donnell, Patrick. "Engendering Paranoia in Contemporary Narrative" in *National Identities and Post-Americanist Narratives*. Ed. Donald Pease. Durham, NC: Duke University Press, 1994. 181–204.

"100 Greatest Movies of All Time." *Total Film*. <http://www.totalfilm.com/features/total_film_presents_the_top_100_movies_of_all_time>. Accessed 22 November 2008.

Owczarski, Kim. "Reshaping the Director as Star" in *Critical Approaches to the Films of M. Night Shyamalan: Spoiler Warnings*. Ed. Jeffrey Andrew Weinstock. New York: Palgrave Macmillan, 2010. 119–35.

Powers, John. "Eyes Wide Open." *LA Weekly.com*. 22 May 2002. <http://www.laweekly.com/film/eyes-wide-open-2134827>. Accessed 3 March 2015.

Pratt, Ray. *Projecting Paranoia: Conspiratorial Visions in American Film*. Lawrence: University of Kansas Press, 2001.

———. "Theorizing Conspiracy." *Theory and Society*. 32.2 (April 2003): 255–71.

Pulver, Andrew. "Martin Scorsese: Master of the Hitchcock Tribute." *The Guardian.com*. 10 March 2010. <http://www.theguardian.com/film/2010/mar/10/martin-scorcese-shutter-island-hitchcock>. Accessed 14 March 2015.

Qi, Shouhua. "The Shift of Emphasis and the Reception of Surprise Ending Stories (1900–1941): a Critical Study." Diss# 9411044. Illinois State University, 1993. Ann Arbor: University of Michigan, 1993.

Rainer, Peter. "Pulling Punches: *Fight Club* Serves up Frustrated Everymen under Extreme Duress." *NY Mag.com*. <http://nymag.com/nymetro/movies/reviews/1248/>. Accessed 22 July 2013.

Raymond, Marc. *Hollywood's New Yorker: The Making of Martin Scorsese*. Albany, NY: SUNY Press, 2013.

Rea, Steven. "M. Night Shyamalan is Popular at the Box-Office, but not with Critics." *Pop Matters.com*. 6 August 2010. <http://www.popmatters.com/article/129269-m.-night-shyamalan-is-popular-at-the-box-office-but-not-with-critics/>. Accessed 27 February 2015.

Rehling, Nicola. *Extra-ordinary Men: White Heterosexual Masculinity in Contemporary Popular Cinema*. Lanham, MD: Lexington Books, 2009.

"Research and Statistics (2007)." *Motion Picture Association of America*. <http://www.mpaa.org/researchStatistics.asp>. Accessed 14 June 2008.

Richter, David H. "Your Cheating Art: Double Dealing in Cinematic Narrative." *Narrative*. 13.1 (January 2005): 11–28.

Roberts, Gillian. "Circulations of Taste: *Titanic*, the Oscars, and the Middlebrow" in *Movie Blockbusters*. Ed. Julian Stringer. London and New York: Routledge, 2003. 155–66.

Ross, Jennifer. "*Lost* Series Finale Somehow Only the 55th Most Watched Ever." *Paste Magazine.com*. 27 May 2010. <http://www.pastemagazine.com/articles/2010/05/thirteen-million-get-lost-in-series-finale.html>. Accessed 23 August 2015.

Saad, Nardine. "Leonardo DiCaprio, Model Toni Garnn Reportedly Split." *LA Times.com*. 11 December 2014. <http://www.latimes.com/entertainment/gossip/la-et-mg-leonardo-dicaprio-toni-garrn-split-art-basel-20141211-story.html>. Accessed 2 April 2015.

Sachs, Ben. "*The Village*: Revisiting a Meaningful Plot Twist." *Chicago Reader.com*. 18 December 2012. <http://www.chicagoreader.com/Bleader/archives/2012/12/18/the-village-revisiting-a-meaningful-plot-twist>. Accessed 25 February 2015.

Sampson, Mike. "Early Lady Review." *JoBlo.com*. 26 June 2006.

Sarris, Andrew. "*Mulholland Dr.* (Film Review)." *New York Observer*. 12 November 2001, 23.

Schatz, Thomas. *Hollywood Genres: Formulas, Filmmaking, and the Studio System*. New York: McGraw-Hill, 1981.

———. "The New Hollywood" in *Film Theory Goes to the Movies*. Eds. Jim Collins, Hilary Radner, and Ava Preacher Collins. London and New York: Routledge, 1993. 8–36.

Schickel, Richard. "Sleepless in Alaska." *Time.com*. 19 May 2002. <http://content.time.com/time/magazine/article/0,9171,238623,00.html>. Accessed 3 March 2015.

Schwarzbaum, Lisa. "*Batman Begins* (Film Review)." *EW.com*. 15 June 2005. <http://www.ew.com/article/2005/06/15/batman-begins>. Accessed 4 March 2015.

———. "*Fight Club* (Film Review)." *EW.com*. 22 October 1999. <http://www.ew.com/article/1999/10/22/fight-club>. Accessed 22 July 2013.

Schweitzer, Kate. "From LSD Brain to Dead Autopilot, *Fringe* Premier Skirts Reality." *Popular Mechanics*. 10 September 2008. <http://www.popularmechanics.com/science/research/4281948.html>. Accessed 26 May 2009.

"Season Program Ratings." *ABC Medianet*. Accessed 19 February 2009.

"The Shutter Island Mystery: A Visual Analysis (and Explanation of the Ending)." *Wistful Writer.com*. <http://wistfulwriter.com/2010/08/the-shutter-island-mystery-a-visual-analysis/>. Accessed 2 August 2015.

Silverstein, Paul A. "An Excess of Truth: Violence, Conspiracy Theorizing and the Algerian Civil War." *Anthropological Quarterly*. 75.4 (Fall 2002): 643–74.

Slotkin, Richard. *Gunfighter Nation: The Myth of the Frontier in Twentieth Century America*. Norman: University of Oklahoma Press, 1998.

Smith, Kyle. "M. Night-Mare." *New York Post.com*. 13 June 2008. <http://nypost.com/2008/06/13/m-night-mare/>. Accessed 25 February 2015.

Snider, Mike. "DVD Feels First Sting of Slipping Sales." *USA Today*. 7 January 2008, Life 1.

Sobchack, Vivian. *Carnal Thoughts: Embodiment and Moving Image Culture*. Berkeley, Los Angeles, and London: University of California Press, 2004.

Solomon, Matthew. *Disappearing Tricks: Silent Film, Houdini, and the New Magic of the Twentieth Century*. Chicago and Urbana: University of Illinois Press, 2010.

Stacey, Jackie. "Masculinity, Masquerade, and Genetic Impersonation: *Gattaca's* Queer Visions." *Signs*. 30.3 (Spring 2005): 1851–77.

Staiger, Janet. *Interpreting Films: Studies in the Historical Reception of American Cinema*. Princeton, NJ: Princeton University Press, 1992.

Stam, Robert. "The Politics of Postmodernism" in *Film and Theory*. Ed. Robert Stam and Toby Miller. Malden, UK: Blackwell Publishers, 2000. 753–57.

Stevens, Dana. "The Deep End." *Slate.com*. 20 July 2006. <http://www.slate.com/articles/arts/movies/2006/07/the_deep_end.html>. Accessed 23 February 2015.

Sterritt, David. "Lynch's Twisty Map to *Mulholland Dr.*" *The Christian Science Monitor*. 12 October 2001, 15.

Stewart, James B. *DisneyWar*. New York: Simon and Schuster, 2005.

Stringer, Julian. "Introduction" in *Movie Blockbusters*. Ed. Julian Stringer. London and New York: Routledge, 2003. 1–14.

Sturken, Marita. "Reenactment, Fantasy, and the Paranoia of History: Oliver Stone's Docudramas." *History & Theory*. 36.4 (December 1997): 64–79.

Taylor, Jonathan. "Shyamalan Documentary a Hoax, Sci Fi Admits." *Los Angeles Times.com*. 19 July 2004. <http://articles.latimes.com/2004/jul/19/entertainment/et-scifi19>. Accessed 27 February 2015.

Todorov, Tzvetan. *The Fantastic: A Structural Approach to a Literary Genre*. Trans. Richard Howard. Ithaca, NY: Cornell University Press, 1975.

———. *Genres in Discourse*. Trans. C. Potter. Cambridge: Cambridge University Press, 1990.

Tudor, Andrew. *Theories of Film*. London: Seeker and Warburg, 1973.

Waller, Gregory. "Introduction: A Century at the Movies" in *Moviegoing in America: A Sourcebook in the History of Film Exhibition*. Ed. Gregory Waller. Malden, UK: Blackwell Publishers, 2001. 1–9.

Wasko, Janet. *How Hollywood Works*. London: Sage Publications, 2003.

Weitzman, Elizabeth. "*Inception* (Film Review)." *NY Daily News.com*. 16 July 2010. <http://www.nydailynews.com/entertainment/tv-movies/inception-review-leonardo-dicaprio-christopher-nolan-blow-minds-article-1.200521>. Accessed 7 March 2015.

West, Harry, and Todd Sanders. "Power Revealed and Concealed in the New World Order" in *Transparency and Conspiracy: Ethnographies of Suspicion in the New World Order*. Eds. Harry West and Todd Sanders. Durham, NC: Duke University Press, 2003. 1–37.

"Whaddaya mean 'We don't know about the box'?." *Salon.com*. 26 October 2001. <http://archive.salon.com/ent/letters/2001/10/26/mulholland_drive/index.html>. Accessed 3 July 2008.

Whipp, Glenn. "*Water* Torture: Is M. Night Shyamalan a Genius or an Egomaniac?; Director's Newest Film Has Hollywood Wondering." *The Daily News of Los Angeles*. 21 July 2006. U6.

Whitty, Stephen. "*The Happening* just doesn't well . . . Happen." *NJ.com*. 12 June 2008. <http://www.nj.com/entertainment/tv/index.ssf/2008/06/the_happening_just_doesnt_well.html>. Accessed 25 February 2015.

Williams, Raymond. *Marxism and Literature*. Oxford and New York: Oxford University Press, 1977.

Wilmington, Michael. "*Fight Club* (Film Review)." 15 October 1999. *Chicago Tribune.com*. <http://articles.chicagotribune.com/1999-10-15/entertainment/9910150001_1_movie-edward-norton-fright-club>. Accessed 22 July 2013.

Wyman, Bill, Max Garrone, and Andy Klein. "Everything you were afraid to ask about *Mulholland Dr.*" *Salon.com*. 23 October 2001. <http://archive.salon.com/ent/movies/feature/2001/10/23/mulholland_drive_analysis/#>. Accessed 3 July 2008.

Index

Page numbers in italics indicate illustrations.